JOAQUÍN ORTEGA

CONTEXTOS SERIES

Irene Vásquez, Richard Santos, and Michael Trujillo, series editors

In keeping with the transdisciplinary mission of the Southwest Hispanic Research Institute (SHRI) at the University of New Mexico, the Contextos Series publishes books that deepen our understanding of the historical, social, political, and cultural issues that impact Latinas and Latinos. Topics may span regional, national, and transnational contexts. We invite scholarship in Chicana and Chicano studies, the social sciences, public policy, the humanities, health and natural science, and other professional fields.

Also available in the Contextos Series:

Making Aztlán: Ideology and Culture of the Chicana and Chicano Movement, 1966–1977 by Juan Gómez-Quiñones and Irene Vásquez

Joaquín Ortega

FORGING PAN-AMERICANISM

AT THE UNIVERSITY OF NEW MEXICO

⇌≗⇌

Russ Davidson

University of New Mexico Press | Albuquerque

ISBN 978-0-8263-6202-5 (cloth)
ISBN 978-0-8263-6203-2 (e-book)

Library of Congress Control Number: 2020944758

COVER PHOTOGRAPH: John Donald Robb Photograph Collection
(box 1, folder 5, PICT 000–497), Center for Southwest Research,
University Libraries, University of New Mexico. Courtesy of CSWR.
TEXT AND COVER DESIGN: Mindy Basinger Hill
Composed in 10.8/14pt Arno Pro

Contents

Color plates follow page 130.

Foreword

As the director of the Center for Regional Studies (CRS), I am delighted to welcome the publication of this comprehensive look at the life and career of Dr. Joaquín Ortega at the University of New Mexico (UNM). I would like to first congratulate Dr. Russ Davidson for this valuable undertaking. The genesis of this project is the result of a series of conversations Russ Davidson had in 2013 with the founding director of the CRS, Dr. Tobías Durán. A knowledgeable researcher with an enduring commitment to regional concerns, Tobías Durán had a keen awareness of how educators like Joaquín Ortega had long worked to make the University of New Mexico responsive to the needs of the residents of the state and the greater Southwest. He was also painfully aware that Ortega's story had been overlooked and underappreciated. While working as a CRS research associate, Russ Davidson resolved to produce "the first full-scale study" of Joaquín Ortega. Over the course of a year, beginning in 2014, Davidson consulted all of the known archival collections to produce a composite view of Ortega as an academic, educator, and administrator. Davidson set out to extract in rich detail the story of how Ortega came to found the School of Inter-American Affairs (SIAA) at UNM, his most lasting contribution to the university. Partway into his work, Davidson reported that the UNM archives (regent's minutes, presidential papers, and SIAA reports) housed at Zimmerman Library "proved extremely helpful" and compensated for the absence of any cataloged personal papers from Ortega. Additional research trips led Davidson to the George I. Sánchez Papers housed in the Benson Latin American Collection at the University of Texas at Austin and to the George P. Hammond Papers at the University of California–Berkeley. The Sánchez Papers included the robust correspondence Ortega maintained with Sánchez, as well as the correspondence Sánchez maintained with other leading thinkers of the time in which Ortega's work in New Mexico is discussed. Davidson's research confirmed Joaquín Ortega's decisive role, placing him as the "the innermost figure" and force behind the School of Inter-American Affairs. Ortega emerges as a leading proponent of the idea that New Mexico could be "the place for scholars everywhere to converge and meet to study the Southwest."

The notion that the University of New Mexico is ideally suited to be a center for regional and hemispheric studies redounds to us as we celebrate the thirtieth anniversary of the founding of the Center for Regional Studies. The regional and hemispheric outlook Ortega espoused underpins the CRS's mission to discover, create, preserve, disseminate, and promote a culture of broad inquiry to increase our understanding of New Mexico, the US-Mexican Borderlands, the Americas, and Spain. At the CRS we are especially delighted by the publication of Russ Davidson's *Joaquín Ortega: Forging Pan-Americanism at the University of New Mexico*. Davidson's monograph could not come at a better time to mark the CRS's thirtieth-year anniversary. The book unites the center's legacy to earlier efforts to make UNM a place of convergence for the study of regions, borders, and hemispheric intersectionality. Hat's off to Dr. Tobías Durán for bringing the CRS into existence and to Dr. Russ Davidson, who has brought the past into conversation with the present and with the future.

Dr. A. Gabriel Meléndez

FORMER DIRECTOR, CENTER FOR REGIONAL STUDIES

UNM DISTINGUISHED PROFESSOR

NOVEMBER 2019

Acknowledgments

The genesis of this essay lies in a conversation I had in 2013 with Tobías Durán, then roughly two years away from his retirement as the founding and longtime director of the Center for Regional Studies (CRS) at the University of New Mexico (UNM). The context now eludes me, but Durán brought up the names of several New Mexican Hispanos who had left their mark on the state in important ways but whose contributions, he believed, had to some extent been overlooked or insufficiently recognized. One of them was Joaquín Ortega. Strictly speaking, of course, as a native of Spain, Joaquín Ortega belonged outside the fold, but he had spent so many years in New Mexico and had worked so diligently to improve intercultural relations in the state and to better the lives of its Spanish-speaking people that we —like all those who knew him in the 1930s and 1940s—were only too glad to grant him honorary status. Or perhaps the genesis lay farther in the past, and, in mentioning Joaquín Ortega's name, Durán had managed to stir up an old interest of mine, one that dates to 1979, when I first glimpsed the oil painting of Ortega that hung on a wall in the building that bears his name, Ortega Hall. In subsequent years, as I passed by that painting (now located in the administrative offices of the Department of Spanish and Portuguese), I would wonder about the man whose image it depicts—who was the person behind that cool, cosmopolitan demeanor, and what had his presence really meant for the university? But my curiosity never led to any concrete investigation. So I am grateful to Tobías Durán, who not only planted the idea of this study but agreed as well to fund the initial research that led to it through the grant of a CRS faculty fellowship. My gratitude also extends to the current director of the CRS, A. Gabriel Meléndez, who has added to the book by writing its foreword and who also granted the funding needed to include its color plates.

Most of the research for this book took place in the University of New Mexico's Center for Southwest Research and Special Collections (CSWR). The center's staff and faculty regularly assisted me in identifying key institutional records and related primary source material. For their efforts and for bringing me a steady stream of boxes and books from the shelves to the table, I am grateful to Cindy

Abel Morris, Audra Bellmore, Nany Brown-Martinez, Christopher Geherin, Wendy Pederson, Samuel Sisneros, Portia Vescio, and four former members of the CSWR, Paulita Aguilar, Claire-Lise Bénaud, Terry Gugliotta, and Mary Alice Tsosie. In addition, Portia Vescio and Cindy Morris aided me greatly by scanning many of the illustrations in the book.

Several others figured in this project, and I am likewise grateful for their contributions. In the CRS: Marina Cadena, for her timely handling of university forms and paperwork; and Aracely Chapa, who took over the reins from Durán as I neared the end of the initial phase of my research. In the CSWR: former director of the center Michael Kelly, an enthusiastic supporter of the project from its earliest stage, and the center's current director, Tomas Jaehn, who has sustained that support; in the main library, Monica Doreme, a specialist in the bibliography and organization of US government documents. My thanks also to those in the University of California–Berkeley's Bancroft Library and the manuscript section of the Benson Latin American Collection at the University of Texas at Austin, as well as to David Null, former director of the university archives at the University of Wisconsin–Madison, his successor, Katie Nash, and the staff of the University of Wisconsin Archives and Records Management for facilitating my access to documents, correspondence, and visual materials. Special thanks to Enrique Lamadrid and Merilee Nason Schmit for bringing to my attention images of Joaquín Ortega that I did not know about, and to Bruce Bolinger (whose father, the linguistics and language scholar Dwight Bolinger, earned his doctoral degree in the UW's Department of Spanish and Portuguese during Joaquín Ortega's tenure as its chairman) for locating and making available an important original photograph of Ortega in his family's collection. My gratitude also to Diane Tyink, museum archivist in UNM's Hibben Center for Archaeology Research; and Hannah Abelbeck, photo archivist at the Palace of the Governors Photo Archives at the New Mexico History Museum, for their assistance in providing a photograph of Edgar Lee Hewett.

Between writing the first and final versions of this book I received many worthy suggestions for additions and improvements from several UNM and New Mexico or New Mexico–affiliated colleagues who did me the service of reading it. For this support I am indebted to: Robert Con Davis Undiano, Felipe Gonzales, Linda Hall, Helen Lucero, A. Gabriel Meléndez, Nick Mills, Suzanne Schadl, Christine Sierra, William Stanley, Michael Trujillo, Theo Walker, and the external reviewers engaged by the University of New Mexico Press. Finally, particular thanks to two colleagues: Irene Vásquez, whose patient, critical reading of the manuscript improved it considerably; and UNM Press Senior Acquisitions Editor Elise McHugh, whose advice—in relation to both the text and illustrations—was indispensable in getting the manuscript ready for printing; and to Kate Davis, copy editor par excellence.

JOAQUÍN ORTEGA

Introduction

When I first set out to research Joaquín Ortega's career at the University of
New Mexico (UNM) and examine how it helped shape the character and development of the institution, I thought the project would be fairly simple and
straightforward, a matter, primarily, of documenting and explaining his role
in orienting the university toward the academic study of Latin America. In
the 1940s, the University of New Mexico—although in certain respects still
confined to the lower rungs of American research universities—gained wide
recognition for the depth and range of its program in Latin American studies.
Its newly created School of Inter-American Affairs (SIAA, 1941) was viewed
as one of the leading centers in the country for the interdisciplinary study of
Latin America and US–Latin American relations. Moreover, from the time the
university's president, James Fulton Zimmerman, first sought his ideas and
advice in the early 1930s, to his appointment and years as director of the SIAA
(1941–1948), the central figure and guiding hand behind this initiative—apart
from Zimmerman himself—was Joaquín Ortega.

A Spaniard who had immigrated to the United States in 1915, Ortega brought a
much-needed energy, resolve, and presence to the twin challenges of advancing
the School of Inter-American Affairs at UNM and of broadening and strengthening the university's program in Latin American studies. He was a seasoned
administrator, having chaired the Department of Spanish and Portuguese at the
University of Wisconsin–Madison for eleven years (1930–1941), was widely traveled in academic circles, and well-thought-of by the leadership of major public
and private foundations and government agencies. Following his appointment at
the University of New Mexico, Ortega quickly chalked up a string of successes.
Some were strictly internal to the university and involved new courses of study
and new degree programs as well as sponsored research and expanded scholarly
activity; others involved the community at large and took the form of innovative outreach programs, conferences, and symposia, all of which engaged civic,
cultural, and religious leaders in discussions of a range of social and economic
issues, with the aim of forging more lasting ties between the university and the

world outside it. His concern that the university needed to be an active presence in the community and had a special obligation to work alongside and with it, to address structural inequalities and help improve life for those on the margins, has not always defined its external relations. Even before he left UNM (1951), Ortega's initiatives on this score were dramatically scaled back. They thus take on greater importance today, when the University of New Mexico has reembraced many of his (and President Zimmerman's) ideas regarding the social mission and responsibilities of the institution.

Ortega was drawn to New Mexico for a number of reasons. The state's landscape and physical environment reminded him of parts of his native country. Furthermore, a century ago and through his time at UNM, fully half the state's population still had Spanish as a first language. The folkways and cultural traditions imprinted across 230 years of Spanish colonial rule, and maintained during the brief period of Mexican rule (1821–1848), were still a vital force. The state's Hispanic heritage was everywhere visible and tangible, its connections to Spain and Latin America still alive, if necessarily diluted to some degree. "Linguistically and culturally New Mexico has as many ties with South as with North America."[1] If this statement was true in the early 1950s, when its author, John H. Burma, undertook research on New Mexico, it was even truer two decades earlier, when Joaquín Ortega began visiting the state. Thus, to be in New Mexico was, in a sense, to be in a far corner of the wider Hispanic world; it resembled "a country within a country," as the Santa Fe writer, Ruth Laughlin Barker, characterized it.[2] These sensibilities and perceptions colored Ortega's outlook on the purpose and functions of the SIAA, leading him to make New Mexico and the Hispanic Southwest as much a focus of the academic mission of the school as the study of the republics to the south, a policy that provoked criticism on the part of some and eventually weakened his hand within the university.

Ortega was also deeply committed to the betterment of the state, and on this matter, too, he believed that the SIAA could play an important role. Many of his efforts and many of the grants he secured were invested in community-based projects aimed at improving the lot of low-income New Mexicans, Hispanic and Anglo-American most prominently, and Native American to a lesser extent. To further this objective, and because he relished the give-and-take of argument and conversation, Ortega cultivated contacts and friendships with a wide circle of New Mexican leaders and luminaries, in the arts, politics, and business community. His conviction that a shared history and heritage existed between the Hispanic Southwest and Latin America meant, on his reading, that they should be studied jointly, as parts of a whole. He also believed that the boundaries that separated the university from the community were artificial and stood in the way of economic and social progress. UNM, and his and President Zimmerman's joint creation in particular, the School of Inter-American Affairs, needed to involve themselves directly in the day-to-day and long-range work of uplifting society. In this regard, too, Ortega would come under criticism, at first muted and later more vocal, but as a rule, he was not one to sit on the sidelines of controversy and strike a neutral pose. More than some of his colleagues, he hewed steadfastly to his principles.

Joaquín Ortega's high profile in the University of New Mexico and the key role he played in helping secure and solidify its standing as a leading center for the study of Latin America warrants a study and a recounting of his career at UNM and his work in New Mexico. Yet it would probably make for dry reading, just the kind of academic exercise that Ortega typically found so tedious and unappealing. As I got further into the story, however, I realized there was more to it than this dimension alone. Ortega was not only a polymath and an erudite scholar; he was also a committed reformer, a man of fierce conviction attuned to the world around him and its more glaring contradictions, ironies, and unful-filled promises. Crucially, he viewed the university as a place for addressing discrimination and social inequalities. As noted earlier, however, his propos-als and reformist impulses were primarily directed toward the Hispanic and Anglo-American communities. Native Americans were not an afterthought to Joaquín Ortega; he often referenced them in his proposals, and he deplored their exploitation and mistreatment. Yet they were rarely the main target, or at the forefront, of his external or university-based projects.

Ortega's personal story and record of achievement thus connect to a larger picture, one in which issues of race, ethnicity, language, cultural heritage, and the making of national identity stand out, along with the span of social, economic, and political divisions they produced in New Mexico. These issues have been of interest to scholars of the Borderlands region and the inland Southwest for many years, underscored—in more recent times—by the motivation to separate fact from fiction. The evolution and interplay of these factors in New Mexico, from the latter part of the nineteenth into the early decades of the twentieth century, has drawn special scrutiny over the last decade and a half.[3] Moreover, the manner in which they intersected with and stamped the character of higher education in the state—with the focus primarily on the University of New Mexico—has also drawn attention. In this latter context, however, only one recent study, the work by Phillip B. Gonzales, *Forced Sacrifice as Ethnic Protest: The Hispano Cause in New Mexico & the Racial Attitude Confrontation of 1933*, examines these issues in depth, and his work is necessarily limited in time and space, because it focuses largely on a single event and its ramifications.[4] Yet the University of New Mexico was not only unshielded from the force of these issues, it also served as a critical site on which they repeatedly played out.

Beginning shortly after it opened its doors in the early 1890s and extending well into the twentieth century, the University of New Mexico—its administrators, faculty, students, and the different constituencies whom it served and to whom it answered—engaged in a debate over the nature and definition of its mission and core identity. In large measure, the debate—which Ortega entered into with typical flair and determination—sprang from the particular history and heritage of the state. Formed out of what had always been the nucleus of colonization and settlement within the northern reaches of the Viceroyalty of New Spain, New Mexico stood apart. In terms of language, ethnicity, cultural and religious practices and customs, patterns of land and water use, social institutions, and "even world view,"[5] no state in the union maintained a stronger connection to Spain, Mexico, and Latin America than New Mexico. In Ortega's own words, "The most cohesive Hispanic population in the United States, the one most faithful to a long and uninterrupted tradition of identification with the soil, is to be found in New Mexico."[6] The strength and persistence of this connection—as manifested, for example, in the high number of native Spanish speakers, the ingrained pattern of subsistence farming on small family-owned plots, and the vitality of extended kinship ties—forced a series of questions on the university. To what extent should its mission and goals, its programs and policies express and promote this heritage and the way it blended—architecturally, culturally, and otherwise—with the traditions of the Native American population? What balance should exist between an imported "Anglo" model of the academic enterprise and one that incorporated and built upon local and regional tradition? How much emphasis should be given and how many resources devoted to creating a focus on a unique Nuevomexicano heritage, or one that encompassed the wider region? And what were the proper geographic limits, since "the Southwest," as Erna Fergusson wrote, "is not, like other sections of the United States, exactly bounded."[7] Thus, figuratively speaking, New Mexico's regional borders had connected to Mexico and Latin America for centuries.

These questions, which went to the heart of defining a clear identity for UNM and deciding how and where its resources should be allocated, were part of a larger debate that took place in New Mexico before and after it gained statehood (1912). Anglo-Americans and Nuevomexicanos had carried out a debate over language, ethnicity, race, and nationality, coalescing around what Erlinda Gonzales-Berry and David Maciel aptly termed "the contested homeland."[8] Broadly speaking, among Anglo-Americans and Nuevomexicanos, three groups—assimilationists, Hispanists,[9] and pluralists—each with its followers and factional bands, maneuvered for power and position. Each sharpened its rhetoric and hardened its position over the first three decades of the twentieth century. For the advocates of assimilation, the overriding task was to "Americanize," that is, "Anglicize," the Spanish-speaking Nuevomexicano. Through the explicit primacy they placed on forging a culturally and linguistically homogeneous society, a majority of the Anglo-American population (whose strength and numbers were rapidly growing) highlighted their ethnocentrism and their will to subordinate other identities and traditions. In the eyes of this community, the Hispanic population could not enjoy the same status, for its members were largely illiterate and belonged to an alien Catholic culture with a different language. Before all else, they had to be brought and absorbed into the "American" mainstream.[10]

The second group, the Hispanists, strongly opposed the "Anglo" definition of what it meant to be an "American." The members of this group defended and fought for their recognition as US citizens within a dual-ethnic society. The leading spokesman and great champion of this party, embodied in the so-called "Native Son movement," was Octaviano Larrazolo, New Mexico's first post-territorial Hispanic governor (1919–1921). Larrazolo and his brethren "argued for the preservation and extension of rights for people of Mexican descent."[11] In this reckoning, both *nativos* (a term that people of Mexican ancestry, born in the region, used at the time to describe themselves) and other New Mexicans of Mexican or Spanish American background and heritage were no less "American" than their "Anglo" counterparts. They did not have to share the same language or culture or learn new customs and practices to belong fully to the nation. This promotion of the "Hispano Cause," as Phillip B. Gonzales called the movement and its periodic mobilizations in New Mexico (and the Southwest more widely) from the 1880s into the 1930s, defended not only the claims and permanence of a separate ethnic identity but the right to a corresponding share of political power as well. By its very nature, of course, the Native Son movement (which, ironically—given its name—did not incorporate the Native American population) accentuated ethnic cleavage. Still, the benefits of this movement outweighed any costs, because it allowed Nuevomexicanos to preserve their native culture and ways against the assimilative current: "The degree and rate of assimilation to Anglo society . . . was slow or nonexistent throughout the territorial period and even afterward."[12] Hispanic resistance to the "Americanizing" project manifested itself through several avenues: political action to preserve rights and privileges, the development of a Spanish-language press and the retention (though slowly weakening) of Spanish as a living language, the continued practice of local Catholic folkways, and the attainment of high-level, statewide political leadership. The adoption of New Mexico's state constitution in 1912 was a watershed moment for the Hispano Cause, because it codified Spanish-language rights in certain spheres of state government and in public education—although much less effectively in the latter case.

To a certain degree, the Hispanist position shaded into and overlapped with the outlook of the third group, the pluralists. Fundamentally anti-assimilationist in tone and substance, the members of this group issued a call for a multicultural society that granted equal recognition and importance to both traditions— Anglo and Hispanic. To their way of thinking, American identity was multifaceted, nonexclusionary, incorporating different ethnicities, races, classes, and cultures. While the English language needed to be emphasized first, there was also room for and, more pointedly, the need to affirm and embrace bilingualism. For pluralists, the "composite American identity of the future," to use Walt Whitman's expression (from *Prose Works*), was still in the process of formation. While Native Americans and their traditions belonged, by definition, within the pluralist fold, in practice they faded into the background because their inclusion was largely rhetorical.

In a further refinement or extension of their thinking, partisans of the pluralist orientation (who included Joaquín Ortega and, as his thinking evolved, James Zimmerman as well) frequently leaned on a manufactured, carefully tailored image and narrative of New Mexico as a kind of tricultural wonderland, a place where three distinct groups—Native American, Anglo-American, and Hispanic, the "heroic triad," as writer and historian Paul Horgan collectively called them— lived side by side on an equal footing, in mutual recognition of their separate but interconnected history and traditions. Of course, to refer to "three" major groups obviously left out the fourth such group in the New World population—people of African ancestry. This omission, however, relied on numerical differences, since in the period under study, their representation in the state of New Mexico was very small, 0.7 percent of the state's total population in 1930, and 0.9 percent in 1940.[13] Still, even when confined to the three main groups, the image was simplistic, misleading, and easily refuted if examined closely.[14] To begin with, while Native Americans were as—if not more—embedded in this encounter as the other two groups, their participation in it was of a different order since they lived a largely segregated life on tribal lands. Moreover, in reality, in everyday life, the three major groups that Anglo promotors of the image portrayed as "distinct" were never as separated or alien from each other as many had depicted. Nonetheless, their coexistence was marked by conflict and contestation, by patterns of accommodation and resistance. As Carey McWilliams put it, in noting the extent of race mixture and cultural fusion among the three groups, "However antagonistically each group may have regarded the other, the plain fact is that they have been in continuous, direct, and often intimate contact in the Southwest for over a century."[15] Identities were often segmented and overlapped to a high degree. For example, the state's native-Spanish-speaking inhabitants—depending on whom they were addressing, what impression they wished to leave, or how they sought to distinguish themselves, by caste and class, from other native Spanish speakers—might refer to themselves as Mexicanos, Nuevomexicanos, Spanish Americans, Hispanos, nativos, or Hispano-Americanos. Although the subtler meanings and distinctions might be lost on the non-Spanish speaker, they were clear enough to those who invoked them. Nevertheless, first celebrated and marketed for touristic and commercial purposes and later, as we will see, for political and academic reasons, the tricultural image, or formulation, eventually took hold in the public mind and infused the rhetoric and imagination of university and political officials.

It is worth detouring briefly to consider the image from a literary vantage point, because writers often treated it more realistically, drawing out the complications and nuances of relations between and within the three main groups. For example, in his novel *Fire in the Night* (1934),[16] Raymond Otis uses one of his main protagonists, Lorenzo de Baca, as a foil to explore the social transformation that took place in Santa Fe, New Mexico (and, implicitly, in other sections of the Old Southwest), in the decades after the city became part of the United States and its Spanish-speaking residents, willingly or not, fell increasingly under the sway of new cultural norms and practices. Lorenzo, a *rico*, or member of the traditional landholding class, and intensely proud of his "pure" Spanish blood, laments the loss of the old order, when each person occupied a fixed place in society and accepted it as his due. With the American annexation, that world steadily disintegrated; in its place came an untethered individualism, founded upon a concept of equality, such that "the teaching and training of centuries was undone." Lorenzo finds himself split. On the one hand, he wants "to be loyal to his people," on the other, to maintain his privileged place in the social scale. In the end, although "his people would resent him and hate him for it," he opts for privilege. The imperative and dictates of class and the desire to be accepted within the right social circles outweigh the bonds of cultural heritage.

While Lorenzo's disquiet seemed to hinge on the question of class and social position, it was actually more encompassing, for just underneath and often rising to the surface lay a series of related issues concerning language and nationality, ethnic identity and labeling, racial stereotyping, and the attendant debate over who was a true "American" and who was not. For New Mexico's Spanish-speaking inhabitants (not to speak of the still-greater victim in this dynamic, the Native American population), the last question was especially vexing, since its effect was to relegate them to being outsiders in a region where they had owned their own land and to thus remind them, in the most visceral way, of all they had lost.

With the end of the Mexican-American War and the adoption of the Treaty of Guadalupe Hidalgo (1848), any Mexican citizen who resided in New Mexico in 1848 and who did not formally declare loyalty to Mexico by 1849 automatically became a US citizen. This right was guaranteed by the terms of the treaty, yet many US authorities as well as many within the US population generally did not honor it, nor did they accept the idea that Mexicans could ever be "Americans." In part, this prejudicial attitude derived from their erroneous belief that "Mexican" denoted or was synonymous with a particular race. To the contrary, however, Mexico comprised multiple racial groups. The inhabitants of New Mexico, prior to the US annexation, were identified, racially and culturally, as Indians (Pueblo, Navajo, Apache, or some other indigenous community), *mestizos* (persons of mixed European and Native American ancestry), *españoles* (Spaniards), Anglo-Americans, and so on.[17] The populations maintained differences in language use, religion, national origin, social practice, and the like, but were united—following independence from Spain in 1821—in one respect: all were citizens of the Mexican republic. In the United States, however, Mexico was construed as a racial monolith. Mexicans, whatever their lineage and appearance, however they might define themselves, were seen as belonging to a single racial group: mestizo. Thus, for most Anglo-Americans, the United States was a "white" nation, while Mexico was not.

Again, we can turn to Otis's novel to glimpse the tensions and misunderstandings fed by such conflicting ideas about race, nationality, and identity. Lorenzo de Baca, descendant of the old Spanish gentry, finds himself driving through the countryside with the transplanted Anglo-American easterner (and object of his desire), Claire Mosely. Exchanging views about where they would like to live, Lorenzo declares that his choice would be Spain, to which Claire replies that his preference makes perfect sense, since "after all, you're a Spaniard, Lorenzo." Parroting the general Anglo-American propensity to obliterate all the nuances and interpolations of race and ethnic ancestry, Lorenzo counters by responding, "No, I'm a Mexican," adding, "Aren't you just a little ashamed to be hob-nobbing with a Mexican? . . . I'll bet you there are people in town who think you lose caste by associating with me." His personal disenchantment bleeds out and colors his image of Santa Fe and, by extension, other New Mexican towns and cities with similar populations. For Lorenzo, because of how it degrades and adulterates age-old customs, traditions, and caste distinctions, indeed an entire way of life— albeit that elements of that way of life now came alive only in memory—the mix of people of such different origins and backgrounds makes the town "a mongrel," tainted and impure.

To brand New Mexico's towns as "mongrelized" was a crude and racialized statement that papered over or dismissed the more subtle realities and fraught aspects of Anglo-Hispano relations and also subsumed the Native American populations. For some, like Ortega, the tricultural formulation served to rec-oncile, or compartmentalize, the legacies of racial hierarchy. Their acceptance and use of it helped him and other university leaders forge a path for Southwest Hispanic and Latin American studies alongside simmering issues of racial and ethnic conflict and division. Men like James Zimmerman and Joaquín Ortega did not deny and were not indifferent to the existence of such conflict and con-troversy in the university. Indeed, if Raymond Otis had wanted to, he could in all plausibility have set his novel on the grounds of the UNM campus.

For this reason, a long line of UNM administrators and faculty either willingly joined or were pulled into the "contested homeland" debate (or its academic variant) as it unfolded during the first half of the twentieth century and reached its apex just before and after World War II. At the center of the discussion was Zimmerman himself. Zimmerman's strategic vision for the university, which he patiently nurtured for more than ten years, was firmly on the side of the cultural pluralists and culminated in the creation of UNM's School of Inter-American Affairs. As earlier explained, the SIAA was founded on the belief—which Zim-merman and Joaquín Ortega shared in common—that the study of the Hispanic Southwest, and of New Mexico in particular, had to be linked, intellectually and programmatically, with the study of Latin America. The rationale for this belief would be elaborated in great detail in the last half decade of Zimmerman's presidency, 1939–1944, but some of its main points were apparent all along to more astute and historically minded observers. First, there were the bonds that reached into the Spanish colonial period, reinforced by the fact of language: more than half of New Mexico's residents continued to have Spanish as their everyday language well into the twentieth century. Second: both in New Mexico and in the nations to the south, diverse cultural groups had been brought into contact by complex historical processes, leading to a system of authoritative social control of one group over the others. As such, New Mexico could be seen as a "living laboratory" for understanding cultural conflict and fusion.[18] In addition, both regions had been shaped by a pattern of development that left a legacy of poverty, malnutrition, illiteracy, and other social and economic ills. With an eye to its own problems of ethnic and intercultural relations, UNM, Zimmerman believed, could maneuver to address and help ameliorate these conditions on various fronts. Moving carefully and incrementally to build a solid core of support, he recruited faculty who were sympathetic to this viewpoint and, with their support and assistance from external sources, converted it into a guiding principle of the university's mission and the centerpiece of its community-based programs.

Unquestionably, Zimmerman's greatest ally in this enterprise was Joaquín Ortega, but there were others in this period who left their mark as well, notably, Francis Kercheville, Paul Walter Jr., Donald Brand, Anita Osuna Carr, France Scholes, George P. Hammond, George I. Sánchez, Arthur L. Campa, Lloyd Tireman, Mela Sedillo Brewster, and a future president of the university, Tom Popejoy. Not all embraced Zimmerman's "Boltonianism" (i.e., the approach toward New World history promoted by University of California professor Herbert Bolton, resting on the idea that the Americas shared a common history and therefore profited from being studied in this light) or his creation of the SIAA with the fervent enthusiasm of Ortega; and some—like Brand—had no affection for the school at all. On balance, however, Zimmerman's ideas about the ties that bound New Mexico to the Hispanic world and how and why these should help shape the future direction of the university enjoyed broad support, including from such leading voices in the community, state legislature, and congressional delegation as Concha Ortiz y Pino, Gilberto Espinosa, William Keleher, Bronson Cutting, and Dennis and David Chávez.

Next to Joaquín Ortega, George Sánchez had the greatest influence on President Zimmerman with respect to the latter's ideas for building a program of inter-American studies at UNM and how the systematic analysis of New Mexico's historical development fit into this complex. Although Sánchez was compelled (for reasons that will become clear) to leave New Mexico before plans for the SIAA came to fruition, his research into the origins and structural conditions of poverty, educational deprivation, and social isolation faced by native New Mexicans—brought together and encapsulated in his landmark study of Taos and its environs, *Forgotten People: A Study of New Mexicans*—laid the ideological foundation for the SIAA and provided the inspiration and critical data for some of its programs.[19] While Ortega never wrote a book like Sánchez's (although he had long planned to), his knowledge of the state and its problems, and his appreciation for its special features and attributes, ran just as deep. Like Sánchez, he was anti-assimilationist and an advocate for what today would be called cultural pluralism. As such, he argued that New Mexico's diverse ethnic and racial groups should be encouraged and allowed to maintain their unique identities, while engaging with each other as part of a larger, democratic society. After assuming the directorship of the SIAA in August 1941, Ortega worked at a feverish pace, and in less than half a decade he had, in a joint effort with Zimmerman, orchestrated the university's emergence and consolidation as one of the nation's premier centers for the study of Latin America and US–Latin American relations. Operating in unison with Zimmerman, he helped carry the university to new heights, fostering scholarly strength and tradition that still characterize the institution.

As alluded to earlier, however, these achievements—notable as they were— are only one element of the story. In helping Zimmerman realize his vision for the university, Ortega also furthered awareness of how the problems of ethnic and racial labeling and stereotyping, language, social exclusion, and claims and counterclaims about national identity played out both at UNM and in the state more broadly. Part of what makes Ortega's views and actions and his career at UNM so interesting and worthy of study is that, despite the ever-growing strength of the assimilationist camp, these issues, and related questions bound up with the tricultural image and its manipulation, were never fully resolved. Quite the opposite, they surfaced again and again, endowing some of his ideas (as well as Zimmerman's) with a very contemporary ring.

For example, in the late 1950s—nearly a decade after Ortega retired from UNM and returned to Spain—a deeply felt argument broke out in public over the use of the terms *Anglo- American, Mexican,* and *Spanish American* by Senator Dennis Chávez. Chávez had used them, in referring to residents of the state, in a talk that he gave to the local chapter of the national Hispanic veterans and civil rights association, the New Mexico American GI Forum, and then subsequently repeated in an interview with *The Albuquerque Tribune*. The editor of the *New Mexico Historical Review* and UNM history professor Frank Reeve objected to Chávez's doing so on the grounds that the terms were archaic and divisive. Their use, he claimed, carried a "sub-surface meaning of dislike," and kept alive "ancestral animosities."[20] Reeve contended that whatever their ancestry, New Mexicans should simply be called "Americans" and underlined his point by paraphrasing President Woodrow Wilson, who had stated at the outbreak of World War I that the time had come to end the use of the hyphen when referring to citizens of the United States. Ezequiel Durán, secretary of the New Mexico American GI Forum, sprang to Chávez's defense. First, the senator had addressed his remarks to a largely Spanish-speaking audience; and second, they had a specific political subtext, namely, the struggle that this group of New Mexicans faced in finding employment *precisely* because its members were perceived as belonging to a different class of Americans. Naïvely or otherwise, Reeve was looking past the problem. "Why is it," wrote Durán, "that a professor who should know the facts about race relations cannot understand the most simple statements relating to discriminatory practices in employment."[21] The *New Mexico Lobo*, UNM's student newspaper, weighed in on the argument, leaning somewhat in favor of Reeve. Chávez's use of the term *Mexicans*, the paper asserted, was at bottom a political maneuver, designed to pressure Governor-Elect John Burroughs into hiring New Mexicans of "Spanish ancestry," who had helped get him elected, into state government jobs. The paper criticized the idea that the party apparatus "owed" these people jobs because of their surnames and ethnicity: "It is not a system of ancestries that runs the government; it is a system of parties."[22] The *Lobo*, however, was evading the heart of Durán's argument—that the manner in which "ancestry" was put to use in New Mexico was anything but politically and economically color-blind. The *Lobo* may have seen Chávez's position as entailing a kind of protopolitical correctness, but Reeve's stand could equally be seen as another instance of denying unpleasant realities and of taking the "accomodationist" line. (The latter, part of a formalized system, or "pact of silence," that proscribed overt discussion of friction and discord in the conduct of Anglo-Hispano relations, is covered in detail in chapter 2.) The disagreements over nomenclature thus exposed widespread resentment on the part of Spanish-speaking New Mexicans and revealed deeper tensions and anxieties relating to identity, discrimination, historical grievance, and national origin among New Mexicans in both the Anglo-American and Hispanic communities.

The exchange between Reeve and Durán had taken place in the public square, but—like the dialogue between Lorenzo de Baca and Claire Mosely—could have as easily been transposed to the UNM campus. Subsequent decades witnessed new iterations and expressions of these long-standing problems, between and across all three of the state's main population groups, and in the epilogue to this book, I summarize and discuss two additional, more recent disputes, one involving representations on the official seal of the university, the other involving a set of murals in the university's main library.

The sentiments and beliefs and the sense of grievance and loss highlighted in the exchange between Chávez and Reeve—stemming from differences of ethnicity, race, and language, which that gave rise to and informed prejudicial attitudes and discriminatory practice—have marked the history of the University of New Mexico from its earliest days. Joaquín Ortega's voice was heard, unreservedly, on all of these issues (although, as earlier noted, less insistently as concerned the situation of Native Americans). He thought deeply about them, first as an outside observer, then as an inside player. Furthermore, his interest was far from purely academic. No armchair intellectual, he proposed remedies and practical solutions and set these down in a series of concise tracts and essays. Shadowing and inspiring all his proposals was the School of Inter-American Affairs, the research and work that it carried out, and the values of cultural pluralism, democratic, community-based social and economic action and reform, and hemispheric solidarity that it sought to promulgate both within and outside of the university.

From the day the SIAA opened in mid-1941 through the seven years of Ortega's directorship, no program in the university maintained a higher profile or had a greater effect on the state than it had. Its programs reached into some of New Mexico's most remote and isolated communities. Today, however, apart from the building that bears his name, there is little if any institutional memory of the man. In part, this lapse is understandable; his time in the university was brief, just under a full decade, and came to an end nearly seventy years ago. The post–World War II years seemingly transformed the state overnight, accelerating the industrialization and urbanization of what had been a heavily rural, agrarian society. UNM was compelled to respond to these changes, expanding its programs, recalibrating its commitments, and distributing its resources accordingly. While the SIAA's central place in the mission of the university was not called into question, its academic program was forced to compete with new priorities. Furthermore, although anything but self-effacing, Ortega also had the trick of leaving few personal traces of himself behind. It would doubtless be easier to render an account of Joaquín Ortega, as I propose to do here, if one had access to his personal papers, but regrettably they seem to have disappeared or been lost. If I were attempting to write a traditional biography, that void would pose a major obstacle, but that is not the aim here. Rather, it is to explain and interpret more fully a singular period in the history of the university and the preeminent part—now largely forgotten—that Joaquín Ortega (in partnership with President Zimmerman) played in shaping its educational image and priorities vis-à-vis the Hispanic community and its larger historical, hemispheric, and cultural context. For that purpose, fortunately, the records of the university—although not systematically preserved until well after the Zimmerman years and also depleted through periodic disasters such as flooding—still contain sufficient material to make the study possible.

This book follows a chronological-topical arrangement. Much of what UNM accomplished in the inter-American field during Ortega's time as the SIAA director grew out of his own ideas and convictions and was directly attributable to him, but the foundation for his work had been established years before. Thus, to better understand the context and why Ortega thought as he did about education, language, hemispheric relations, and the state of minorities in New Mexico, it is important to review UNM's history prior to James Zimmerman's appointment as president and Ortega's as the SIAA director. Chapter 1 traces the history and growth of the university during the four preceding presidencies (1901–1927), when, still in the first phase of development, its leaders made a series of attempts to institutionalize Southwest Hispanic and Latin American studies as part of an effort to clarify how local and regional history and tradition should help define the character of the university and influence its growth. These attempts, which shared many features in common, secured the support of key political and civic figures in the community as well as the attention of outside agencies, but for various reasons they proved unsuccessful.

Chapters 2 and 3 cover the years of Zimmerman's presidency (1927–1944) and explore how and why the study of the Hispanic Southwest and Latin America emerged as core programs of the university, central to its sense of mission and purpose; why the two fields were considered as one, with New Mexico conveniently being viewed as "little Latin America;" and how these developments led the School of Inter-American Affairs to institute community-based projects in New Mexico aimed at improving the lives of disadvantaged segments of the Hispanic population. The university in this period made great strides in a number of areas and finally succeeded in placing its Southwest and Latin American studies programs on a solid institutional footing. The crowning achievement was the founding of the SIAA in 1941. Chapters 2 and 3 explain the strategies that Zimmerman employed to manage this success, the principal individuals—besides Joaquín Ortega—with and through whom he worked, and the stresses, strains, and outright (though limited) opposition that accompanied the effort. Ortega's ideas and plans furnished the main framework for the SIAA's activities and projects, several of which are described in some detail. The two chapters also describe and analyze the tensions and conflicts that underlay relations between Hispanic and Anglo-American students at UNM, how these manifested themselves and were treated within the university, and how they were viewed and dealt with by the larger community. Through its academic and extracurricular activities and its external work, the SIAA sought to confront and combat such discord. Joaquín Ortega was not a blind optimist, but he held out hope that New Mexico, with its particular history and heritage—and here he exploited the tricultural formulation—could become, as he called it, a "synthesis of the Americas" and offer a living example to the rest of the hemisphere of the Pan-American ideal. Chapter 4 analyzes in depth two pillars of Ortega's thinking in this regard, bilingualism and cultural pluralism (and the politics surrounding them), as brought out in three of his most trenchant writings, while also tracing the ideas and contributions of others who focused on these issues, notably the UNM Hispanic-folklore specialist and professor of Spanish language and literature Arthur L. Campa. Chapter 5 brings us to the end of story, the postwar years, when the University of New Mexico faced a set of new challenges and Ortega's star inevitably faded, analyzing how and why this happened and also describing how this cosmopolitan Spaniard briefly reoriented his career at UNM before his health and spirit finally gave out. Chapter 6, the conclusion, provides a final assessment of Ortega—the scholar, the reformer, and the man, as reflected in the different stages of his career.

Terminology

A last word in this introduction concerns the choice of terms used to describe people of varying ethnic identity and national background. In the nineteenth century and through the period under study in the twentieth, the term *Anglo*, or *Anglo-American*, was typically employed as a catchall; Italians, Germans, Jews, Nordic people, and others who demonstrably were not of Anglo heritage were still lumped into this category. More recently, the term *Euro-American* has come to replace it, since it more accurately describes this segment of the national (and in this case New Mexico's) population. Contemporary usage notwithstanding, I have frequently opted for the out-of-date *Anglo*, since that was the designation used by everyone who figures in this study and thus better reflects their own cast of mind. The cases of the terms *Hispano*, *Nuevomexicano*, and *Hispano-Americano* are more problematic, in that they sometimes presuppose private and intracommunal understandings. Apart from terms found in a direct quotation (such as *Mexican*, or *Mexican American*) or where the text dictates otherwise (e.g., *nativo*), I have followed the practice of using all three terms, depending on what best suits the context. On first use in each chapter, Spanish words and expressions with no common English equivalents have been italicized and, where called for, defined or explained. Finally, all translations from the Spanish are mine.

CHAPTER ONE

⬱

Forging a Distinctive Identity
and Emphasis for UNM

The Partial Successes of the Pre-Zimmerman Years

It has been claimed that "from the outset . . . university officials foresaw the growing importance of and interest in Spanish and Hispanic culture of the Southwest."[1] In broad measure, the claim stands up. Although uneven, the trajectory of the University of New Mexico pointed in this direction. Certainly, the early leaders of UNM were not blind; all around them, in city and in countryside, many essential features of a social and economic landscape laid down centuries before still survived, in whole or in part. This link to the colonial past was especially true for the rural communities of New Mexico's Middle and Upper Rio Grande Valley, where peoples' lives continued to revolve around subsistence farming on small family-owned plots, and—despite the breakup and loss of many communal lands—the cohesion and structure of village life remained largely intact. Nonetheless, although the university's leaders lived and worked in a state whose population, in 1900, was more than 50 percent native-Spanish-speaking and whose history belonged disproportionately to its Spanish Empire period, they sent mixed signals about the need to emphasize the Spanish language and Southwestern and Spanish American history.

Created in 1889 through a bill passed in the territorial legislature, with its first students admitted three years later, UNM struggled over the next decade simply to organize itself as a functioning university. However, the decision to situate it several miles away from either Albuquerque's heavily Spanish-speaking Old Town or nearby village of Barelas, its 65-to-5 ratio of Anglo to Hispanic students in the inaugural class, its 4 Anglos versus 1 Hispano on the first Board of Regents, and its core curriculum of Greek, Latin, mathematics, and English literature and composition demonstrated two things: the degree to which the Hispanic community was generally unprepared and unencouraged at that time to take advantage of higher education and the ascendancy of the Anglo elite in managing the affairs of the territory.[2] In the minds of the regents, UNM's energies needed to be focused on helping New Mexico modernize, that is, become more like the rest of the nation, so that it could finally take its place as one of the states of the union. During these initial years, the agenda for the university was thus skewed toward serving the interests of the Anglo merchant and financial class, with which many Hispano ricos—accommodating themselves to the new balance of power and seeking their share of a growing economy—had aligned themselves politically. The Hispanic elite, however, strongly objected to some of the cultural implications of modernization, in particular the belief that Hispanos could never be "true" Americans until they forsook Spanish and embraced the English language. The insistence on eliminating Spanish in favor of English met a wall of resistance. Language was the greatest marker of Hispanic identity, so it had to be protected, kept vibrant and alive. Hispanic civic and political leaders rallied around this issue. When the constitution of the new state of New Mexico was adopted, they prevailed (trading favors with more pluralist-minded Anglos who also wanted Hispanos' political support) in getting protection for the Spanish language and certain allied rights and privileges incorporated into it.[3]

The Hispanic concern with the defense of heritage found a strong echo in Santa Fe in this period (roughly 1910–1930), one that reverberated far beyond the region. As Ian Frazier put it so well: "About a hundred years ago, footloose men and women of a certain romantic disposition discovered the American Southwest and were blown away. The dramatic landscape, the largely intact Native American culture, the atmosphere of ancient mysteries preserved in the dry desert air—all combined to put a powerful charm on their minds. . . . Some of the newcomers quickly succeeded in making others throughout the U.S. excited about the Southwest and eager to go there."[4] Building on this enthusiasm, a circle of scholars, writers, poets, artists, and civic boosters established a series of recurring public programs and festivals in the state capital that would reawaken and promote interest in Spanish and Native American arts and culture. Moreover, organizations were set up to give these events permanent presence and structure. Among the more prominent patrons of this movement, called the "Spanish revival" by Charles Montgomery, were Edgar Lee Hewett, who started the Santa Fe Fiesta in 1919; Mary Austin and Frank Applegate, who with other supporters founded the Spanish Colonial Arts Society in 1929; and a large group, led by John Gaw Meem, Carlos Vierra, Gustave Baumann, Alice Corbin, William Penhallow Henderson, and Mary Austin, who established the Old Santa Fe Association in 1926. The opening of the School of American Archaeology in

1907, renamed the School of American Research (SAR) in 1917, was—in broad measure—an earlier expression of this interest. Hewett was its first director and also served as the director of the Museum of New Mexico, created by the territorial legislature in 1909. If the Spanish revival, the fascination with Native American culture, and the "surge of adoration" for the region had one champion who stood above the others, that person might have been Edgar Lee Hewett: "He was able to tap into, and promote, the Southwestern desire for a cultural identity equivalent to that touted in the East."[5] Some years later, Hewett would reach an agreement with President Zimmerman that formalized a relationship between the SAR and UNM and also made him the founding chair of UNM's Department of Archaeology and Anthropology. Still, those developments lay in the future. At this juncture, to what extent and in what ways did the spirit that animated Santa Fe's quest to rediscover New Mexico's Spanish roots, to appreciate its history before the American annexation, and to proclaim a distinctive regional identity for the state permeate the University of New Mexico?

The answer is: "fitfully." Each of the four presidents who led the institution between 1901 and 1927 responded in somewhat different ways, but all shared one trait in common: they adhered by and large to the assimilationist line and devoted little attention, if any, to building an institutional environment in which Hispanic students, by finding clear resonances of their own history and culture, could feel equally at home.[6]

The Tight Presidency (1901–1909)

One of the first signs that UNM would create a distinct identity for itself by calling on a unique feature of the state appeared during the presidency of William Tight. Tight's imprint on the university would be felt most strongly in its physical appearance and infrastructure. It is scarcely an exaggeration to say that upon arriving in Albuquerque, he found UNM "to be little more than a name."[7] Tight had to build a university virtually from scratch. The campus site was barren, devoid of trees and plantings, and stood in dire need of classroom buildings and housing for its students. Wanting to know and experience the territory into which he had moved, Tight made frequent excursions to Native American pueblos near and distant. Like the literati in Santa Fe, he was soon entranced by the simple, stark beauty of their adobe structures. Furthermore, his admiration was not passive; he made a close study of Native American architecture, motivated to grasp the details of its design, materials, and methods of construction. He took numerous photographs of pueblo structures and studied their lines, walls, and windows. Inspired by what he saw and learned, Tight decided to "New Mexicanize" the university by adopting the Pueblo Revival style as its unifying architectural motif. Initially, he faced widespread opposition but gradually won over a portion of the critics to his viewpoint—that this style fit perfectly into the surroundings of the university and satisfied requirements of climate, convenience, and economy. It was molded to the communal life of the school, and its form harmonized with the characteristic landscape of New Mexico, "with its boundless plains and the towering mesas and their steep declivities and table like tops."[8]

What is more, Tight's interest was not to be different simply for the sake of being different; it was a way to demonstrate respect for antiquity and tradition, a means of recognizing and honoring something organic in the territory and region. As one architectural critic put it rather loftily, Tight, a native Ohioan, sought "to preserve the building art of a vanishing race and so perpetuate the memory of the most ancient civilization upon this continent."[9] Tight oversaw the planning and construction of four campus structures: a heating plant, two dormitories, and a central administration building. Noting that all of their decorations—exterior and interior—consisted of Native American pictorial art and symbols, the critic continued in the same vein, declaring that the walls of these buildings would serve as "ethnological records." At the same time, the use of Native American architecture, as adapted by the Spanish, was also a way to strike out in a new direction and create something "unique, attractive and distinctly appropriate, a way of breaking . . . with the commonplace and striking the unusual—a new-old style which would make the University of New Mexico absolutely distinctive in college architecture the world over."[10] There was some truth to this claim, or at least to the fact that Tight's bold move achieved notice beyond the borders of the United States. In 1908 the university received a request for descriptions and photographs of its buildings from one Victor Jorbin of Paris, France.[11] Jorbin's interest had evidently been piqued by articles published in "eastern magazines of this country."[12]

Although Tight's own research interests extended into South America (as a geomorphologist, he had a special interest in studying the glacial geography of the Bolivian plateau), they did not lead him to envision a focus, even an elementary one, for Hispanic or Latin American studies in the university. In keeping with the regents' priorities, he oriented the curriculum toward the goal of "modernizing" New Mexico, strengthening the offerings in the sciences, engineering, and music, while displaying minimal concern for creating a more inclusive student body. The curriculum did include Spanish, but the emphasis, in the area of languages and literature, was clearly on Latin and Greek. Still, the addition of a course in 1909 titled "The History of New Mexico" reflected Tight's interest in Southwestern culture and constituted the first step toward incorporating the study of regional history into the university's teaching program.[13] Tight was a popular figure but, for political reasons, was dismissed by the regents in 1909.

The Edward McQueen Gray Presidency (1909–1912)

Things quickly changed under Tight's successor, Edward McQueen Gray, who served as president from 1909 until 1912. Scottish by origin, the University of London–educated Gray was a confirmed Europeanist, grounded in the classics, and one of his first actions as president was to dismiss a young professor of romance languages, Aurelio Espinosa Sr. (see fig. 1). Espinosa was a highly qualified scholar, closely associated with the University of Chicago, from which he received his doctoral degree and where he taught Spanish during three summer quarters (1907–1909) and was made a fellow for the 1908–1909 academic year. A successful member of the UNM faculty since 1902, Espinosa returned to the university from Chicago in 1910 only to be told by Gray that he was "unfit to properly teach the elementary Spanish and French classes" and that his services were no longer needed.[14] Espinosa had been reappointed in 1909 for the next academic year, with no apparent dissenting view, but unhappily for him, he did not fit into Gray's plan to uplift the university by bringing its curriculum into line with that found at long-established universities. Indeed, unbeknownst to Espinosa, soon after his appointment Gray set about recruiting and hiring two new faculty in the languages area, one in the Greek and Latin section and another to teach German. He then replaced Espinosa with a new hire at the instructor level, a non-native speaker of Spanish. Shaken by Gray's action, Espinosa made one attempt to go over his authority by appealing to the Board of Regents, but the regents—on this occasion and contrary to Espinosa's expectations—supported Gray, and Espinosa was gone.[15] His fatal error—in Gray's eyes—was to focus his research on the study of New Mexican folklore and Spanish dialectology, a new and "wonderfully rich and interesting" field of study, which "should aid greatly in writing an adequate account of the territory's past since the Spaniards first appeared on the scene."[16] Rich and interesting it may have been, but not so for Gray. Such interest, for him, was emblematic of UNM's inward-looking ways and intellectual provincialism. In line with this bias, the course on New Mexico history that Tight had introduced was dropped from the curriculum.[17] The irony of Gray's dismissal of Espinosa is that Espinosa, unlike many on the UNM faculty, had an impeccable record of scholarly excellence. He embodied the high standards that Gray sought to instill in the university.

The loss of Espinosa and the elimination of the course on New Mexico history epitomized one side of Gray—his Eurocentrism and attachment to rigid preconceptions. Yet, as we will see, there was another side to Gray. He was a hard person to pin down, an odd combination of the refined classicist, possessing the mannerisms and ways of speech of the man who had left Britain but not "Britishness," versus the man who was eager to experience life as it was lived in the American West and the territory of New Mexico. Gray had immigrated to New Mexico with a group of English settlers and developed a genuine affection for the land. He owned a farm near Loving and later moved to Carlsbad, where he took a keen interest in local affairs and strove to improve conditions for the town's workers. Later, after his return to England, he composed poems about New Mexico, calling it "El Estado del Sol" (the sun-drenched state) and professed to miss it.[18] During his four years as UNM president, he traveled widely around New Mexico to give presentations and promote the university.

Nevertheless, Gray's evident fondness for New Mexico did not extend to full acceptance of the architectural aesthetic decreed by his predecessor. Gray moved to repudiate, in part, Tight's embrace of the Pueblo Revival model, electing to mingle it with the California Mission style, which he preferred for what he considered its more cosmopolitan and softening qualities. Furthermore, the opposition (some of which appears to have been racially tinged) to Pueblo Revival architecture as the model for the university had not dissipated entirely, and Gray tapped into it: He "found many good people in Albuquerque to side with him, people who had always been a little horrified at the idea of adapting the cliff dwellings to the uses of 'White folks.'"[19] But like Tight before him and the presidents who succeeded him, Gray was able to play off the considerable interest that the novel architecture of the UNM campus elicited across the United States and abroad. For example, in August 1911, Gray wrote to a certain James L. Rodgers to acknowledge receipt of a copy of "P.B.T." that Rogers had sent to him. Whatever this was, it included information on how the architectural distinction of the University of New Mexico "had penetrated as far as Argentina." In his reply, Gray mentioned that illustrations of UNM's buildings had also appeared in some Brazilian publications, adding that "as we feel particularly in touch with the

FIGURE 1 "Aurelio Espinosa in front of a building on the Stanford
University campus," 1923. A successful UNM faculty member since 1902
and pioneering student of Spanish dialectology in New Mexico, Espinosa
was dismissed by President Gray in 1910 on the grounds that he was unfit
to teach elementary Spanish. Espinosa was immediately hired by Stanford
University, where he had a long and distinguished career, serving as
chairman of its Department of Romance Languages from 1933 until his
retirement in 1947. Aurelio Espinosa and Family Papers (MSS 999, box 6,
folder 5), Center for Southwest Research, University Libraries, University
of New Mexico. Photo by Helen V. Terry. Courtesy of CSWR.

South American Republics I cannot but think that there is some appropriateness in their thus noticing us."[20]

This suggestion by Gray that a special connection existed between New Mexico and the Latin American nations anticipated an initiative he put forward near the end of his tenure as president. That end, as it happened, was close at hand. In hiring Gray, the regents had thought they would open UNM to more worldly influences, but Gray had clearly carried his remit too far and, in doing so, rubbed too many people the wrong way. Dissatisfaction spread among the faculty with how Gray was managing the university. By the end of 1911, a majority of the regents had come around to that view and lost faith in Gray. The following year he was terminated.

Just before he left, however, Gray made a surprising move, one that denoted a change of heart and a conversion to Tight's belief in the value of cultivating the multiracial, multiethnic heritage of New Mexico. In a piece titled "The Spanish Language in New Mexico: A National Resource," Gray proposed that UNM should establish a Spanish American college.[21] In laying out his reasons, he first struck the familiar note of "modernization." The college he had in mind would help promote the welfare of the state and enhance its status as it prepared to join the union. Posing the rhetorical question—What were the special resources at the disposal of New Mexicans?—Gray answered: the Spanish language. Unfortunately, because Spanish had been depreciated by the Anglo population and its use actively suppressed by the federal government, it came to be devalued as well by those who possessed it. This was a great mistake; bilingualism was an invaluable asset. Still arguing the practical side of his proposal, Gray asked: How could New Mexico best exploit this capability? He saw two possibilities: first— and this became a leitmotif down to and through Zimmerman's presidency—it needed to recognize how important relations with the Latin American republics would increasingly be to the United States in the commercial, diplomatic, and political spheres. Second, it needed to leverage its strategic advantage, since in New Mexico the Spanish language had greater currency and importance in the life of its people than was the case in any other state.

Gray tried to ground his argument and reasoning in pragmatism and hard facts. Cultivation of the language could lead to jobs in businesses, corporations, and different areas of government service. The opportunity existed, but would New Mexico seize it? The course of action that Gray advocated was a federal appropriation to establish and endow a Spanish American college in the university that would utilize this inheritance of New Mexicans. In Gray's words: "The

Spanish American College would become, not merely for New Mexico, but for the United States, the training ground and place of preparation for active service in the Latin American countries."[22] He had apparently discussed the idea with and claimed to have received endorsement for it from the Chilean and Brazilian ambassadors to the United States as well as from President Taft.[23] Gray thought the time was ripe, since New Mexico was now a state. His proposal generated a great deal of interest, but, in the end, funding could not be secured. As war clouds began to gather over Europe, Washington's customary disinterest in Latin America asserted itself.

As we have seen, Gray framed his proposal around practical arguments that he felt would strike a chord with all the factions that had clamored and fought for statehood. There was a more radical side to it, however, an argument grounded in moral considerations and in the wish to address historical grievances. His plan, Gray stressed, "would go far to obliterate the lines of division which have too long marred . . . the state, and to wipe out the memory of past misunderstandings and distrust. The state of New Mexico . . . must, to a large extent, stand or fall according to the manner in which the question of race and language is handled by its citizens."[24] Thus going full circle, Gray wrote, apropos of the issue of according Spanish full equality of treatment: "The right of the Spanish American citizens [i.e., Nuevomexicanos] to the unrestricted development of his [*sic*] racial inheritance in language is incontestable, and the direction of our duty must lie in the freest concession of that right and the most generous grant of opportunity for its exercise."[25] One wonders what Aurelio Espinosa, now embarked on a long career as a Spanish professor at Stanford University, chose to make of this belated declaration. Gray's eleventh-hour insight into the multiple benefits of preserving and cultivating the Spanish language in New Mexico made his dismissal of Espinosa look even more rash and misconceived. Espinosa, moreover, was a native Nuevomexicano (born in southern Colorado). He thus grasped, both intuitively and intellectually, how and why regional studies might at least be worked into the university's curriculum, if not made central to them. Had Gray possessed a more open outlook at the beginning of his presidency, he would likely have seen Espinosa's interest in researching the history and development of the Spanish language and Hispanic culture in the region as a field worthy not only of scholarly investigation but as one with the practical application that he now heralded.

The David Ross Boyd Presidency (1912–1919)

Gray was succeeded as president of UNM by David Ross Boyd, whose tenure lasted from 1912 until his resignation in 1919. Boyd was a study in contrast to Gray, very different in temperament and training. He had served as president of the University of Oklahoma from its opening in 1892 until 1908. Although he lacked Gray's scholarly credentials and reputation, Boyd brought a fund of successful experience in campus construction and design, student recruitment, private fund-raising and lobbying for federal grants, and the development of extension services and outreach programs to tie the university to the tax-paying community. Gray's firing had left UNM, in the words of a local judge, Clarence M. Botts, "a school little known and less respected."[26] Boyd's immediate challenges, as he saw them, were to expand the campus, which was still confined to its original twenty acres, fund and carry out the construction of new buildings, increase enrollment, and create a constituency and base of support for the university that reached beyond Albuquerque and its environs.

Even more indicative, however, of how Boyd would construe his role and mission as UNM president were the four years that he spent, between 1908 and 1912, supervising the educational work of the Women's Board of Home Missions of the Presbyterian Church. This work had led him to travel the state, visiting all of the board's mission schools in the New Mexico territory. He thus was "no stranger to the bilingualism of New Mexico."[27] Nonetheless, his extensive contact with Hispanic culture in New Mexico did not lead him to believe that it stood on an equal footing with Anglo culture or make him at all sympathetic to the Hispano Cause. On the contrary, he was assimilationist to the core, a belief that he expressed in a variety of ways.

For example, newly arrived in Albuquerque, Boyd wrote to a friend (and Home Missions board official) in New York, M. C. Allaben, that he was trying to get an athletic park built near the university, to be used by UNM, the local high school, the Indian School, and the Menaul School (a Presbyterian mission school for Hispanic boys and young men), so that the town could "develop a real American interest in at least football and baseball. They are very much needed, for the amusements that are provided here consist largely of fake prizefights and picture shows."[28] Boyd may have left his position with the Home Missions board, but he continued to think and, to some extent, act as though he were still in the board's employ, declaring in another letter to Allaben: "As soon as things settle down here, I think the work among the Mexicans ought to be thoroughly organized and pushed."²⁹ For Boyd, the missionary schools were the source of moral and material improvement for the native population and the proper model for education: "[A]lmost in every instance where a Mexican family showed improvement in home surroundings and public spirit in the community," he wrote to Katherine Birdsall, an officer of the Home Missions board, "they had been trained in the Mission Schools . . . supported by our [illegible] Churches."³⁰ As these references indicate, Boyd drew a sharp distinction between the Anglo and the Hispanic populations of New Mexico. Like so many of his compatriots, he viewed the latter as a different people; to him they were "Mexicans" and needed to be acculturated and assimilated into "American" society and, critically important, make English their primary language.

Given his wide travels around the state (by his own account, he was out on the road approximately two-thirds of the time, trying to generate greater awareness of and support for the university) and extensive dealings with Spanish-speaking New Mexicans, Boyd was surprisingly naïve about Hispano-Anglo relations. The relative absence of overt expressions of hostility and grievance led him to the simplistic conclusion that relations between the two groups were optimal. "The educational work in this state," he wrote to a friend and colleague in 1915, "is very interesting. We have a population of about 180,000 Spanish Americans, or Mexicans, and probably the same number, or a little more, of Americans. It is remarkable how well the two races are getting on together. The leading men among both peoples are studiously and very effectively doing everything they can to allay and extinguish all race prejudice. Indeed, little prejudice exists except among the recent comers of both races."³¹ Ironically, at almost the identical moment, Aurelio Espinosa authored a rebuttal to an article that had appeared in *The San Francisco Call*, denigrating the Spanish and Portuguese as "miserable failures among the nations." Espinosa wrote, "It must be very painful, even to our Anglo-Saxon Americans, to live in a part of America where Spanish tradition, blood, and culture are everywhere evident. In question of racial prejudice, we in the United States have advanced very little. Indeed, racial prejudice [of which Espinosa knew personally more than a little] is in some respects becoming more and more pronounced."³² Although Espinosa was reacting to conditions that he found in California, it is difficult not to surmise that he would not have had New Mexico in mind as well.

One might say that Boyd's view of Hispano-Anglo relations contained the early flowering of the tricultural image. Interestingly, that same idealized view eventually seeped into his decisions about the architectural style of campus buildings. Initially, he adhered to Tight's belief that UNM should not mimic outside styles, but instead evolve an authentic local style born of indigenous influences and tradition. In 1913, he wrote to an acquaintance that "he [Tight] was hampered by lack of funds, so that he could not carry out his ideas thoroughly … but he did a splendid thing. The idea of having the grouping of the buildings, the style of architecture and position in the landscape [and] surroundings to represent, as much as possible, the historic background of the state, was most commendable."[33] By 1915, however, Boyd had moved into Gray's camp, announcing that the architectural plan for the campus would follow a hybrid scheme and combine the original Pueblo Revival style with the features of California Mission architecture. With this compromise, Boyd convinced himself that "he had mastered whatever difficulties previous UNM administrations had faced about New Mexico's Hispanic and Indian cultures."[34] It was a way of acknowledging the powerful impact that they had had, and continued to have, on the built environment. For Boyd, the mixture and blending of the two styles would be the architectural expression of the harmony that he predicted would soon come to characterize social relations between UNM's Anglo and Hispanic students.

He may have been wrong on this score, but Boyd was serious about wanting to recruit Hispanic students and build up their enrollment at UNM.[35] That concern was matched by his recognition that UNM's academic program was deficient in not offering any courses on local and regional history or archaeology for either the pre-Colombian or Spanish colonial eras. Anticipating Zimmerman's later moves, Boyd saw the utility of working out some relationship between the School of American Archaeology in Santa Fe (it had not yet become the independent and renamed School of American Research) and the University of New Mexico. While nothing concrete actually came to fruition that officially tied the two institutions together, Boyd and Edgar Hewett did work toward that end. Boyd was particularly anxious to incorporate some relevant history courses into the UNM curriculum. In 1913, he wrote to Ralph Twitchell, a leading authority on New Mexico history and archival resources, in connection with the appearance of Twitchell's new journal, *Old Santa Fe*, that once he could get the "history work" organized better, he would like to have "the very interesting local history of the state" properly "exploited," that is, integrated into UNM's courses of study.[36]

Two years later, in 1915, he not only succeeded on this front but considerably broadened the scope of "history work" to encompass Spanish America. Boyd never issued the kind of plea that Gray did with respect to arguing for bilingualism in New Mexico, with its implicit endorsement of cultural pluralism ("the question of race and language")—that would have directly contradicted his full-blown assimilationist views—but he made several moves (like the cultivation of Hewett) that kept a certain momentum going. Perhaps the most notable was his decision, in 1915, to add Roscoe Hill to the Department of History faculty. Hill taught at UNM from 1915 to 1917 and again from 1919 to 1920. During the interim between these two appointments he served as president of the Spanish-American Normal School in El Rito, New Mexico. Hill was the first Latin Americanist historian at UNM and possessed excellent qualifications. He had lived in Cuba for some five years (1904–1908), where he served as head of a foreign Christian missionary society school, had later been employed (1911–1913) by the Carnegie Institution's Department of History to research documents in the Archive of the Indies, and had lectured in Latin American history and Spanish history at New York University, Columbia University, and the University of California–Berkeley.

Prior to his arrival, the UNM Department of History was top-heavy with courses on European history, with minor attention paid to US history, and—as earlier noted—not a single course on the Southwest or Latin America. Hill turned this concentration around.[37] In a letter he wrote when he applied for reappointment to UNM in 1919, Hill cogently explained why New Mexico's historical ties to Latin America offered it a special opportunity, a chance to stand out in the scholarly world. As he stated, "The early history of the Southwest is bound up with that of Spanish America. It offers a wide field for research and New Mexico should be a center for this work. As yet little has been done in this state towards developing this line of research."[38]

Whether Hill had planted this idea earlier with President Boyd, or whether the impetus came from some other source, Boyd revived Gray's parting proposal and called, in 1915, for the creation at UNM of a School of Latin American Affairs. For Boyd, however, while the school might indirectly have scholarly research as a goal, its real purpose was practical—to train students for careers in business, diplomacy, and government service, for which the ability to speak Spanish came into play, and not just any students, but Hispanic students in particular. The percentage of such students at the University of New Mexico was still pathetically small—barely more than 2 percent at a time when total enrollment was still in the low hundreds. Although, as we have seen, Boyd deceived himself into thinking that relations between Anglos and Hispanos in New Mexico, because they were not often openly discussed, were essentially problem free, he was anxious to address the underrepresentation of Nuevomexicanos in the university. The School of Latin American Affairs, he felt, could be an effective recruiting tool. Boyd understood that Hispanic youth were likely to feel more positive about attending UNM if their heritage was given a prominent place. Through the proposed school, people across New Mexico would see that the university indeed existed as "the servant of all the people," not just the Anglo elite.[39] In this connection, Boyd dispatched Hill to Guadalupe County in eastern New Mexico, where he addressed audiences in Spanish on "opportunity in education." The *Albuquerque Evening Herald* reported that Hispanic attendees "felt gratified that the university could and should send a speaker to address them in their own language."[40] The school could also draw attention to UNM on the national level and contribute to the improvement of inter-American relations. A little more than a decade later, Frank Reeve, then a graduate student at UNM and later a member of its history department, summed up Boyd's ambitions for the school as follows: "A School of Latin American Affairs was organized in 1915 for the purpose of developing and strengthening the relations between the United States and Latin America; also, to meet the needs of the native [by which Reeve meant Hispanic, not Native American] population of New Mexico."[41] To this end, special courses were outlined in Latin American affairs. Boyd's proposed school, however, was never more than embryonic. It fell victim to the same combination of factors that had doomed Gray's: the country was now even closer to its entry into World War I; nationalist sentiment ran high; from the East Coast to the West Coast universities felt strong pressure to orient their curricula in ways that would emphasize "Americanness" and patriotism. The nation's attention was thus focused elsewhere, and securing funding for a proposal that centered on benefiting the interests of New Mexico's Spanish-speaking population was simply not a realistic proposition. In New Mexico, not even the Mexican-born governor, Octaviano Larrazolo, an otherwise eloquent spokesman for the Hispano Cause, could be persuaded to support it, given the state's bleak finances. Rejected in his appeal for a major increase in UNM's budget, Boyd resigned as president of the university.

The David Spence Hill Presidency (1919–1927)

The man tapped to succeed Boyd was David Spence Hill, an educational psychologist whose past work, because it dealt with the causes of failure on the part of school- and college-age students, would, so the regents thought, enable him to find ways to "modernize" the university by applying more rigorous standards of evaluation and better techniques for learning and instruction. In this way, the university could play a lead role in producing a more educated citizenry, who in turn would possess the knowledge and skills to advance the state's economic growth and prosperity.

Like Boyd, Hill believed resolutely that Anglo culture was more advanced, but he took this belief even further by deeming it to be the inevitable result of "racial differences." Steeped in pseudoscientific theories of the day, Hill subscribed to the notion that Euro-Americans were inherently superior to other people. His bias emerged right after his appointment. While in Chicago for the 1919 conference of the National Association of State Universities, Hill met with Abraham Flexner, director of the Rockefeller Foundation's General Education Board (GEB). Like Gray and Boyd before him, Hill sought to attract private support to UNM. In his meeting with Flexner, Hill drew attention to the heavy concentration of Hispanos in New Mexico. UNM and the state in general, he stressed, faced two problems with educating native New Mexicans: first, very few secured a high school education (as he put it, he encountered in the state a population that was "unusually illiterate"), and, second, this drawback compounded "the unusual difficulties presented by problems of race, finance, and . . . by enormous distances."[42] Aware of the Rockefeller Foundation's long record of support for black colleges, Hill informed Flexner that "the peculiar racial problems in this state are not dissimilar to the problems of race and politics now urgent in the Southern States." He hoped, he told Flexner, that when the GEB allocated funds for fiscal year 1921, it would take into special account "the strategic position of this state from the standpoints of education and 'Americanization.'"[43] For reasons not made clear, however, UNM's application to the GEB did not succeed.

Consistent with his view that the most pervasive psychological issue in New Mexico was "racial differences," Hill had a very low opinion of Hispanic peoples in general. He saw them as "incapable of self-government."[44] Although he had never been south of El Paso, Hill was convinced that "some races [living in what he characterized as the "tissue-paper" republics of Latin America] are still in their childhood in matters of finance."[45] Yet, for all that he dismissed the region as a political and cultural backwater, Hill wasted little time in developing plans for introducing and expanding Latin American course offerings, and his proposals to the federal government and private foundations always referred to UNM's strong commitment to Latin American studies.[46] On the recommendation of Herbert Bolton, David Hill filled Roscoe Hill's vacant position by hiring a recent graduate of the Berkeley program, Charles Coan. In accepting his appointment, Coan indicated that he planned to offer a course titled "History of the New

World" and that it "would naturally be based on his [Bolton's] syllabus."[47] Hill replied that he thought this an "excellent" idea. Hill also took a keen interest in following the studies of a UNM graduate and native-Spanish-speaking New Mexican, Anita Osuna Carr (see fig. 2). Interestingly, Osuna Carr had worked as a teaching fellow for Aurelio Espinosa at Stanford University while pursuing a master's degree in romance languages. In 1922, Hill invited her to return to UNM as an instructor in Spanish. She initially rejected his offer, but they subsequently came to an agreement. She was the first Hispanic woman to receive a permanent faculty appointment at UNM, gaining the rank of assistant professor in 1925.[48] The regents were very much in favor of Osuna Carr's appointment, as they thought it could strengthen the university's ties to the community.

The schedule of classes for the period 1920–1927 shows that some progress, albeit modest, was indeed made toward expanding the number and range of courses pertaining to Latin America and the Southwest as well as to Spanish language and literature.[49] For example, in 1920 the university offered only three courses in Spanish versus eleven in English. The real strength of the curriculum during these years lay in the physical and natural sciences, electrical and chemical engineering, home economics, and English literature. In 1922–1923, however, Spanish began to gain ground, with seven courses offered, and by 1926–1927, it had pulled more or less even with English, though the latter had greater depth and specialization through courses offered on individual authors. The curriculum in history, too, saw some noteworthy development in line with Hill's desire to broaden it. In addition to standard courses in the American and European fields, Charles Coan taught a new seminar in New Mexico history as well as a course titled "History of the Arid Southwest." It does not appear, though, that he managed at any point to introduce Bolton's "History of the New World." The history section was further strengthened by the hiring, in 1925, of the Harvard-educated France V. Scholes. The addition of Scholes (who began a long, rich, and productive association with UNM, though one interrupted for many years—see chapter 2) gave Coan room to offer courses on the history of Spain and South America. A course on Mexican history was added during the first semester of the 1926–1927 academic year. By this time, there was a clear shift away from Europe to the New World, and while Scholes left in the fall of that year to take up a research position with the Carnegie Institution, his departure did not stop this new momentum.

Hill's efforts to build up course offerings in Spanish and in Southwestern and Latin American studies were paralleled by the recurrence of efforts to develop a

FIGURE 2 *left* Anita Osuna Carr, 1937. Hired by President Hill in the early 1920s, Osuna Carr was the first Hispanic woman to receive a permanent faculty appointment at the University of New Mexico. She specialized in studying the problems of bicultural, bilingual education, with a particular focus on assembling collections of children's literature. Anita Osuna Carr Collection (PICT 2019–012, unprocessed, image no. 003), Center for Southwest Research, University Libraries, University of New Mexico. Photo courtesy of Quito Osuna Carr. Courtesy of CSWR.

FIGURE 3 *right* "Edgar Lee Hewett with bear cub at Corralitos Ranch, Chihuahua, Mexico," 1922. President Zimmerman's two immediate predecessors, David Ross Boyd and David Spence Hill, saw the potential advantages of cultivating Hewett, with the aim of forging some relationship between the School of American Archaeology (renamed the School of American Research and, today, the School for Advanced Research), which Hewett directed, and UNM. Zimmerman brought these overtures to a successful conclusion in 1927. Photo by Kenneth Chapman, courtesy of Palace of the Governors Photo Archives (NMHM/DCA), neg. no. 22440.

formal connection between the university and the School of American Research. The prospect was actively discussed in 1920, with Hill stating, "the university desires that each of its students have a general knowledge of the remarkable ethnological and archaeological background of the history of New Mexico."[50] He expressed the hope that Edgar Hewett (see fig. 3) would accept appointment as a "non-resident lecturer" in the graduate school (which was just getting off the ground). Hewett was receptive to the idea, although it is not clear if such an arrangement was actually worked out at this juncture.

Hill also tried to take advantage of the presence of outside scholars who came to New Mexico to do fieldwork. For example, in the summer of 1924, word came to him that the Harvard archaeologist Alfred Kidder was in the state excavating ruins in the Pecos area for the National Geographic Society. Hill lost no time in writing him to ask if he would deliver a lecture at UNM. Kidder gladly obliged and gave four additional lectures at UNM during the following summer. Hill's concern that UNM students acquire an understanding and appreciation of New Mexico's past (whatever his thoughts about the meaning and effects of its "racial differences") was also evident in the invitations that he extended to local officials to present lectures on Hispanic and Native American culture. When the construction of Sara Raynolds Hall (at that time for home economics) was completed in 1921 (in modified Spanish Pueblo style), Hill wanted portraits for its walls that expressed the "uniqueness of New Mexico," and he contacted the artists Ernest Blumenschein and Gustave Baumann for this purpose.

Like Boyd, Hill saw the gross underrepresentation of Hispanos in the university as a serious problem that needed remedying. Although hardly a scientific measure, the analysis of the student body by surname provides one gauge of the severe imbalance between the two groups.[51] The university's annual report for the period November 1918–December 1919, for example, lists 364 enrollees, of whom a mere 9, or 2.47 percent, were Hispanic.[52] Using the same measure, multiyear statistics on candidates for degrees offer a similar picture: 3 of 33 in 1922, 0 of 25 in 1924, 2 of 44 in 1925, 1 of 48 in 1926, and 2 of 43 in 1927.[53] Their consistently low numbers were attributable to several factors. For Hill, given his racialized views, social and environmental factors went only so far in explaining the inadequate preparation of Hispanos for academic participation and success. Nonetheless, he also cited a pattern of neglect by the federal government, which after annexation had made no investment in bringing education to native New Mexicans or to offering them any other benefits of membership in the American community, as it had done in Puerto Rico, Hawaii, and the Philippines.

His solution for this welter of problems was to resurrect a version of the failed schemes of Gray and Boyd and propose, in 1922, the creation at UNM of a "School of Spanish Literature and Life." Hill explained its purposes as:

(a) study and conversation of Spanish literature and culture as it exists in New Mexico;

(b) the training of teachers in Spanish language and literature, both for their specific work and also in the ideals of the United States;

(c) preparation of young men and women for business or governmental service in Spanish-speaking countries; and

(d) research into conditions affecting the welfare of the Spanish-speaking people in New Mexico as related to the whole population of the state and of the nation. I have reference to sociological surveys . . . studies of vocations in agriculture, commerce, manufacture, mining, etc., as affecting the Spanish-American people.[54]

The wording, or language, of Hill's proposal might lead one to think that he had developed a more pluralist-minded outlook, but such was not really the case. The intent behind the school was not to instill Spanish-speaking students with a renewed sense of pride in their cultural heritage, but rather to pull them into the American mainstream. Hill's cultural blinders had boxed him in; he had never known how to integrate the university into the life of the state. All the same, he knew that his proposal stood a much better chance of success if it had the support of the Hispanic community. To that end, Hill secured endorsements for his proposal from five prominent members of the Hispanic elite: Antonio Sedillo, Octaviano Larrazolo, Benigno Cárdenas Hernández, Adelina "Nina" Otero-Warren, and Dennis Chávez, as well as from Governor Merritt Mechem. Their reasons for supporting the proposal, however, were specific to each. For example, one of the more enthusiastic proponents was Antonio Sedillo, who served in the New Mexico legislature and on the UNM Board of Regents during the 1920s. For Sedillo, the school would not only spotlight Hispanic history and culture, reinforce the Spanish language, and promote closer relations between the United States and its sister republics to the south but, of equal importance, would help fulfill one of his prime goals: the "Americanization" of Nuevomexicanos. "Here," as he wrote to Hill, "is also a fertile field for the thorough Americanization of our citizenship."[55] Another supporter was the former governor and future US representative and senator Octaviano Larrazolo. In Larrazolo's case, the particular virtue of Hill's proposal was the possibility it offered for correcting the monolingualism of Euro-Americans. Their English-only attitude, in his judgment, created a barrier to forging stronger commercial and cultural relations with Mexico and the South American countries. He contrasted the inability of most North Americans to speak with Latin Americans "in their own tongue" and, by extension, the failure of the US government to cultivate friendly commercial relations with the Latin American countries to the success, on both counts, of Germans and the German government. Still another promoter of the school was Adelina "Nina" Otero-Warren. Her motivations for supporting Hill's proposal were similar to Sedillo's and Larrazolo's in some respects, but also different in spirit. Otero-Warren was a prominent figure on the Santa Fe political and cultural scene, a pioneering state-level suffragette and educational leader and also a foremost advocate of the "Spanish revival." Far from recasting the mind-set of Hispanic youth and developing a vanguard for the Americanization of Nuevomexicanos, Otero-Warren saw in the proposed school an opportunity to revive and enrich Hispanic arts and crafts and folkloric traditions and to spread awareness and appreciation of them among Anglo groups. To her way of thinking, the need for education and cultural sensitivity belonged as much if not more to the non-Hispanic as to the Hispanic populations. Finally, Dennis Chávez—then practicing law in Albuquerque and newly elected to the state House of Representatives—offered yet another perspective on Hill's proposal. In his view, if the school could be established, its most valuable contribution would lie in the studies that it carried out of the impoverished social and economic conditions under which a great many Spanish-speaking New Mexicans lived. In this respect, as we will see, Chávez was a forerunner to a number of intellectuals and activists, such as George Sánchez, Joaquín Ortega, and Paul Walter Jr., who advocated and carved out a role for the University of New Mexico in community-based research and activity.

Armed with such support, varied as it might be, Hill submitted his proposal to the Carnegie Foundation for the Advancement of Teaching. Its president, Henry Smith Pritchett, had visited UNM earlier in 1922, and Hill —based on his conversations with Pritchett—had reason to think the foundation might be receptive to his proposal. In the end, however, although Pritchett and the Carnegie Foundation's trustees found the proposal worthy of serious consideration, they did not fund it, partly because of other commitments as well as its steep cost (a $280,000 endowment, or more than $4,000,000 in 2017 dollars—half to come from the state of New Mexico, half as a match from the Carnegie Foundation) and partly because, in their judgment, it did not spell out in sufficient depth or detail just how it would benefit Spanish-speaking New Mexicans on the local level or how the research component would work. Hill's proposal thus went the way of its two predecessors. In some respects, the weakness that the Carnegie Foundation had identified in this latest proposal could also be found in the first two. Each of the three had its strong points, but they all relied too heavily on airy generalizations and platitudes. It was fine to talk about capitalizing on the Spanish-speaking abilities of native New Mexicans to help further relations with Latin America and to drive up the number of Hispanic students at UNM by pointing to enhanced employment prospects in that part of the world, but how would these initiatives filter out and down to address the long-standing needs of Spanish-speaking communities in the state? That question and others like it had not been worked into the equation, nor had the complexities and challenges of ethnic identity and intercultural relations, either in UNM or in New Mexico as a whole, been laid out empirically.

By 1927, David Spence Hill had fallen out of favor with the regents, and they elected to replace him. Slowly but surely, the next decade would bring a more sophisticated approach on the part of university administrators, an approach based on the principle—borne out in field studies (although perhaps exaggerated to a certain degree)—that the regional and the hemispheric were intertwined and shared numerous elements in common. The conviction that the Hispanic Southwest and Spanish America not only deserved to be studied in depth but—insofar as certain past and present conditions were concerned—needed to be studied comparatively, within the context of their shared history, became for a time an article of faith for many and was woven into the fabric of the university. Its greatest and most persuasive champion would be Joaquín Ortega.

⩸

CHAPTER TWO

Developing the Southwest–
Latin America Focus, 1927–1940

When Joaquín Ortega made his annual Easter recess visit to New Mexico in 1931 and met James Zimmerman for the first time, the university was still in its early formative stage. Only four years had elapsed since David Spence Hill's departure, and the country was now mired in the Great Depression. A poor state had slid even deeper into poverty. The dawn of a new era for the University of New Mexico, one of growth and expansion, would apparently have to await better times. Refreshingly, however, the regents' appointment of Zimmerman in 1927 as the next president upset this calculus. Zimmerman possessed all the necessary qualities for successfully leading a university. He valued learning and the academic life, had a cosmopolitan outlook, believed in the mission of educating young men and women, and knew how to navigate among competing factions and—to the extent possible—unite them in pursuit of a common vision. Moreover, he understood the role of the institution in promoting the advancement of the state and realized the importance of "networking" on a local, regional, and national scale to gain support and funding for special initiatives. Although a product of the lower Midwest, he was the right person for the University of New Mexico because he cared about the state, genuinely valued the amalgam of cultures that historically defined it, and—after some early stumbles—tried on various fronts to introduce a similar diversity in the institution.

The man Ortega met and with whom he conversed for several hours had devised a new blueprint for the university. More than a decade later, Ortega recalled that meeting, during which Zimmerman had elaborated on his ideas for building UNM to, as Ortega put it, "academic size." As Ortega continued: "He also mentioned the inter-cultural problem of our state and was convinced of the need of solving it through a determined effort of education of the minority and the majority, so that the state could play the role it should in inter-American relations. He saw the international possibilities of New Mexico as the converging point of the three main ethnic groups of this hemisphere."[1] While Zimmerman had made a series of important points to Ortega, one in particular stands out: his implied belief that the state's ability to assume an important role in the area of inter-American relations was contingent on solving the existing problem of intercultural relations within New Mexico. Others would soon call Zimmerman's attention to UNM's own failings in this regard.

In sketching a broad vision for the future direction of UNM during his inauguration as president in September 1927, Zimmerman (see fig. 4) had emphasized some of the same ideas as he did four years on in his meeting with Ortega, if perhaps phrasing them a little differently. He stressed:

Indian art, architecture, and art in general have a distinct place in the intellectual life of New Mexico, and should therefore find a place in the university. I . . . urge permanent and advanced study of them in the future. . . . A more exhaustive study of Southwestern history, which links New Mexico with the early phases of the expansion of Europe, will furnish valuable illustration of many important frontier problems. . . . Our important relations with Mexico and other Latin-American nations constitute a chapter in American diplomacy and foreign service which our students should not only know, but in which because of our language relations, they should have special training for leadership, both in commerce and diplomacy.[2]

Developing the Core Program

In announcing that he wanted to expand the university's focus on Native American and Southwestern studies and also promote an engagement with Latin America, Zimmerman at least had some foundation on which to build. It will be recalled that President Hill had made three faculty hires in those two fields, plus one in Spanish: Roscoe Hill, who was rehired in 1919 only to resign precipitously a year later, to take up a position in the Library of Congress; Charles Coan (the replacement for Roscoe Hill), France Scholes (see fig. 5), and Anita Osuna Carr. Osuna Carr soon became a mainstay of the team that Zimmerman assembled to advance the Southwest–Latin American initiative, and Coan most certainly would have as well, but his time at UNM was not destined to last much longer. Scholes, who emerged as one of the country's preeminent scholars in the field of colonial New Mexican history, would have two careers at UNM. Although the first ended in 1931 and the second commenced only in 1945, he remained in

FIGURE 4 "James F. Zimmerman seated at his desk." University of New Mexico Student Publications Board Records (UNMA 146, box 5), Center for Southwest Research, University Libraries, University of New Mexico. Courtesy of CSWR.

close contact with President Zimmerman throughout the 1930s and early 1940s and greatly assisted the university in strengthening its Hispanic Southwest and Latin American programs.

Seeking to fulfill his inaugural pledge, Zimmerman significantly increased the number of faculty who specialized in the Southwest and Latin America. Among those hired in the first seven years after he became president were Lloyd S. Tireman (education), Edgar Lee Hewett (anthropology/archaeology), Lansing Bloom (history), Donald Brand (anthropology and geography), Francis M. Kercheville (Spanish language and literature), Arthur L. Campa (Spanish language and Southwest Hispanic folklore), Clyde Kluckhohn (anthropology/archaeology), and Mela Sedillo (Hispanic arts and crafts). As will be seen, all of these teachers turn up as important figures in this story, and several later intertwine closely with Joaquín Ortega in his sometimes-embattled efforts to implement the full range of programs eventually offered by UNM's School of

Inter-American Affairs. The number and range of courses and allied programs devoted to the Southwest and Latin America quickly expanded as well.[3]

Tireman's interest lay in the problem of minority and rural education, along with the problem of Spanish-speaking students in New Mexico; that is, the problems faced, as he put it, by children "who are in the midst of a two-language environment."[4] In 1930, when the San José Demonstration and Experimental School was begun under the administration of UNM, he became its director.[5] Campa, Kercheville, Kluckhohn, and Sedillo (see plate 1) all joined the faculty at approximately the same time: 1931–1932. Kercheville, a protégé of Ortega's at the University of Wisconsin, was also keenly interested in the problems of bilingual education, from preschool to university level. He was one of the first to face squarely the issue of cultural relations at UNM and endeavored through various initiatives to bridge the gap between Hispanic and Anglo students. Campa graduated from UNM in 1928. Earlier supported through a fellowship funded by Senator Bronson Cutting, he returned as an instructor in 1932 to open the field of Southwestern folklore in the university. Under his direction, the program in folklore, as taught during the 1930s in the Department of Romance Languages, became the largest of its kind in the United States.[6] Brand's interests spanned the Southwest and Latin America. He wrote on such topics as "New Mexico's prehistory," "pottery types in Northern Mexico," "prehistoric trade in the Southwest," and the "origin and cultivation of New World cultivated plants."[7]

FIGURE 5   France V. Scholes. Although on the UNM faculty only sporadically during the 1920s until 1931, Scholes remained in close touch with President Zimmerman and returned permanently to UNM in 1946. His painstaking archival research and the publications that flowed from it helped secure the UNM Department of History's high reputation in the field of Spanish colonial history. He was a strong supporter of Joaquín Ortega and the School of Inter-American Affairs. France V. Scholes Pictorial Collection (box 1, folder 1, PICT 0000–360), Center for Southwest Research, University Libraries, University of New Mexico. Courtesy of CSWR.

He was thus in the very mold that the program initially grew into, a broad canvas of anthropological, archaeological, linguistic, historical, and geographic research with, in his case, Mexico, Peru, and the American Southwest as interrelated areas of study. The case of Edgar Hewett, which relates to Bloom and Kluckhohn as well, is especially important because it exemplifies how Zimmerman, operating with and from a very limited budget and resource base, sought from the start (as had presidents Gray, Boyd, and Hill before him) to forge alliances and capitalize on relationships with external agencies and offices as a way of building his Southwest–Latin America focus within the university and gaining support without. Somewhat paradoxically, as this focus was sharpened, it also further exposed and accentuated ethnic and racial tensions and cleavages within the university.[8]

The passage of years and the steady advance of the university enabled Zimmerman to fulfill the ambitions that Tight, Boyd, and Hill had entertained to create some official tie between UNM and the Santa Fe branch of the Archaeological Institute of America and its successor, the independent School of American Research. During the spring and summer of 1927, Zimmerman and Hewett, aided by Paul Walter, associate director of the SAR and a man of considerable influence in Santa Fe business and political circles, entered into discussions about creating a formal partnership between the university and the School of American Research. Both parties stood to gain through such a cooperative venture, especially UNM. With the resources of the SAR added to the university's budget, Zimmerman was able to realize one of his major goals, the founding of a freestanding Department of Archaeology and Anthropology. The SAR's core mission was to preserve and study the unique cultural heritage of the Southwest, but its archaeological work also extended into Mexico, Guatemala, and South America. The Museum of New Mexico, established by the territorial legislature in 1909 and focused both on preserving the artistic traditions of Native Americans in the Southwest and on documenting and interpreting the history of New Mexico and the region, was also under its wing. Thus, in one stroke Zimmerman could map UNM more effectively onto this full complex of interests. Under the arrangement, Hewett joined the faculty and became the first chairman of the Department of Anthropology and Archaeology. Other SAR faculty were similarly made faculty of the new UNM department, a move that was justified as reducing by half the cost of setting up the department. Hewett was a controversial figure in the archaeological profession, dismissed as an ill-trained amateur and roundly disliked by some of his counterparts in the principal East Coast universities, but he had a national reputation, so the new department gained immediate recognition and prestige and quickly attracted students from around the country. There were other benefits to the affiliation as well. In Zimmerman's view, a UNM-SAR alliance would improve the university's chances of quickly securing accreditation for its graduate program, strengthen its standing before the state legislature, and give him further entrée to the art colony in Santa Fe.[9] The SAR conducted excavations and summer field schools at different pueblo sites in New Mexico, thereby affording students in the department valuable opportunities for fieldwork, and the SAR in turn gained greater academic respectability. Hewett agreed to organize a museum in the university to house materials collected from sites for laboratory and classroom use. Publications resulting from the combined work of the university and the School of American Research were to bear the imprint of both institutions.[10] In addition, as part of their focus on the region, both Zimmerman and Hewett shared an interest in acquiring archaeological properties throughout the state to protect them from exploitation by the eastern universities. The two institutions obtained ownership, either through purchase or donation, of important sites at Pecos, Quarai, Gran Quivira, Abo, Jemez, Paako, Coronado Monument, and especially Chaco Canyon.[11]

The UNM-SAR affiliation also facilitated the hiring of Clyde Kluckhohn and Lansing Bloom. Bloom began his work in archaeology and later branched into history. A veteran staff member of the SAR, he also served as assistant director of the Museum of New Mexico and editor of the *New Mexico Historical Review* (*NMHR*). In 1928, a year after Hewett joined the university, Charles Coan unexpectedly died, creating a vacancy in the history department. Spurred on by Hewett, Zimmerman and France Scholes agreed that Bloom was the logical choice to succeed Coan. It was this series of developments that brought the *NMHR* to UNM—another instance of Zimmerman's enterprising approach in building the institutional framework for a program in Spanish Borderlands–colonial Latin American history and aligning it with a growing specialization in Southwest and New World anthropology and archaeology. With Zimmerman's encouragement and active support, Bloom and Scholes (soon to be joined by George P. Hammond) began what became known as the New Mexico Archives Collection, a massive, many-years project aimed at identifying and reproducing material in foreign archives that documented New Mexico's colonial history—still another tangible expression of Zimmerman's larger vision for the university.

Kluckhohn had a very different allure than Bloom had. With an undergraduate degree in Greek from Princeton and advanced work in the classics (which he studied as a Rhodes Scholar at Oxford), he would have conformed perfectly to

Edward Gray's image of the ideal UNM professor. But Kluckhohn then branched off into anthropology, taking up advanced study in the subject at the University of Vienna. Already familiar with New Mexico from time spent in the state, he accepted an assistant professorship in the university's Department of Anthropology and Archaeology in 1932 while simultaneously serving as a research associate in the SAR. His tenure at UNM was brief, since he left in 1934 to pursue doctoral work at Harvard. While the loss of Kluckhohn deprived UNM of a brilliant young scholar, it was compensated for (at least partially) in two ways. First, he was replaced by another highly qualified scholar, Donald Brand; and, second, he continued to visit and correspond with Zimmerman and to use his connections into the East Coast world of government agencies and private foundations to help advance Zimmerman's ambitions for the university.

As the number of faculty and the span of courses devoted to the study of the Southwest, Mexico, and Spanish America continued to grow, branching out from the core in history, anthropology and archaeology, and language and literature into other fields, such as philosophy, biology, and the fine arts, Zimmerman reiterated his message that the university should avoid the trap of imitating the model of older, larger, and wealthier public universities, but, instead, should carve out a distinctive identity grounded in the special qualities and characteristics of New Mexico that its history and location had given it and that set it apart.[12] These characteristics might find expression in multiple forms; in language, art, architecture, music, religious practice, or in modes of land and water use, but ultimately they all came back to one prime, unifying feature: New Mexico—to recall Joaquín Ortega's paraphrasing of Zimmerman's idea—as the "converging point of the three main ethnic groups of the hemisphere," in other words, Paul Horgan's "heroic triad" dressed up for service to the academic world. The tricultural formulation was the taproot feeding all the shoots of regionalism in its distinctive New Mexican form: "There is in this environment," wrote Zimmerman, "abundant material for intensive study in the history, customs, language, literature, and art of at least two great racial and cultural groups of mankind, the Indian and the Spanish. Both share a common environment with a third racial group with its achievements in our modern industrial era.... Our environment, our history, and above all our diversified racial and cultural elements, provide us first hand a laboratory in the humanistic and social sciences upon which we may well concentrate our best efforts."[13]

In 1937, Clyde Kluckhohn, now living in Cambridge, Massachusetts, but still a presence in New Mexico, published a short article in *The New Mexico Quar-*

terly ratifying Zimmerman's strategy and plan for charting the future direction of UNM. Moreover, his description of the tricultural formulation, of that which made New Mexico distinct, captured the view of it held by many of his colleagues both inside the state and elsewhere: "Southwestern culture is a composite, of a still vibrant Pueblo Indian culture, a partially successfully resistant Spanish American life—important to keep alive—to which are added the pioneering Anglo-American—largely gone—and the contemporary Anglo-American."[14]

While one could hardly disagree that New Mexico represented the confluence of three principal ethnic groups, there was much room for disagreement, as we will see, about the degree to which they had blended or remained separate in different spheres of life and culture. Furthermore, New Mexico as the meeting ground of these groups created a different kind of meeting ground, one composed of historians, art historians, ethnologists, and archaeologists, who found the ideal territory and laboratory for their investigations. In these years, and going back to the first decades of the twentieth century, a virtual honor roll of academicians from both coasts repeatedly visited New Mexico, drawn to the state and the Southwest as a culture area. Among the more notable were Frederick W. Hodge, Alfred Tozzer, Alfred Kidder, E. A. Hooten, Sylvanus Morley, Herbert Priestly, and Herbert Bolton. Zimmerman was on personal terms with them, and they in turn commended his efforts to build a program of distinction in Southwest and inter-American studies. Their recurring presence in New Mexico and their interaction with Zimmerman helped him refine and sharpen his focus on regional studies. And when opportune, they interceded with foundations and lobbied government agencies to help secure funding for Zimmerman's projects. France Scholes, too, often visited New Mexico during the interim between his two UNM appointments and offered his services to the university on behalf of its burgeoning research interests in Southwest and Spanish colonial history.[15]

While Zimmerman's appreciation for New Mexico's "diversified racial and cultural elements" was genuine (although not without traces of paternalism), he was initially confounded by the educational challenges of dealing with them. Like his predecessors, he was exasperated with what he perceived as "Hispanic[s'] intractability in accepting the benefits of twentieth century America,"[16] that is—to put the matter in simpler terms—their continued reluctance to fully adapt to or embrace Anglo ideas and practices. He had as yet only a superficial grasp of the complicated nature of Hispanos' supposed "intractability." It was by degrees that Zimmerman moved from an assimilationist-oriented position to a pluralist one. Time, experience, and exposure to the ideas and thinking of individuals such as Joaquín Ortega and George Sánchez would give him a greater respect for the virtues of pluralism and a deeper, more nuanced understanding of the obstacles that blocked the path to acculturation by many Nuevomexicanos.

Zimmerman strongly regretted the loss of France Scholes, who had joined the Division of History in the Carnegie Institution in Washington, DC, and in 1935 tried to lure Scholes back to UNM. One enthusiast for this idea (doubtless there were many) was Clyde Kluckhohn. Informed by Zimmerman of this possibility, Kluckhohn wrote from Cambridge in May 1935, "I hope very much indeed that Scholes will find it possible to accept your offer. . . . I know that you and he together would soon bring the University's research and scholarly program to an enviably high level."[17] But it was not to be, as Zimmerman wrote back to Kluckhohn in the following month: "I failed to get Scholes. . . . Now I have got to find another man. I am negotiating with Hammond at the present time."[18] The Hammond to whom he referred was George P. Hammond, who, like Scholes, was a specialist in the history of New Mexico's early colonial period and—though still relatively young—had gained wide recognition for his work. Hammond was attracted to the idea of relocating to New Mexico, and when Zimmerman offered to make him the dean of graduate studies as well as chair of the history department, he accepted. Hammond saw great possibilities for realizing Zimmerman's vision for the university, or at least aspects of it, as did his mentor at the University of California–Berkeley, Herbert Bolton. In writing to Hammond to congratulate him on his appointment at UNM, Bolton invoked the image, and reality, of New Mexico as the meeting ground of both academics and denizens of high culture in general: "New Mexico," he wrote, "is a region of much interest to many groups of scholarly and cultivated persons, and it ought to be possible to get money, perhaps from private sources, to enable you to build up a very great center of learning."[19] Hammond may have been encouraged by these words, but he knew very well that New Mexico was not California and that Albuquerque was not Berkeley, hence the building up of a "very great center of learning" was bound to be an arduous affair.

For Zimmerman, another feather in Hammond's cap was his position as editor of the Quivira Society, a scholarly project founded in 1929 to publish English translations of writings that documented the early history of the southwestern part of the United States and of northern Mexico. As Hammond wrote to Zimmerman when the two were still negotiating terms, "I would naturally bring the Quivira Society [and its prestige, he could have added] along, were I to join your staff."[20] Having the society headquartered in UNM's history department, coupled with the NMHR, significantly elevated the university's profile among scholars of the Spanish colonial and postcolonial periods. Zimmerman's hope was to build a program in Southwest and Spanish colonial history that would rank with the best. To this end, even as he was recruiting Hammond, he was also trying to bring another leading figure in the field, Carlos Castañeda, from the University of Texas to UNM. According to Zimmerman, Castañeda was very eager to join the UNM history department (although for the first year his appointment would be half-time in romance languages), but the official offer reached him a few days too late, so he remained at the University of Texas.[21] Had it come about, the combination of Hammond and Castañeda at UNM (with Lansing Bloom acting as a kind of second-tier figure) would have been a powerful one.

There was a very interesting component to Hammond's orientation toward teaching Latin American history, one that complemented and served the purposes of Zimmerman's evolving ideas of how UNM might maneuver to play an important role in furthering the goal of hemispheric solidarity, especially as embodied in President Roosevelt's recently announced Good Neighbor Policy. Hammond, like Charles Coan before him, was a disciple of Herbert Bolton. As such, he subscribed to Bolton's concept of a "greater America," meaning that the Americas—North and South—had a common history on the highest plane. In Bolton's view, a history that encompassed all of the Americas allowed us to get beyond narrow, constricted national histories, thus opening the way to comprehending more fully the history and culture of the entire region. The "multinational" history of the Southwest was the history of the Americas, or certainly key elements of that history, in microcosm.

Hammond was a confirmed "Boltonian." As he wrote to Bolton in April 1935, shortly after listening to a presentation by the latter: "It was a great pleasure to hear you present once again some of the ideas which are fundamental in a proper approach to the history of the Americas. Even though we were brought up on the doctrine, it is worthwhile to have it reemphasized."[22] On the eve of his move to New Mexico, Hammond made it clear that he intended to inculcate his students with the same ideas: "In regard to my teaching program for next year, I would like to introduce one new course, the 'History of the Americas.' This is the course that Dr. Bolton has made famous, and it is being offered in a great many colleges and universities across the land. . . . I feel that it will fit into the program of the University of New Mexico very well, in view of the State's close contact with the Latin American countries."[23] This last point helps explain why Bolton's approach would hold considerable appeal for Zimmerman. The United

States was seeking commercial opportunities and a stronger presence in Latin America; its footprint in the region was growing. With the strength of its living connections to Latin America, New Mexico, through the pipeline of its flagship university, could take advantage of the federal government's desire to forge closer commercial and diplomatic ties with its neighbors to the south.[24] Bolton's ideas provided an intellectual bedrock on which to anchor and rationalize these practical objectives within the academic context. In addition, they opened a window onto attempts to make greater sense of the multicultural, pluralistic society of New Mexico and the Southwest.

If American history, in its broadest sense, transcended national boundaries and the US government considered it imperative to deepen and extend its relations with Latin America, then all the more reason why UNM should strengthen and expand its concentration in the inter-American field. Zimmerman, now supported by a growing body of like-minded faculty, proceeded along these very lines. He had lost out on bringing Carlos Castañeda to UNM, but operating on the principle that the history department occupied a central place in his plans, Zimmerman added another Latin Americanist, Dorothy Woodward, to its ranks in 1935, right on the heels of hiring Hammond. More hires followed in fine arts, government, education, romance languages, and other fields, as the momentum carried through the 1930s. By the end of the decade, the curriculum had expanded considerably and become far more specialized. For example, the 1938 course list included an anthropology seminar in "New World Cultivated Plants and Primitive Agriculture," a history department course on "Source Material for the Spanish Colonial Period," and a seminar on the history of the Southwest and the Americas; also included was a course on Mexican civilization in the Spanish section of modern languages, as well as courses on "*lo popular*" in Hispanic literature and the *modernista* movement in Spanish America; a course on Hispanic thought was offered in the philosophy department.[25] For Zimmerman, however, it was not just a matter of increasing the number of Southwest and Latin America–oriented faculty. That was fine as far it went, but his greater goal was to create advanced degrees and programs on the master's and PhD levels and to build a library collection that would support and sustain such programs.

UNM's library holdings in the relevant areas (and overall as well) were still very meager. As Hammond wrote to his friend and fellow Quivira Society board member, bookman, and Southwest bibliophile Henry Wagner, in reference to the state's planned Coronado Cuarto Centennial: "We are even dreaming of the establishment of a 'Coronado Library' here at the University, which, if dreams come true, shall be our 'Bancroft Library.' We are in such desperate need of material on the Spanish Southwest and Mexico that one hardly knows where to turn. At least half a dozen of our departments in the University are interested, in some way or another, in this area."[26] Addressing this problem was a high priority for Zimmerman. In the early 1930s, he had tried to acquire the six-thousand-volume library—rich in primary and secondary materials—of Mexican historian and belletrist Luis González Obregón.[27] Having learned of its availability from France Scholes, Zimmerman inquired of E. Dana Johnson, editor of Bronson Cutting's newspaper *Santa Fe New Mexican*, whether the senator—a strong booster of Hispanic culture—might help underwrite its purchase. Cutting was not prepared to go that far, so the effort fell through, but Zimmerman persisted. During this same period, parts of the extensive Spanish and Mexican literature and history collection belonging to Thomas B. Catron began to be deposited in the library. At the end of the decade, aided by Hammond and two influential New Mexicans, David Chávez and William Keleher, Zimmerman succeeded in obtaining an outstanding collection of Mexicana for the library, the nine-thousand-volume Paul Van de Velde Collection. In addition, the remaining parts of the Catron Collection were also deposited in UNM's library, and Zimmerman's outreach to foundations and government agencies brought in a steady flow of more material focused on the Southwest and Latin America. Still, as essential as it was to build up library holdings, the need to do so commanded less of Zimmerman's attention than his desire to create a research center for studies on the Southwest and Latin America and to institute advanced-degree programs in targeted fields.

One of Zimmerman's first moves in the latter direction came in 1934 when he sought endorsement from the university's graduate committee for his plan to begin PhD-level work at UNM in Spanish and anthropology. The way he phrased and explained the request was telling. He tried to negate any thought that the impetus for the selection of those fields had come from the departments themselves. Rather, he explained, it was the logical outgrowth "of the general University policy for advancing research in fields that are related to our New Mexican and southwestern area," a policy, as he noted, that "was advocated strongly by Dr. Tight in the earliest days of the University's history."[28] In other words, he was only implementing an emphasis on regional studies that had been identified as a university goal decades before. The university now had the critical mass to move ahead in these fields (soon expanded, upon Hammond's arrival, to include history). In addition, he tried to allay fears on the part of some that the expansion of university programs in this fashion would diminish the importance of the undergraduate curriculum.[29] The articulation of a hierarchy of interests according certain areas of study more prominence than others continued to be reinforced and filtered down below the graduate level. In 1937, the faculty's Committee on the Expansion of Upper Division Courses issued a set of draft principles that, if adopted, would govern decisions affecting the size and strength of individual departments—whether they should be candidates for expansion or not. The document represented a clear vindication of Zimmerman's belief that the university's competitive advantage, and possibilities for achieving distinction, resided (at least in the 1930s) in emphasizing those qualities and characteristics that made New Mexico stand out from the rest of the country. The committee capped its report by spelling out the particular subject areas in which it believed the university's "special opportunities" for sustained excellence lay. These were archaeology, anthropology, art, ethnobotany, geology, history (regional), and Spanish. Conversely, it concluded that other fields should accept a more limited profile within the university.[30]

While Zimmerman could call on a core of the faculty to support these recommendations, they appeared, understandably, to cause considerable unease among the rest of the faculty. When the committee issued its final report, the document repeated the general observation that the university enjoyed certain special opportunities arising from its location in the American Southwest but pointedly omitted the listing of any preferred subject areas or fields of study.[31] In a letter to Herbert Bolton written around the time the committee finished its work, Hammond noted that the university's commitment to emphasizing regional studies was not receiving the acclaim of everyone on campus: "The University administration, at least, is quite clear in its own mind that the development of the University should be in the field of Southwestern interest in general. Kluckhohn . . . emphasizes the same thought in his article in the Quarterly. Our science men may not be very happy over this policy, yet if this idea is broadly interpreted it should take care of them as well."[32] One such unhappy science man was Fred Allen, a professor of biology. In direct opposition to Kluckhohn's logic, Allen argued that UNM's commitment to regionalism was parochial and would consign the university to mediocrity. He feared that biology students who aspired to go on to medical school would be denied the full range of courses they needed in such fields as bacteriology and zoology. His outspokenness caused Edward Castetter, the chair of the department, to initiate the process of firing him, a move supported by Zimmerman. Allen appealed to the American Association of University Professors, which sent an investigative team to Albuquerque. The AAUP representatives found a certain degree of dissatisfaction over Zimmerman's insistence that, wherever possible, faculty engage in Southwest-focused research—the better to obtain federal and private foundation grants.[33]

Confronting Ethnic Tensions and Divisions Within the University

The attempt to define areas of special emphasis and to determine the proper balance in upper-division and graduate-level courses across departments was important, but the arguments for one viewpoint or another were basically internal to the university, a matter to be debated and settled by its faculty and academic administrators (and in some regard its Board of Regents). Zimmerman's administrative skills, the convincing logic behind his thinking, and the wide respect he enjoyed among the faculty enabled him for the most part to command the terms of this debate as well as its outcome. While setbacks might occur, these were short-lived, and Zimmerman made steady progress toward realizing his goal of building UNM into a recognized center for the interdisciplinary, interrelated study of the Southwest and Latin America. The high point and culmination of this effort, the creation of UNM's School of Inter-American Affairs, was only a few years away.

But Zimmerman faced another set of issues that was far larger than the reach of his own persuasive personality, had deeper meaning and resonances, and could not be managed and resolved on the basis of effective strategic planning for academic growth. These issues were rooted in the disadvantaged position that New Mexico's native-Spanish-speaking population had long occupied, in most spheres of life, in relation to its Anglo counterpart, and—in the most immediate and direct sense—stemmed from the sharp divide that existed on the UNM campus between Hispanic and Anglo students. This divide left the Hispanic students, who were many fewer in number, isolated and marginalized, the victims of discriminatory practices—some more subtle in nature, others more overt—that excluded them from participation and membership in clubs, the Greek societies, and social events. In the early 1920s, the disparity in numbers between Anglo and Hispanic students in the university was striking. For example, in 1922 only 4.5 percent of the student body was of Hispanic descent in a state whose overall population was more than 50 percent Hispanic. By 1928, the percentage of Hispanos among total student enrollees had nearly tripled, to 12.6 percent (123 of 990), and by 1932 had reached 16 percent (314 of 1,940 students)—a significant increase but still dismally low in relation to the percentage of Hispanos in the New Mexico population as a whole.[34]

The exclusion of Hispanic students from various areas of campus life underscored the perception on the part of the Hispanic community that UNM served as a bastion of Anglo privilege and, consciously or not, stood for the belief that American identity, "Americanness," was contained and expressed in the values and traditions of the white, overwhelmingly Protestant population of the nation as a whole. In Phillip Gonzales's concise summation: "[T]hroughout the state Spanish Americans associated conditions at the university with a history of Anglo dominance and the denigration of their heritage."[35]

Zimmerman was hardly ignorant of this situation and its wider dimensions, as he had evidently made clear to Joaquín Ortega, when outlining his view of the state of the university and the challenges it faced during the conversation the two held in 1931. But we needn't simply take Ortega's word in this matter. Zimmerman's awareness of the so-called "inter-cultural problem" of the state, the gulf that separated Hispanic and Anglo students within UNM, and how these related to the goal of fostering better relations between the United States and the countries of Latin America—a project in which Zimmerman envisioned a central role for UNM—were all tied together in a speech he gave in 1932 to the Institute of World Affairs at the University of Southern California and subsequently published in *The New Mexico Quarterly*.[36] Tacking away in this case from the Boltonian current, Zimmerman began his piece, the theme of which was the promotion of the Pan-American ideal, by noting the disparities between the United States and Latin America as measured by their differences in language, custom, and "Anglo Saxon versus Latin traditions." On the one hand, he maintained, focusing on "social and cultural elements" can be a way of evading more troublesome economic and political issues, but on the other, it can offer nations equal ground on which to meet. Comprehending the literature, music, and art of other peoples fosters greater insight and understanding. Zimmerman cited Dwight Morrow, US ambassador to Mexico from 1927 to 1930, as the epitome of the diplomat who lived this creed and sought to "use the cultural approach," by means of which he came truly to understand the Mexican people. He wanted UNM to take up this challenge and described some of its early endeavors in this regard, but he indicated that the field had barely been cultivated. Tremendous ignorance still existed on both sides. Pivoting to the American Southwest, Zimmerman contended that conditions in this region mimicked those on the hemispheric level. We need, he claimed, to "get into real contact with the Spanish-speaking people in our states," strive "to understand their ideas and ideals, and indeed their entire philosophy of life," as expressed in folklore, literature, art, and habits of life and thought.[37] He went on to note that Anglo and Spanish relations at UNM were characterized by substantial misunderstanding and prejudice, and in what seems slightly attenuated fashion he acknowledged that, in promoting Pan-Americanism, the United States faced the same challenges at home that it confronted beyond its borders: "Here then we have with our own states of the Southwest the central problems of Pan Americanism on its social and cultural side."[38] Zimmerman concluded by citing the interventions that UNM had thus far made to help bridge the gap and to promote better understanding and relations between the two groups.

Before describing these, however, it is worth dwelling for a moment on the theme of Pan-Americanism, because Zimmerman's critics were not about to let him get away with what, from their perspective, were little more than soothing platitudes and diplomatic niceties, when what was called for was a full-scale cleansing at UNM and its sister institutions around the state of all their practices and organizations that underpinned and helped sustain the unequal treatment of Hispanic students. One of the key broadsides against Zimmerman came from Juan Clancy, Hispanic on his mother's side and a onetime schoolteacher in the Pecos River Valley town of Anton Chico. Clancy had also served in the New Mexico legislature and long concerned himself with the inequities that characterized the state system of public education. In his eyes, Zimmerman's call for Pan-Americanism was offensive because it was constructed on false or hypocritical grounds. In effect, he was using the Spanish-speaking population of New Mexico for his own ends—building a high-minded case for goodwill and understanding between the United States and Latin America—while actually doing very little to eliminate the injustices visited on Hispanic students on his own campus. On this reading, Zimmerman's entreaties amounted to little more than symbolic politics. As another of his critics, Ernest García, summed it up: "Pan Americanism should start in the very portals of Mr. Zimmerman's institution."[39]

Although these remarks by Clancy and García were directed specifically at Zimmerman and issues surrounding higher education, they could be extrapolated to apply more broadly to discrimination and unequal treatment experienced by Spanish-speaking New Mexicans within society generally. It is possible that some of the hostility expressed toward Zimmerman, who, after all, had gone on record as faulting the university on the matter of ethnic and race relations, reflected his concentration, as exemplified in *The New Mexico Quarterly* article, on art, music, and literature as the vehicles to improve intercultural relations, while skirting more problematic, deeply embedded questions of social and economic injustices. Some years later, utilizing the ideas and recommendations first of George Sánchez and then of Joaquín Ortega (and, to be inclusive, of others), Zimmerman did broaden his focus, consciously placing UNM at the center of community-based projects aimed at improving the lot of poor Hispanic families and revitalizing their traditional arts and crafts. Nonetheless, for advocates of the Hispano Cause, recognition that the indignities and prejudice experienced on all levels by the majority of Nuevomexicanos arose from long-standing structural and societal defects made promotion of Pan-Americanism and the Good Neighbor Policy ring rather hollow. An appraisal of the Good Neighbor Policy by George Sánchez (who in the period 1932–1933 was a firm ally of Zimmerman's) brought out its contradictions and explained why Latin Americans might look at it with a jaundiced eye:

> Probably the most serious obstacle to good neighborliness between the United States and Mexico [he was originally writing for a Mexican audience] is to be found in the situation confronting Spanish-speaking people in the United States. Some twenty per cent of these people are nationals of Mexico and a majority of them are second and third generation immigrants from that country. The government of Mexico, and Mexicans generally, are acutely aware that this sector of the population of the United States is not only a socially and economically underprivileged group here but that it is constantly being subjected to discriminatory practices and prejudicial attitudes that not only increase the underprivileged character of their situation but that is in direct contra-distinction to official protestations of amity, democracy, reciprocity, and mutual respect. This state of affairs casts a somber shadow upon the Good Neighbor Policy and constitutes cause for dangerous mental reservations in dealings between Mexico and the United States. Furthermore, the rest of Latin America is not unaware of this situation and of the tense feelings resulting therefrom. . . . Latin America is wary of the possibility that as the Pan American movement develops, her peoples and cultures may be subjected to the traditional "color line" of her northern neighbor and she looks with live interest upon evidence of the application of Jim Crowism to Latin Americans in the United States.[40]

As tentative or limited as they might have been, what concrete steps did Zimmerman and the UNM community take in the early 1930s to improve relations between Hispanic and Anglo students, ease ethnic tensions within the university, and provide leadership on the state level in addressing these and related problems? The record is thin, confined principally to three initiatives that Zimmerman listed in his *New Mexico Quarterly* article. The first one, founding the San José Demonstration and Experimental School in a Spanish-speaking district of southern Albuquerque in 1930 for the purpose of training bilingual teachers, with Lloyd Tireman (see fig. 6) as its director, had the virtue of engaging community support to meet an important need. The school's supporters and its board of directors hoped that it "would be a focal point of cultural integration."[41] But even on this score, whether he deserved it or not, Zimmerman came in for criticism. So far as the school's mission was concerned, one of his leading critics was fellow board member Mary Austin, who thought him largely ignorant of the "history, culture, capabilities, racial and social background of the children."[42] Austin, of course, deemed herself an expert extraordinaire in these matters and believed that Zimmerman, along with some others on the board, were overly mechanistic in their approach, convinced that "an educational problem is solved when it can be reduced to a tidy statistical chart." [43] This criticism seems highly exaggerated. One could as well have indicted George Sánchez or Lloyd Tireman or many others with a clear understanding of the challenges of bilingual education, simply because they collected hard data and employed empirical methodologies. Even under the best of circumstances, bilingual education was as much an art as a science, demanding trial and error. Tireman himself was very honest about these difficulties, admitting to a visiting program officer of the Rockefeller Foundation's General Education Board (GEB)—which helped fund the San José Demonstration and Experimental School—"considerable uncertainty as to the best way of handling language problems in the New Mexico Public Schools."[44] Despite its challenges, the school did make progress, and three years later, building on its example, Zimmerman tried to interest the GEB in funding a national research center at UNM for bilingual education. The board, however, turned him down.

The second initiative—development of a concentrated focus on the study of Spanish history and folklore at UNM—was a start in the right direction, but, for critics like Clancy and García, while doubtless welcome as a way of placing the Hispanic experience in the heart of the university curriculum, it was more in the nature of window dressing. The third venture, establishing a bilingual club at UNM and, as an offshoot, a series of Pan-American conferences, had more potential. The club's main purpose was to build a cultural bridge and

FIGURE 6 Lloyd Tireman. Tireman was a Zimmerman loyalist and strongly subscribed to the UNM president's belief in the social mission of the university. An innovator in the field of bicultural, bilingual education, he founded the San José Demonstration School in 1930 and helped start the Nambé Community School in 1937. In its broad sweep, the latter shared much in common with UNM's Taos County Adult Education Project. Faculty Files Collection (UNMA 152, box 28, folder: Lloyd Tireman), Center for Southwest Research, University Libraries, University of New Mexico. Courtesy of CSWR.

improve understanding between English- and Spanish-speaking students at UNM. The conferences were designed to explore the interconnections, historical and contemporary, between New Mexico, the Southwest, and Latin America, with speakers drawn both from the UNM faculty and from the wider community. Moreover, these conferences, which were held annually for at least five years (1932–1936) and were open to the public, did not shy away from discussion of controversial or politically sensitive topics. Like the San José school, albeit in a more ephemeral way, they helped give the university a more visible presence in the community. For example, the program of the 1932 conference included presentations on "Fusion of Best Elements in Cultures of the Southwest," by the prominent Albuquerque judge and political figure John Simms; "Educational Problems of Bi-Lingualism," by George I. Sánchez, then serving in his role as director of research for the State Department of Education; "Rural Schools of Mexico," by Lloyd Tireman; and an address (the topic was not specified) by US Congressman Dennis Chávez.[45]

The moving spirit behind the Bi-Lingual Club was Spanish professor and Department of Romance Languages chairman Francis Kercheville. Kercheville had a long tenure at UNM and, as the decades wore on, a not particularly happy one, but in these first years he was full of energy and ideas, some of which he directed toward forging a more inclusive environment in the university. Before Kercheville's arrival in 1931, UNM had begun an effort in this direction through its Casa Española, an intensive Spanish-language summer session that offered lectures and programs on Spain and Spanish America, conducted entirely in Spanish, with students living together. Implicit in its organization was the idea that a program of summer courses focused on the Hispanic world would give students a more cosmopolitan outlook and a greater appreciation of New Mexico's cultural complexities. The Bi-Lingual Club, on the other hand, was born out of the explicit recognition that the cultural and ethnic divide that existed on the campus hobbled the university and needed to be addressed openly, on its own terms. With Kercheville as its faculty sponsor, the club's purpose, as explained by two of its members, was "not to accentuate differences but to preserve the best elements of our cultural heritage and to encourage those students who are fortunate enough to possess a practical knowledge of Spanish to polish it up and make it more effective, without any intention to slight the significance of the English cultural heritage, but to develop both uniformly and employ the Bi-Lingual Club as a means, as a cultural-bridge to this end."[46] George Sánchez (who had been a member of the Casa Española faculty as a visiting instructor of Spanish and education) was a notable influence on the Hispanic students in the club; his early investigations into the problems faced by Spanish-speaking students in the public schools and the historical impediments blocking any effective process of acculturation helped sharpen their understanding of the Hispano Cause.[47] Of course, by its very nature and aims, the Bi-Lingual Club represented an instance of the "cultural approach," (but, in this case, one that was unequivocally pluralist in spirit and substance). Although his thinking became more diversified, Kercheville at first was a strong advocate of this orientation. Some of the ideas that Zimmerman presented in his Institute of World Affairs speech came in fact from him. He, too, saw UNM's potential to be a spearhead in the implementation of Pan-Americanism on the policy level and began early in the decade of the thirties to work up proposals for a university institute that would guide and coordinate such an effort.

The ethnic cleavages at UNM, however, were too deep and ingrained to be solved by such well-meaning gestures as a bilingual club. Carolyn Zeleny, who observed and analyzed conditions at UNM in the early 1940s, found that "the system of social separatism at the University of New Mexico is very marked. The two groups rarely mix."[48] Prejudices and exclusion operated in all corners of university life; for example, at social events ("Spanish-Americans are only allowed to attend one of the University dances of the year") and in the Greek letter societies ("Such organizations as fraternities and sororities have strict rules never to admit Spanish-Americans").[49] The pattern and habits of separation in part grew out of cultural and class differences but were also attributable to racial attitudes. In documenting that Hispanos were by and large of one mind in viewing UNM as a "hotbed" of racial discrimination, Phillip Gonzales later corroborated what Zeleny had observed (and to some extent learned anecdotally) many years earlier. On this point it is worth quoting her at some length:

> At the University the unwritten code of race relations does not permit an Anglo girl to date a Spanish-American boy. In the summer of 1941 there was only one girl who appeared somewhat to escape the full force of prejudice, a member of a prominent Spanish family, whose looks and manner did not distinguish her in any way from the Anglos. The fact that many immigrant newcomers of Jewish, Italian and other backgrounds are more freely admitted to the social life of the University is a source of intense resentment among the Spanish-Americans, and many avoid the university on that account.[50]

These practices were indeed a source of great resentment on the part of Hispanos, both within the university and among the wider community, but for reasons soon to be discussed, they generally contained their resentments within a larger framework of accommodation, only sporadically voicing protest and opposition through popular gatherings or assemblies known as *juntas de indignación* (mass meetings of indignation, or mass protest meetings).[51]

In 1933, the Hispanos' sense of wrongdoing committed against them, their feelings of grievance and indignation, their frustration with negative stereotyping and prejudice and with being marginalized in their own homeland, boiled over as the result of a proposed survey to measure the racial attitudes of white students toward Spanish Americans. The controversy that erupted not only exposed UNM to the condemnation of the Hispanic community as well as many Anglo leaders but injected the university even more directly into the swirl of state politics. The survey, based on a well-known model called the Thurstone scale, was prepared by a recently hired instructor of psychology, Richard Page. Page's survey was to be sent to three thousand New Mexico high school students as a means of gauging the degree of racial prejudice they held, or did not hold, toward Spanish American classmates. George Sánchez viewed Page's project as legitimate research relating to issues in public education, and, in his capacity as director of research in the State Department of Education, he allowed Page (unwisely, as it turned out) to use the departmental mailing list and agreed to distribute the survey through his office. Zimmerman knew of plans for the survey, had cautioned Page about the content and terminology of the scale (which included racially charged terms like *greaser*) and warned him that it could bring offense, but he had not taken any concrete steps to discourage its distribution. Governor Arthur Seligman learned of the survey prior to its mailing and informed the press, which proceeded to run with the story. Seligman had repeatedly clashed with Sánchez, who used his position in the Department of Education to critique the inequities inherent in the state's method of funding local school districts, heavily Spanish-speaking districts in particular, and to push for a range of educational reforms. Zimmerman (working with allies in state government and the educational establishment) had maneuvered both to get Sánchez's department established and to have Sánchez installed as its director, and Seligman strongly disliked him and the university for this and other reasons. As Sánchez recalled many years later, "Seligman saw that [the racial attitude scale and survey] as a way of getting rid of J. F. Z. [James Fulton Zimmerman], so he called a press conference and said Zimmerman and the U. had insulted our 'great Spanish Americans, glorious, ennobled citizens,' and all that crap."[52] When word of the proposed survey spread, members of the Hispanic community rose up in protest, calling—through the device of the juntas de indignación—for the firing of Page, Sánchez, and Zimmerman.

While other incidents had occurred at UNM that offended Hispanos' pride and dignity, none so galvanized the Nuevomexicano community into action like the Richard Page affair.[53] Feelings ran so high that a public inquiry was held, called by the regents, to investigate and lay bare all of the facts surrounding Page's survey.[54] The investigating panel was composed of three members of the Hispanic elite—Gilberto Espinosa (a prominent lawyer and brother of Aurelio Espinosa), Mauricio Miera (chairman in the early 1930s of the state's Progressive Party and also a leading Republican Party figure in New Mexico), and Camilo Padilla (well-known educator, editor, publisher, and holder of civic offices in Santa Fe)—and two non-Hispanos, Lloyd Tireman and Vincent Tolle, the latter president of the New Mexico Educational Association. They sought to probe more fully into ethnic and racial tensions and antagonisms in the university and to document how these played out in student clubs, organizations, and the fraternity system. Although grilled extensively by the panel and with his leadership in question, Zimmerman nonetheless managed to come through the episode relatively unscathed. Since he could have prohibited Page's use of the scale by virtue of his position and authority, he was criticized for not doing so. The committee rendered a harsher verdict on Sánchez, censuring him for having "failed to exercise the knowledge he should have of his own people."[55] Vilified by some for acting as a kind of fifth column and betrayer of the Hispano Cause, Sánchez was in a precarious position. Seligman would have liked to capitalize on this opportunity to rid state government of his presence, but Sánchez had his supporters among the political class, chief among them Senator Bronson Cutting. The strong support Cutting enjoyed from New Mexico's Hispanic population translated into votes that Seligman needed, and so Sánchez was able to weather the storm and retain his position in the Department of Education. His division had been set up through a four-year grant awarded by the General Education Board of the Rockefeller Foundation. The grant was due to end in mid-1935. Sánchez tried to secure new funding from the legislature but failed, and so he resigned in May 1935. He left the state to conduct research and do consultancy work elsewhere but would come back into the picture in 1938–1940 as a key figure in designing and implementing the initial phase of a new UNM program that fed into Zimmerman and Ortega's inter-American initiative. Page was not so fortunate. Already found guilty in the public bar of having grossly insulted Hispanic sensitivities, and further judged by the panel to have committed a serious professional blunder, he resigned from the university, once the panel issued its report, and slipped away from New Mexico.

While the panel had called for Page's dismissal, it focused its attention on the larger problem of anti-Hispanic feeling at UNM. Its report, echoing Zeleny's finding, emphasized that "the almost unanimous expression of every witness indicated that at UNM there now exists and has for a number of years, a most distressing social relationship [between Anglos and Hispanos]," and traced this problem to the pernicious discrimination practiced by fraternities and sororities.[56] More dramatically, the report not only condemned surveys such as Page's for the black eye they gave to legitimate scientific research but also called for a prohibition against "social research involving the Spanish-speaking people of New Mexico."[57] To make New Mexican citizens of Spanish ancestry the subject of social surveys, the report maintained, was to violate their dignity. Needless to say, the call, which appalled the faculty at large, was not heeded, but it revealed the degree to which the affair had inflamed Hispanic sentiment.

In the first instance, the furor that erupted over the racial-attitude survey was a public relations disaster for the university, an embarrassment that tested the loyalty of its friends and supporters. For example, Mary Austin (as we have seen, no great admirer of Zimmerman), who had been nominated to receive an honorary degree at the 1933 commencement, wrote to Zimmerman that she might have to withdraw her name depending "a little upon the outcome of this very unfortunate matter of race prejudice questionnaire, which should never have been broached. . . . It will set us back in public opinion for years."[58] If nothing else, the proposed survey and the reaction it provoked had revealed the extent to which Anglo and Hispanic students went their separate ways, remaining largely within the social boundaries of their own group. It would take a particular kind of obtuseness not to have noticed this pattern, yet George Hammond, the university's dean of graduate studies, appeared to be oblivious to it. In a letter that he wrote to Hammond, Henry Wagner reported that according to a mutual friend "the racial feeling among students at UNM was intolerable."[59] Hammond assured Wagner that he had "certainly not noted any racial feeling that could be called either disagreeable or intolerable. Quite the contrary, in fact."[60] In this respect, Hammond clearly sailed along on the surface of things, and he was not—when it came to this matter—a purely one-man camp. While the social distance between the two groups of students may not have proved, in and of itself, the existence of racial animosity or discrimination, a number of faculty nonetheless questioned whether ethnic and racial tensions and divisions on the campus were as bad as portrayed in the press and by outside interests.

At a different remove, however, the controversy posed a more wide-ranging threat. First, it demonstrated that deep-seated frustrations and resentments could quickly flare up in the face of perceived insults to Hispanic ethnic pride and cultural heritage. Such open expression of wounded feelings in turn exposed the sharp divide that still separated New Mexico's Hispanic and Anglo communities. Together, these factors called into question the credibility of the tricultural formulation. As a partial frame in which to grasp the "inter-cultural problem of the state," as Ortega had described one of Zimmerman's concerns, one could take Sánchez's explanation of how Latin Americans viewed the Good Neighbor Policy of the United States and, in place of the former, substitute the state's Spanish-speaking *nativos*, while substituting the Anglo power structure in New Mexico for the federal government. A facile equivalency, perhaps, but one not altogether lacking in accuracy. Whether Horgan's "heroic triad"—the idea of New Mexico as the land where three main and discreet ethnic groups lived side by side in harmony—was true or not, or was primarily a myth (a question that will be taken up later), was less important than understanding the role it had played and continued to play in helping tamp down and contain the conflicts and disagreements that inevitably arose between Hispanos and Anglos.

By the time Richard Page devised his racial-attitude survey, relations between the two groups in the state of New Mexico were markedly unequal. This imbalance was partly the result of sheer numbers. Between 1870 and 1930, or over a period of two generations, the Hispanic percentage of the population declined from more than 80 percent to slightly above or below 50 percent.[61] Even faster, however, than the pace of their population increase, Anglo business and commercial interests came to dominate the urban and rural landscape. Yet, in New Mexico prior to and after the attainment of statehood, wealthy and well-entrenched Hispanic families managed to maintain a toehold on political power and representation, forming alliances with Anglo politicians and dealmakers who sought their votes, while also finding success in the new capitalist economy. Although Anglo interests were unmistakably ascendant, the two groups frequently cooperated when they saw a mutual advantage in doing so. This pragmatic arrangement not only worked to help keep ethnic hostilities and their overt expression in check but required that the two groups adhere to a certain etiquette and vocabulary in dealing with each other. As Charles Montgomery writes, "Along with negotiating the distribution of wealth and votes . . . they achieved a rhetorical compromise, a way to talk about New Mexico and its people that was acceptable—and seemingly beneficial—to both groups."[62]

In her description and study of this accommodative balance, or system of trade-offs, Zeleny had put the case more bluntly: "A complex pattern has developed which out of deference to the pride and sensitivity of the Spanish-Americans forbids overtly discriminatory practices or mention in intergroup situations of the generally inferior position of the group."[63] So in this scheme, while prejudice and discrimination obviously existed, the "rhetorical compromise" discouraged any frank discussion or analysis of the problem. To function as intended, the compromise required the imposition and observance of what Zeleny called the "conspiracy of silence," an informal, tacit understanding of the permissible limits governing public discourse about issues of race and ethnicity in New Mexico.[64] On the Hispanic side, a mass protest meeting was one form of signaling that the boundaries had been breached.

New to the state and uninitiated in these ways, Richard Page had crossed a line. Part of the virulent reaction against him was that his survey "offended inter-group ethics."[65] Once it erupted, the racial-attitude-survey controversy had to play out, but the investigation that closed the loop on the controversy was itself a violation of the code, an infringement upon the "conspiracy of silence." Moreover, by revealing through a public inquiry the institutionalized discrimination suffered by Hispanic students at UNM and the depth of resentment this treatment engendered in the Hispanic community more widely, it could also have damaged the image of New Mexico as the "land of the three cultures" living side by side in harmony. The fact that it did not, indeed that it actually reinforced the image, may at first glance seem wholly unlikely. On deeper reflection, however, the reinvestment in the image made perfect sense, because the rationale that drove the Hispano-Anglo accommodation had not evaporated. Once the protest had run its course and justice was seen to have been done (via the public interrogation of Zimmerman, the scolding of Sánchez, and the banishment of Page), the informal pact of silence would need to be restored. There would have to be a reversion to the status quo ante. This dynamic could be seen, for example, in the public and private reactions of Gilberto Espinosa (see fig. 7), who presided over the inquiry. Publicly, in his declarations and questioning of witnesses, he took a militant stand, inveighing strongly against the failures of Zimmerman and others to work more aggressively to break the mold of ethnic and racial discrimination in the university; even suggesting—before the investigating panel had convened—that it would be better if Zimmerman were relieved of his duties as president.[66] Yet simultaneously with this move, he also wrote to Zimmerman, in the tone of a semiconfidante, advising him that the interests of both groups—Hispanos and Anglos—were best served when the university resisted the impulse to confront and remediate these problems directly. In the matter of intergroup relations, progress would come about in its own good time and could not be forced or legislated. Espinosa's prescription for the university was a retreat into the ivory tower: "Let's forget this Spanish American and Anglo business," he urged Zimmerman. "Let the University of New Mexico put forth its effort to legitimate lines of education and forget social and racial problems which are solving themselves and will if they are left alone and not continually agitated."[67] Even for purely scholarly initiatives, the rules of the game applied. Writing about the oppressed conditions under which many New Mexican Hispanos lived, the rural poor among them especially, was not objectionable as long as such writing fell within acceptable bounds and did not touch a raw nerve or strike the wrong note, as Joaquín Ortega would learn some ten years hence, when a proposal he submitted was branded "dangerous" and summarily rejected.

A second set of developments occurred, during the last years of the 1930s, that highlighted the sensitive nature of Hispano-Anglo relations and the considerable importance that prominent voices placed on avoiding public discussion of potentially troublesome topics in the interests of preserving the accommodative

FIGURE 7 "Gilberto Espinosa [man in the middle with striped tie] at a party in 1982."
Espinosa chaired the 1933 investigation into an aborted research project, organized by a
junior UNM psychology professor, designed to survey the racial attitudes of whites toward
Hispanos in New Mexico. When word about the proposed survey leaked out, it caused
an uproar, earning a reprimand from the investigating panel for President Zimmerman,
a denunciation of George Sánchez by his fellow Hispanos, and the resignation from the
university by the hapless professor Richard Page. Dennis Chávez Pictorial Collection
(PICT 0000–394), Center for Southwest Research, University Libraries, University of
New Mexico. Courtesy of CSWR.

balance. The belief that the close, living connections between New Mexico and
the Latin American nations afforded the state (and the Southwest as a whole) a
special role in promoting hemispheric solidarity and—as the country watched
Hitler's rise to power—countering Nazi propaganda and the influence of German nationals living in South America was also linked to these developments.
In 1935, the New Mexico legislature passed a bill creating an entity called the
New Mexico Fourth Centennial Coronado Corporation, to plan and organize
events around the four-hundredth anniversary of the expedition led by the
Spanish conquistador Francisco Vázquez de Coronado and his entry, in 1540,
into present-day New Mexico. Zimmerman was elected president of the corpo-

ration; Erna Fergusson, vice president; and Gilberto Espinosa, secretary. Other leading members included Benigno Hernández, a former two-term (1915–1917 and 1919–1921) US congressman and longtime New Mexico political figure; Paul Walter; and Henry Dendahl, president of the Santa Fe Chamber of Commerce. Later in the decade, the corporation was renamed the Coronado Cuarto Centennial Commission (CCCC), and Clinton P. Anderson, future senator from New Mexico, was appointed its managing director.

The events and activities organized by the commission were chiefly fourfold: (1) publication of books and pamphlets, (2) staging of spectacles and pageants for the public, (3) establishment and extension of museums, and (4) promotion of folk festivals. The commission tried, in this fourth category, to manipulate and work in the tricultural formulation, so that the festivals would incorporate "survivals [in music, song, and dance] of the Indian traditions which existed before Coronado's coming, Spanish traditions which grew up later, and the rich traditions of the Anglo which were superimposed on the two existing civilizations." The celebration was also seen as a chance to promote the Good Neighbor Policy and Pan-Americanism, counter negative propaganda against the United States in the Latin American republics, and spread the idea that "we are not a wholly alien nation." There was a further benefit, in that "The 1940 celebration will bring to their attention the fact that there is within the United States a great area . . . covering tremendous territory . . . where we find ourselves tied to the people of the other American Republics by a common tradition of conquest, a common use of the Spanish language and Spanish place names, a similar history of missionary endeavor in [sic] behalf of Christianity, and a common interest in the native arts and crafts." These descriptions of what the commemoration hoped to accomplish had a decidedly boosterish ring, airbrushing away all of the darker aspects and legacies of the conquest and early contact periods. They were part of a summary history of the formation and labors of the CCCC, a document not credited to any particular individual, but whose language and prose style almost certainly pointed to George Hammond.[68] While Hammond (and others of a similar bent) did not directly repudiate the tricultural formulation, the celebration, in his view, was less an occasion to highlight the multicultural heritage or ethnic parity of New Mexico than an opportunity to focus on the spread of European civilization and to advance the New Mexico–Latin America connection. "As the state of New Mexico," he wrote in 1939, "is preparing to celebrate the coming of the white man [Hispanic people at this time were considered "white" for the purposes of the US Census] and his civilization to the Southwest, there is a need of stressing our cultural, political, and economic relations with the peoples of the Latin American nations."[69] The University of New Mexico, Hammond felt, had positioned itself to become the leading center for Latin American studies in the American West, if not in much of the United States, and the CCCC could serve as a powerful aid in furthering this development.

An alternate view of how the 1940 celebration might serve the ideals of Pan-Americanism was offered by Dennis Chávez during a speech that he delivered in the US Senate in April 1937. He used the plan for commemorating Coronado's *entrada* to make the case for a true equality of relationship between the United States and Latin America and for the special role that New Mexico and the Hispanic Southwest could play in forging it. A serious attempt to cultivate the friendship of Latin America, he argued, would mean replacing "the swaggering attitude, both official and commercial, that has characterized our relations with these nations in the past," with a genuine appreciation of a "culture which is in many ways totally different than our own. A culture introduced four hundred fifty years ago has proved so strong and lasting that it exists even to this day. The Southwestern descendants [of the early explorers and settlers] retain the language, the customs and psychology of their kindred folks of the South. . . . New Mexico and the Spanish Southwest is a linguistic and ethnological treasure house." Anticipating a thesis soon developed and propounded by Joaquín Ortega, Chávez went on to conclude that "it is possible to form from there a ploughshare on which will turn the success of our Latin American policy."[70]

The political crosscurrents of the Cuarto Centennial were thornier, however, than either Hammond, from his side, or Chávez, from his, might want to entertain. This reality was illustrated by an exchange that took place in 1938 between Zimmerman and R. H. Faxon, secretary of the Raton, New Mexico, Chamber of Commerce. Faxon objected, as did a number of state officials, to the prominent place that the CCCC planned to give to Mexico in the various celebratory activities, writing to Zimmerman that "in the light of the terrible things that Cárdenas [Lázaro Cárdenas, Mexico's president] and his labor and Communist and even Nazi cohorts are doing in Old Mexico, with expropriation and what-not, . . . is it proper to play him up so much in connection with this Centennial? In other words, is the time propitious to go so strongly on Old Mexico?"[71] Zimmerman tried to mollify Faxon and short-circuit the issue, responding, "I appreciate what you say about the Mexican situation, but in light of the efforts of our own government to get along better with Cárdenas, I imagine our cultural efforts will not do any harm."[72] The CCCC, and especially Zimmerman as its president, needed the support of local leaders such as Faxon to lobby the legislature to appropriate funds for the celebration.

The reluctance of both Hispanic and Anglo leaders to risk upsetting the accommodative balance by engaging in open discussion of socially and politically sensitive issues was apparent in a disagreement that occurred among commission members in 1939. Two years earlier, Zimmerman had not only responded positively to the message conveyed in Chávez's speech but also linked it directly to home in a more fundamental way, telling the senator that he thought the commemoration could have "tremendous value in helping us solve many of our difficult problems in New Mexico."[73] While on a trip to the East Coast in August 1939—a trip made in part to lobby for government support on behalf of CCCC activities—he elaborated more fully on this belief in a letter he penned to Clinton Anderson. The centennial, Zimmerman wrote, should stress "the great human factor of the Sp. Am. people. . . . I think 1½ or 2 million descendants of Spanish leaders on low economic, social, educational etc. level would have national human appeal. Besides we shouldn't overlook our obligation to set our own Anglo citizens to thinking seriously on this subject."[74]

One means of accomplishing that was to organize a week-long conference devoted, among other things, to "scientific reports on rural life, agriculture, land use, health, education etc." He informed Anderson that officials in the State Department's Division of Cultural Relations and Secretary of Agriculture Henry Wallace, as well as persons close to Wallace, were supportive of the idea and would provide technical advice and assistance. Zimmerman closed his letter by reemphasizing the need to use the occasion of the Coronado Cuarto Centennial to confront actual problems and not just entertain the public and further scholarly interests: "Despite historical work, pageantry and other phases, I feel that we must face these larger human issues at some point in 1940."[75] In September 1939—now back in New Mexico—Zimmerman set the wheels in motion, conferring with Clinton Anderson and Gilberto Espinosa, and the three agreed that the idea was worthwhile and should be pursued. George Sánchez was then deputed to prepare a memorandum outlining the desirability of a conference that would address "vital current questions" bearing on the Spanish-speaking population of New Mexico and the Southwest. Yet, as subsequent events demonstrated, it appears that Espinosa was only rhetorically supportive of the idea. The proposed conference was discussed "at length" by commission members at their October 16, 1939, meeting. On the surface, the prospects for the conference seemed positive. Anderson made the formal recommendation "that Dr. Zimmerman, Dr. Sánchez, Gilberto Espinosa, and Mrs. Ruth Alexander, and three additional persons be appointed as a committee to frame suggestions and discuss limits for a cultural conference along the line suggested by President Zimmerman."[76] Immediately thereafter, however, another commission member, Benigno Hernández, moved that the conference idea be tabled indefinitely. His motion was seconded by Mrs. Alexander, and it carried. Zimmerman (and, presumably, Anderson) had been outflanked. The conference he envisioned was not meant, of course, to focus primarily on "cultural" matters but rather on the nexus of problems faced by the state's Hispanic population, that is, the very "social and racial problems" that should not, as Espinosa had earlier recommended to Zimmerman, be "continually agitated." For most CCCC members, all of whom represented the upper tier of Hispanic and Anglo society, such a conference would likely violate the accepted rules of discourse and had, therefore, to be rejected.

As incidents like these made clear, the trope of the "heroic triad" could be tailored to a variety of uses. In the wake of the racial-attitude survey and through the Coronado Cuarto Centennial celebration (apart from the more Eurocentric orientation of people like George Hammond) came a strengthened belief on the part of the university that the tricultural heritage of the state should more than ever be at the core of its identity and that its academic program should place special emphasis on conducting research into the historical and cultural backgrounds of Anglo, Hispanic, and Native American peoples. As Phillip Gonzales noted, the idea of New Mexico as the meeting ground of these three cultures became ingrained in the state, turned into a kind of official dogma in its political culture, and fashioned into a public relations slogan as a spur to tourism.[77] A decade and a half after the 1933 confrontation, Erna Fergusson pointed out the risk inherent in the reification of this inaccurate slogan. The image, she wrote to Herbert Weinstock, her editor at Alfred Knopf, had taken on the qualities of a museum piece, had become—as it were—a mere artifact.[78]

From the Cultural Approach to Programs for Social and Economic Amelioration: The Taos County Project and Its Background Study

The message was not lost on Zimmerman that to achieve success, a campaign for Pan-Americanism in New Mexico would need to embrace more than art, literature, and music. The "soft power" of the cultural approach, while effective in its own way, was insufficient. In his Institute of World Affairs address, UNM's president had stressed that to make the Pan-American ideal a reality in the Southwest, it was necessary "to get into real contact with the Spanish-speaking people in our states." By "real contact" he meant more than a deep understanding of the worldview and way of life of the native-Spanish-speaking population; it meant coming to terms with and helping to alleviate the impoverished conditions under which so many of its communities lived. Zimmerman, of course, was not alone among university personnel in recognizing this need. One who clearly saw the need, and did not limit its scope simply to the state of New Mexico, was Paul Walter Jr., director of the University of New Mexico Press from 1930 to 1933 (and future professor of sociology at UNM). When *The New Mexico Quarterly* was launched by the UNM Press in 1931, Walter saw "the big problem brought about by the larger Mexican and Spanish-American population in the states" as one of the main subjects it should cover. It got to the essence of "New Mexico's opportunity and responsibility in connection with the question as a whole rather than in our own state alone."[79] Walter had identified an issue of paramount importance. Nonetheless, realization of the need for applied research and direct action was slow in coming on the part of some. In 1936, for example, a plan outlined by Francis Kercheville restated the case that Hispanic studies should be emphasized at UNM as a natural outgrowth of the state's special history and the positive advantages resulting therefrom: "Conditions here are quite different in many respects because New Mexico is unique in many of her advantages. There is no reason why the University of New Mexico should be asked to follow exactly the path taken by older institutions. This thought has been expressed many times by the Administration."[80]

As university leadership was beginning to grasp in a more fundamental way, however, the special history of the state that gave it qualities (at the core of which was the three-cultures motif) so different from other states in the union also left it with serious *dis*advantages as well. Nobody described and explained these better, insofar as they characterized the lives of many Nuevomexicanos, than George Sánchez. Summarizing the gap that separated New Mexico's Anglo citizens and major segments of its Hispanic population, Sánchez put his finger on both the cause and the effect: "They [the Hispanos] battle their own cultural inadequacy. They are unprepared to act in their new environment—unprepared because of centuries of isolation. They have no tradition of competition, of education, or of Western civilization beyond the sixteenth century. The New Mexican is not yet an American culturally, the Treaty of Guadalupe notwithstanding. . . . The

American of Spanish descent, the New Mexican reflects that tradition and that heritage [i.e., a distinctly Spanish heritage tempered by generations of adaptation to a new land, which created particularized patterns of social and economic life]."[81] Elaborating further on the problem of cultural deprivation, Sánchez wrote with respect to the mass of rural New Mexicans and also of many town and city Hispanos: "Almost a hundred years after becoming American citizens, a broad gap still separates [them] from the culture which surrounds them. In lieu of adequate instruction, they have clung to their language, their customs, their agricultural practices."[82]

One of the more serious handicaps facing rural Nuevomexicanos was their deficient and in some cases all-but-nonexistent level of education, a situation that traced back to the nineteenth and early twentieth century (indeed back into the colonial period), when federal and territorial authorities neglected the issue and people did not want to tax themselves for this purpose, thus leaving education in a great many communities either in the hands of the church or to private initiative. Subsequently, when the public school system was established, schools in rural areas were chronically and systematically underfunded. Their failures, however, derived not only from the schools themselves but also because they were replicas of the schools one would find in, for example, Massachusetts or Washington state or Indiana. Children were taught in English by English-speaking teachers whose methods were those used by teachers elsewhere in the country. The children, however, came to school at age six speaking Spanish: "They think in Spanish, play in Spanish, talk in Spanish, everywhere except in their recitations."[83] The education that children received was thus as strange to them as its language of instruction.

Cognizant of this problem and responding to the reformist call of the New Deal, UNM made one of its first significant moves beyond the "cultural approach" by taking the lead in organizing and mounting a rural education and community-action-demonstration project in Taos County. The county, located in the mountainous far north of the state, had been chosen for specific demographic and socioeconomic reasons. When the project got underway in January 1936, over 90 percent of its population of fifteen thousand was of "Spanish" descent.[84] The majority in this group lived in small communities, nestled in valleys that were isolated from each other by uplands and ridges. The Native American population numbered some eight hundred. The majority of the approximately thousand-strong Anglo population resided in the village of Taos, whereas the Hispanos were for the most part farmers, who, if they were fortunate, might also raise and earn a small amount of money from a few sheep, cattle, and hogs. They lived on small subsistence farmsteads containing less than one acre of land per individual. Thus a family of six (the average size of farm families) was forced to make a living from only five to six acres of land. The main crops were wheat and alfalfa, most of which went for domestic consumption. Virtually no cash crops were produced. The per capita wealth was extremely small, the standard of living low, with an annual cash income per family of around one hundred dollars. Illiteracy was high—15.5 percent in 1930. Young people on average did not complete elementary school. Among young and old alike, functional education and market-oriented practical skills were drastically lacking. Recreational and cultural activities were limited, confined essentially to weddings, wakes, fiestas, and dances. Finally, health conditions were very bad: Taos County had the highest infant mortality rate of any county in the nation.

The Taos County Adult Education Project was a cooperative venture on the part of UNM, which drew on the resources of the Harwood Foundation and a number of state agencies and boards. It also received financial support and technical assistance from the state organization of the Works Progress Administration (under the supervision of Tom Popejoy, then the assistant state administrator of emergency education) and one of the Works Progress Administration's (WPA's) divisions, the National Youth Administration.[85] The Harwood Foundation had come into UNM's sole possession in 1936–1937, as a gift from Taos artist and doyen Lucy Harwood (1867–1938). The foundation's physical plant, located in Taos, consisted of a library, art gallery, auditorium, offices, and some furnished apartments. In addition to its program in adult education, the project had four general aims: to provide for occupational rehabilitation and improvement, to set up a program of health education and service, to begin a recreational program for children and young adults (employing young people as leaders and assistants), and to foment a sense and spirit of community responsibility and empowerment for social progress.[86]

Vocational education was at the heart of the project and included such things as conservation of soil and water, improvement of livestock and farm methods and products, and cooperative enterprises involving both production and marketing. The agricultural program was matched to a program of domestic education and services that focused on such activities as preserving food, home planning and economy, clothing and feeding the family, and strengthening and sustaining home relationships. Revitalizing people's handicraft skills (partly for personal use and enjoyment and partly to create a source of cash income from salable surplus goods) also received attention, with instruction in fashioning and decorating articles of wood, wool, leather, and tin, using native raw materials. In the area of health, attention was placed on childcare, food and water sanitation, instruction about and treatment of disease, personal health and hygiene, and work toward establishing operable community clinics as well as a central hospital in Taos. Another vital component of the project was teaching literacy in both English and Spanish along with instruction in practical arithmetic and other basic subjects, so that participants acquired the specific knowledge necessary as a background for the various program activities.

Nine communities (seven strictly rural in character) and five hundred individuals were involved in this first phase of the Taos County Adult Education Project. They were served by seventeen workers, all of whom (with the exception of the project director and the librarian) were unemployed teachers (by and large of Hispanic ethnicity) selected from the Taos County relief rolls. The project was premised on the belief that transformative change would only come about through community-based action. Ultimately, it was the people themselves who had to exert control over their own lives. They needed to understand that outside assistance was offered not as charity, "but as leadership and guidance; that the real success of the enterprise depends on their interest and energy" and that the project's activities had to emerge from "the realized needs and desires of the people themselves." To this end, "Every effort will be made to stir the people to self-improvement, to train and use local leadership, and to assist the people to set up what they feel is their own program."[87] It was classic community-development work, and the same thinking would soon inform several of the programs designed and implemented by Joaquín Ortega for UNM's School of Inter-American Affairs.

The project, of course, was important and valuable in its own right. It had two corollary aspects, however—one political, the other cultural—that gave it greater significance, both for UNM and for the larger society. Politically, it signaled an understanding on the university's part that it needed to enhance its image and reputation among certain sectors of the New Mexico population. As many within the Hispanic community saw it, the development of higher education had worked to the disadvantage of promoting education for the "common people" of the territory and state.[88] For these people, a university education was not within reach; they were unprepared to enjoy its benefits. For poor Hispanos, who had been relegated to the margins of the capitalist economy and society, the diversion of a portion of New Mexico's limited resources to higher education did nothing, seemingly, to help them improve their lot. This perception, or its legacy, was something Zimmerman needed to combat, and a project like the adult-education initiative undertaken in Taos County was one way to do that. Even a proven friend of the university like Dennis Chávez (see fig. 8), who was on good terms with Zimmerman, viewed it as too elitist and aloof, not striving hard enough to work for the social and economic betterment of the mass of New Mexicans. In a letter to his brother, Judge David Chávez, he expressed his disappointment in the university's weak record on this score:

> I still maintain that the University is not doing its full share for the people of the state and the Regents should interest themselves in the social problems of the people of the state. The vast portion of the population that needs help should be given some attention. This matter of social welfare is a new thing and only lately have the people become conscious of it. There should be a Department in the State University to train our boys and girls to meet this problem so that they can become availalabe [sic] to carry on the program with-out the necessity of importing people from other states. They talk about buildings and a good faculty, which, of course, is proper, but the main item should be the uplifting of that portion of the population that needs attention and this has been wholly neglected in the past.[89]

The soon-to-be-created School of Inter-American Affairs would take up this challenge and make community-based work a central part of its mission and purpose. Even before he had the formal structure of the SIAA in place, however, Zimmerman tried to work these angles and build political support whenever he could. One such instance occurred in late 1936, when the Albuquerque branch of the League of United Latin American Citizens (LULAC) adopted a resolution urging the university, in light of New Mexico's "large contingent of Latin-American population," to establish a program to train Spanish-speaking New Mexicans for diplomatic service in Mexico and South America. According to LULAC, these youth would be particularly well suited for such service because of their language abilities and their "traditions." The resolution also endorsed such a program as a way to foster good relations between the United States and the Latin American republics and, finally, requested that the university work with the Carnegie Foundation to secure its designation of UNM as a recognized center for such instruction.[90] Sounding like his predecessors Edward Gray, David Ross Boyd, and David Spence Hill, and consistent with his own pronouncements,

FIGURE 8 Dennis Chávez. Chávez
took a keen interest in the affairs of the
University of New Mexico. While he
supported President Zimmerman and
the institution, and especially the role it
sought to play in promoting hemispheric
solidarity and President Roosevelt's Good
Neighbor Policy, he also prodded it to be
more creative and assertive in undertaking
programs aimed at improving the lives
and working conditions of historically
disadvantaged groups in New Mexico.
Dennis Chávez Pictorial Collection (PICT
0000–394), Center for Southwest Research,
University Libraries, University of New
Mexico. Courtesy of CSWR.

Zimmerman responded that he was in full agreement with the points raised by
LULAC: "[I]t is my personal belief that we should give special training in public
service, especially that relating to the Latin American republics." Moreover, he
added that he had discussed the matter with Senator Chávez, who had agreed
to advocate for such a program with the US State Department.[91]

If Zimmerman grasped the political ramifications and importance of the
Taos County Project, he was no less aware of how it related not only to the
"inter-cultural problem of the state" but to how it revealed the survival and force
of misconceptions and distorted ideas about the identity of New Mexicans of
Hispanic blood and origin and their place within the American body politic. A
series of letters exchanged in late 1937–early 1938 between Zimmerman; J. T. Reid,
the director of the project and also of UNM's Extension Division; Morse Cartwright, the director of the American Association for Adult Education (AAAE);
and Frederick P. Keppel, president of the Carnegie Corporation, brought this
matter into relief.

The university was trying to secure a grant from the Carnegie Corporation
that would allow it to extend and deepen the adult-education project in Taos
County. As part of this process, it had hoped that Cartwright's association would
recommend approval of the project to the Carnegie Corporation. As Cartwright explained to Reid, however, the AAAE was unwilling to do so for two
reasons.[92] One was purely technical, involving the scale and scope of proposed

operations, which it considered to be too large. That problem could be easily fixed. The other reason, however, stemmed from misguided notions held by the association or, certainly it appeared, by Cartwright, that the population to be served by the project was not really eligible for this kind of support because it was not integral to the social fabric of the nation. Cartwright, surely, understood that these people were United States citizens. Still, he construed them as being "Mexicans," and therefore somehow not fully "American." They presented, he had written to Reid, "a special problem and one not directly applicable to adult education problems generally in American life."[93] Dismayed by Cartwright's line of thinking and the apparent ignorance and small-mindedness underlying it, Reid responded by explaining that the approximately three million Spanish-speaking people living in the Southwest and California were American citizens whose problems were no more "special" than those afflicting "the Negro of the South, the Indian, the farmer, the factory-worker, the youth of the land . . . for whom special programs have been instituted already," programs that had yet to be extended to the Spanish-speaking people of the border states. "Nowhere," Reid emphasized, "[is there] a well-formulated program of adult education for these so-called 'Mexican' people." He strained to point out, "In our literature for a century, the 'Mexican' has been the villain; few have had the courage to isolate him as a group in our society and fight for his worth as a citizen and his needs as a fellow-man. Such a thing we would like to do here in New Mexico."[94] Reid had made a strong and compelling case for the project, drawing on historical and contemporary data, and Zimmerman tried—as diplomatically as possible—to induce Frederick Keppel to override the AAAE and support it.[95] For the time being, however, Reid's counterargument fell on deaf ears. Cartwright was not ready to revise his opinion, and the Carnegie Corporation—while not guided by the same thinking as the AAAE—was not disposed as yet to fund a new phase of the Taos County Adult Education Project. Two years hence, persuaded by additional data furnished by the university, it would be disposed, as would Cartwright.

The university had carved out a promising role for itself with the Taos County Project and all the players in this affair; Zimmerman, Reid, the Harwood Foundation Governing Board, and others with a stake in it were not about to give up on their attempts to secure additional funding. Their way forward in making a stronger case was to study the community and its needs more deeply and scientifically, and the person chosen to conduct the study was George Sánchez. Sánchez, it will be recalled, had left the state in 1935, first to do field research in the South for the Julius Rosenwald Foundation, and later to work as a consultant to the Ministry of Education in Venezuela. Anxious to return to New Mexico, he composed a long letter to Zimmerman in January 1938, in which he discussed his ideas for a research project in New Mexico that would focus on "rural sociology, southwestern economics, the local share-cropping mess, culture contacts and the incorporation of the Spanish-speaking population into the New Deal type of modern agrarianism, etc. Its chief function should be research and field studies."[96] In addition to registering his desire to lead such a study, Sánchez mentioned that he had been in touch with mutual contacts at the General Education Board of the Rockefeller Foundation, who had indicated that the board might be inclined to fund the project. He also stressed that if it got off the ground, the project could form the basis for creating a Southwestern institute at UNM, incorporating teaching, research, and outreach functions.

Zimmerman, of course, had been thinking along very similar lines. He responded promptly in the affirmative, letting Sánchez know that Paul Walter Jr., by then on the faculty of UNM's Department of Sociology, had been working up a proposal much like his.[97] Zimmerman was in full accord with all of the elements of Sánchez's proposal, including the idea that Sánchez direct the study, with one exception: he liked the idea of the institute but thought it too ambitious for the university under present circumstances. Other faculty, too, were very supportive of the proposal, and it was widely discussed across the university. Kercheville, in particular, was a partisan of Sánchez's ideas, which, he tried to impress upon Zimmerman, were simply the latest iteration of what he had been advocating since the early 1930s—an institute that would allow the university to leverage the inherent strengths that the state's history and location gave it. But where Sánchez's ideas were always well formulated and intensely focused, Kercheville's were often rambling, verbose, and vague. Furthermore, as Kercheville made clear in a letter that he wrote to Zimmerman in July 1938, the institute that he had in mind went well beyond the boundaries of New Mexico. He began by endorsing the choice of Sánchez to direct it: "I was just wondering if it would be possible to organize the Spanish Institute or some Institute of Hispanic Studies with Sanchez [sic] as Director. I am sure he would be a good man for Director and the logical one."[98] Kercheville then moved on to describe what he was really after:

> I understand Tireman and others have also proposed some such plan [i.e., cre-
> ating an institute]. With the cooperation of the departments of history, anthro-

pology, education, economics, English, Spanish and Hispanic Studies [by the latter, he meant the courses taught within the Spanish Department that focused on Latin America and the Hispanic Southwest], I believe we could make a good start on the work in Inter-American affairs, foreign services, language and linguistic problems, etc. which I know you have planned for the University of New Mexico as parts of her real distinctive and vital contribution and destiny. Perhaps finances will not permit the proposal at present.

Kercheville was correct on the last point, and as time would soon tell, his ideas about the focus and framework of a UNM institute were also largely on the mark.

As it turned out, it was not the General Education Board but the Carnegie Corporation—with the AAAE now in agreement—that funded Sánchez's study. Supported by Zimmerman, Sánchez had returned to New Mexico in 1938, with an appointment in UNM's Department of Education. The Carnegie grant, which began in February 1939, was directly linked to the Taos County Adult Education Project, thus allowing Sánchez to conduct his field research in that section of New Mexico. His study of the educational and socioeconomic conditions prevalent in the county was published in 1940 by the University of New Mexico Press as *Forgotten People: A Study of New Mexicans*.[99] It was one of the finest pieces of social science research to come out of the Southwest in this period. As John Nieto-Phillips has pointed out, the book can be read as a kind of manifesto for the Hispano Cause; an appeal, "for Nuevomexicanos to organize around such causes as land and water struggles, political rights, and bilingual education."[100] The book was a personal triumph for Sánchez and the object of much scholarly praise.[101] By now, Sánchez had a long list of important publications to his credit, and he firmly believed that he warranted promotion to a full professorship, with commensurable salary and benefits. Zimmerman believed the same, but for political reasons was unable to grant Sánchez what he wanted. Sánchez's earlier campaign (1931–1935) to rework the structure and financing of public education in New Mexico (which had helped bring about much needed reforms) had antagonized entrenched interests and weakened Zimmerman's political hand. From that point on, Zimmerman was forced to balance his support for Sánchez against the strong anti-Sánchez sentiment that still persisted. Another factor possibly worked against Sánchez: for all the critical praise that *Forgotten People* earned, it may also have made some people uncomfortable by disturbing the "conspiracy of silence." In this regard Carolyn Zeleny reported that "it was hard to discover what the reaction of authorities had been to the ethnic issues raised

by George I. Sanchez [sic] in his book *Forgotten People* [and other writings]
... which points out clearly their subordinate status."[102] Forced to deal, on the
one hand, with a president who felt that his hands were tied and insufficiently
"accomodationist," on the other, to suit his political foes, Sánchez accepted the
offer of a full professorship at the University of Texas at Austin and left UNM
after the spring semester of 1940.[103] Thirty years later, writing to his UNM friend
and professional colleague Frank Angel, Sánchez—as was his wont—recalled
these developments in typically off-color fashion: "Zimmerman had promised
[sic] me a Professorship when my job in Santa Fe [i.e., Taos] ended. When it did,
he backed down and offered me a job as an assistant [underlining in original] to
Dean Nanninga. I told him, Popejoy, and others to kiss my ass. I had several contract offers in my pocket! I chose a full professorship at Texas—on my terms."[104]

George Sánchez (see fig. 9) may have been gone, but the results of his work
remained. His report, based on rigorous empirical research, was instrumental
in convincing the Carnegie Corporation to approve a two-year grant that began
in 1940 in support of a second, enlarged phase of the Taos County Adult Education Project. Morse Cartwright underscored this link in his March 1940 letter
to Zimmerman, notifying him that the university's proposal had won approval:
"The conditions brought to light by Dr. Sánchez's survey, together with the
feeling on the part of the Executive Board of this association and the trustees
of the Corporation of the importance of an experiment and demonstration for
Spanish-speaking Americans led to the favorable result."[105] Interestingly, the
Hispanos of Taos County were no longer called "Mexicans" by Cartwright, but
"Spanish-speaking Americans." The architecture and content of the project were
directly based on Sánchez's findings and the recommendations that came out of
them. The project in turn served as a springboard to the creation of the School
of Inter-American Affairs in late 1941.

In the first instance, Sánchez's book had presented an indelible portrait of the
marginal existence lived by so many Spanish-speaking residents of the county,
and, what is more, explained the relevancy of their chronic problems of "language, poverty, and isolation" to the nation as a whole. It did something else as
well, however—something that perhaps helps reveal why Morse Cartwright
thought these people constituted a "special problem." In lucid, uncluttered
prose, it evoked the cultural no-man's-land in which the nativos of Taos County
dwelled. An article that Sánchez published, titled "New Mexicans and Acculturation," described the predicament: "New Mexicans [shorthand for the citizens of
Spanish descent in New Mexico]," he wrote, "represent one of the most puzzling

FIGURE 9   George I. Sánchez. Before political factionalism and his own hard-charging style forced him to leave New Mexico and UNM in 1940, Sánchez—on different fronts and through various channels—was one of the leading proponents in the state of the Hispano Cause. He supported the creation of the School of Inter-American Affairs, offering advice to both Zimmerman and Ortega on how best to situate it within the university. Faculty Files Collection (UNMA 152, box 24, folder: George Sánchez), Center for Southwest Research, University Libraries, University of New Mexico. Courtesy of CSWR.

cultural problems in the nation. . . . Today, New Mexicans constitute a cultural group which is in the anomalous situation of being native American of native American descent and which, withal, is not typically American," because "the circumstances of history have molded the culture of these people into forms and patterns which set them apart from their fellow citizens."[106]

Finally, Sanchez's book *Forgotten People* was valuable in another way. Like the "three cultures" motif, it could be put to a variety of uses. One of these was to clear a space for a refinement of the Boltonian superstructure. If the Americas shared a common history, then New Mexico, in the human landscape and time-honored ways of its Middle and Upper Rio Grande Valley villages and towns, was the place where the Americas intersected most vividly. It was where the two regions—the Hispanic Southwest and Latin America—in some respects merged into one and became parts of the same equation. Joaquín Ortega would stretch this thesis to the limit, by asserting that the study of their respective histories and of many of their contemporary socioeconomic problems was best subsumed in a single center or institute, one that encompassed *inter*-American affairs. The emergent SIAA may not have become the "very great center of research" whose possibility Herbert Bolton had dangled before George Hammond, but for a brief period it came close.

⟆ ⬩ ⟆

CHAPTER THREE

"Little Latin America"

The SIAA in Theory and Practice

Just as Zimmerman had inherited a foundation on which to build an expanded and a more sophisticated program focusing on the Hispanic Southwest and Latin America, so too did his chief partner in this enterprise, Joaquín Ortega. By the time George Sánchez left for Texas, Ortega had been coming periodically from Madison, Wisconsin, to New Mexico for a decade. He had gained a wide-ranging knowledge of the state and had come to know a number of its leading politicians and civic personalities, Anglo and Hispano alike, in Albuquerque, Santa Fe, and elsewhere in the state. Furthermore, not only did he visit for longer periods of time in the last years of the 1930s but he also acquired a greater awareness and understanding of the University of New Mexico academic program, as well as life on the campus, by teaching summer-session classes during the three years prior to his appointment as the SIAA director. In addition, he was able to observe and follow closely the progress that Zimmerman and the university had made in bringing UNM more directly into the community.

As examples of UNM's outreach and its ability to secure extramural funding to collaborate with state and local boards and agencies to document and improve the living conditions of rural Nuevomexicanos, the Taos County Adult Education Project and George Sánchez's field research were of great value to him. But the program had also made significant strides inside the university. In 1940, the year before the SIAA was established with Ortega as its director, UNM was one of only four universities in the country that offered an interdepartmental major in Latin American studies. The degree program had been officially established in 1939. More impressive still was that UNM offered two such majors: one in the "cultural field," involving history, Spanish, and four other departments; and a second in government and Spanish, designed for those interested in diplomatic service and commercial work. Some of this advancement could be credited to Francis Kercheville (see fig. 10), who, prior to Ortega's relocation to New Mexico in 1941, perhaps did more cheerleading and organizational planning on behalf of Zimmerman's Southwest–Latin American initiative than any faculty member besides George Hammond. Typical of Kercheville's endeavors—both strengths and weaknesses—was a plan that he submitted in 1937–1938 that included proposals for teaching Spanish in the grade schools and promoting bilingualism; creating loan libraries and a translation and lecture bureau to serve Spanish-speaking communities in the state; setting up a summer field school in Mexico to teach Spanish; and, in line with Zimmerman's long-range plan, establishing an institute of inter-American affairs at UNM. These were all worthy proposals, but—as was customary with Kercheville—none ever got past the "big ideas" stage needed to be elaborated in detail. This flaw was especially notable with respect to the proposed institute. Kercheville could never quite decide whether to call it the Institute for Inter-American Affairs or the Institute for Hispanic Studies. This uncertainty about its name reflected an uncertainty about its scope and purpose—whether to put the focus primarily on New Mexico or on the wider Hispanic world. Kercheville never tied the two regions together—historically and contemporaneously—as persuasively and effectively as Ortega would later.

FIGURE 10 Francis Kercheville. Kercheville bemoaned the decline of the Spanish language in New Mexico and, over a long and sometimes fractious career at UNM, formulated a series of plans to revive and preserve it as an everyday, living language. He believed in the virtues and value of bilingualism. While a student at the University of Wisconsin, he had been mentored by Joaquín Ortega and later helped arrange Ortega's invitations to teach in the UNM summer school. Ortega's appointment as director of the School of Inter-American Affairs, however, put a considerable strain on their relationship. Kercheville felt that President Zimmerman never adequately recognized, publicly, the foundational work he had done to make the school a reality. Faculty Files Collection (UNMA 152, box 15, folder: Francis Kercheville), Center for Southwest Research, University Libraries, University of New Mexico. Courtesy of CSWR.

Nevertheless, his energy and enthusiasm and his initiatives—poorly defined as they were—helped stimulate the discussion that Zimmerman needed to carry his plans forward.

We have already seen that Zimmerman carefully nurtured his contacts with private foundations, such as the Rockefeller and the Carnegie, both of which had a stipulated interest in supporting a range of scholarly and community-oriented projects focused on Latin America and the American Southwest. In addition, he actively networked to represent UNM in both academic circles and in the halls of government, so the university would be in a position to benefit from the growing interest in Latin America brought on by the course of international events.

In 1939, for example, Zimmerman informed the regents that Secretary Cordell Hull had invited him, along with a select group of other educational leaders, to participate in a conference being organized by the Cultural Relations Division of the Department of State, aimed at the "development of university facilities which will make for a better understanding between our country and the other American republics to the south of us. The conference will present a broad program dealing with all the aspects of inter-American education activities."[1] The advent of World War II, capped by Hitler's invasion of Poland in September 1939, led Zimmerman to intertwine the themes of national-security preparedness and "hemispheric solidarity" with the 1930s New Deal emphasis on ethnicity and regionalism already in place. The final steps toward formalizing a Latin American studies program at UNM and creating an institute through which to advance and coordinate it were propelled at least in part by these developments affecting the international order. In turn, Zimmerman drew attention to the public-service career opportunities resulting from the new interest on the part of federal agencies in hiring graduates knowledgeable about Latin America and Latin American affairs. He clearly saw the prospect of future funding for the university in this area, and he was correct. Moreover, Zimmerman's ability to stay in close contact with State Department personnel and earn their support for UNM projects was enhanced by his willingness to play a leadership role in regional and national professional societies, such as the Association of American Colleges (AAC) and the National Association of State Universities (NASU). The latter was especially interested in expanding educational ties with Latin America and, in 1942, selected Zimmerman to represent it on a trip to the Southern Hemisphere to recruit Latin American universities to join it. Contending that "many benefits in inter-American educational cooperation will ensue from this widening of the scope of the organization," the NASU's goal was that Zimmerman's trip would result in the standardization of enrollment procedures among member institutions and the compilation of a general directory of institutions of higher education in the Americas. For its part, the AAC had formed the Commission on Cultural Relations with Latin American Countries, which Zimmerman chaired in the years 1940–1941. The commission was charged, among its other tasks, with organizing a committee to develop a model curriculum for the study of Latin American history and society in US colleges and universities, "based upon the work now being done in many of the best institutions in the country."[2] As its chairman, Zimmerman had the authority to appoint the members of the committee, and he named five persons from the UNM faculty.[3] The model curriculum looked very much like the nucleus of courses then being taught at UNM. Furthermore, since George Hammond was on the committee, the suggested curriculum was bound to have (as it did) a Boltonian orientation.[4]

As the result of all these actions and initiatives, both internal and external, Zimmerman had succeeded by 1940 in winning recognition for the university as one of the nation's leading academic centers for the study of Southwest and New World archaeology and ethnology and Latin American and Spanish Borderlands history and for its strong institutional programs in other fields. These included Spanish literature and language, biology, political science, and philosophy, which had developed special concentrations on the region of the Southwest and Latin America. Robert L. Kelly, who delivered UNM's 1941 commencement address, called attention (if a little bombastically) to the university's rising stature in this regard: "The University of New Mexico," remarked Kelly, "has embarked upon a great and new unifying enterprise—the enterprise of helping to bind together with ourselves the people of Latin America. . . . Here in your curriculum, from anthropology straight through to zoology, is a program of integration of the learning, the aspiration and the hopes of the peoples of the Western Hemisphere."[5]

Riding this momentum, and with the foundation now solidly secured and the regents in agreement, Zimmerman considered it propitious to seek additional funding from the legislature to expand the Latin American studies program at UNM and create the School of Inter-American Affairs. Accordingly, a "Proposed budget for biennium 1941–43" identified "Pan Americanism" as a new budget line for the university.[6] This description was as nebulous as one of Kercheville's proposals, but the budget requests gradually came into sharper focus. In April 1941, Zimmerman sent a memorandum to the regents summarizing recommendations voted by the deans and others, one of which was to devote special attention to the program in inter-American relations. A sum of $25,000 was requested for what was called "Pan American Relationship Studies."[7] The definitive move came a year later, when the university budget for the 1941–1942 fiscal year included an appropriation in the amount of $10,500 (or some $165,000 in 2017 dollars) for the "School of Inter-American Affairs"—to operate as a stand-alone unit under the umbrella of the College of Arts and Sciences.[8] This appropriation and related budget items were shepherded through the state legislature's Appropriations and Finance Committee by majority whip Concha Ortiz y Pino, a firm supporter of the university and a partisan of both the Spanish revival and the Hispano Cause. As she succinctly summed up her role many years later: "I carried legislation through for the establishing of the School of Inter-American Affairs."[9] At their May 31, 1941, meeting, the regents were advised by Zimmerman that he had offered the directorship of the new school to Joaquín Ortega, who had spent the spring semester and summer session at UNM as a visiting professor in the Spanish department. Ortega, Zimmerman indicated, would make a final decision after conferring with colleagues and upper-level administrators at his current institution, the University of Wisconsin. By August his appointment was made official.[10] In a listing of new UNM faculty, Ortega was described as follows: "For twenty-five years was head of the Department of Spanish at the University of Wisconsin. For three summers Dr. Ortega has been with us and is known to most of the faculty and to the Regents."[11]

Known to almost all the faculty, yes, but not necessarily beloved or warmly welcomed by all.[12] Short of explicit testimony by Zimmerman himself, we cannot know precisely why he favored Ortega to be the school's first director, but circumstances strongly suggest several reasons. First, Zimmerman had known Ortega for ten years and had developed a close rapport with him. He respected the work Ortega had done in building the University of Wisconsin's Spanish department into one of the best, if not *the* best, in the country—an effort that took imagination, high ambition, intellectual prowess, and administrative and fund-raising skills. He also understood and valued Ortega's great fondness for New Mexico and his attachment to the state and its people. Zimmerman was likely convinced that Ortega, who had advised other universities with an interest in developing Latin American and Iberian studies programs, had the knowledge, skills, and ambition to make the SIAA a success. Indeed, at the conclusion of the spring 1941 semester, on the basis of his own analysis of the existing teaching and research program in the inter-American field at UNM, undertaken at the express invitation of Zimmerman, Ortega had laid out a complete plan for the structure and operations of the proposed school. Foreshadowing the industriousness he would show as the SIAA director, he also supplied Zimmerman with a list of special projects that Zimmerman could carry with him to Washington for possible funding, including proposals for a statewide bilingual conference (on which he collaborated with Concha Ortiz y Pino) to advance research into the teaching of Spanish in the public schools; a Latin American artist-in-residence program and a major grant-in-aid for building up library collections (both were later funded and implemented); and, perhaps most interesting of all, the prospectus for a school of Indian affairs at UNM. Although this latter proposal did not advance beyond the initial planning stage, it nonetheless indicated an awareness of the direct link between Latin American and Native American studies.

Second, there were rivalries and politics internal to UNM that argued (as we shall see) for hiring someone from the outside, someone with the skills and experience to bring opposing factions together and "reconcile contradictions."[13] Partly because of the provincialism and obdurate ways of some parties, and partly because of Ortega's own prideful personality, this task proved more difficult than Zimmerman might have predicted. For better or worse, however (and, personalities aside, it was almost entirely for the better) his choice was made. Enticed by the prospect of making a new start in a social and physical environment that shared much in common with his native land, Ortega pulled up roots in Madison, Wisconsin, and moved with his wife, son, and daughter to New Mexico to spend the last phase of his academic life.

When this move occurred, Ortega was forty-nine and had lived in the United States for twenty-six years, the last five as a US citizen. He was a native of Andalucía, Spain, born in 1892 in the town of Ronda, which lies about sixty miles west of the Mediterranean coastal city of Málaga. While Ortega's early years and family background are an empty slate, he clearly had a predilection for hard work and self-advancement. Between 1909 (when he was just seventeen) and 1915, he worked as a journalist, serving as Spanish correspondent for several Buenos Aires newspapers, while also serving in the Spanish medical corps (Sanidad Militar) in 1913.[14] According to Ortega, the Paleolithic caves of La Pileta, which had been discovered in 1905 and contained a range of well-preserved prehistoric art, lay on his family's property.[15] He spent considerable time during this same 1909–1915 period examining and helping excavate portions of the caves. Ortega earned two postsecondary degrees in Spain—a bachelor's degree from the University of Granada and a professional degree from a business school in Málaga—both awarded in 1914. In 1915, he was hired as a technical assistant within the Spanish Tariff Commission in Madrid, a position that he parlayed into a Spanish government fellowship that allowed him to pursue graduate study in the United States.[16] He began at the University of Michigan in 1915 and transferred the following year to the University of Wisconsin, where he enrolled as a candidate for the MA degree in romance languages and was also made an assistant instructor in Spanish. He was awarded the master's degree a year later, along with a full instructorship.

Joaquín Ortega (see fig. 11) and the University of Wisconsin were apparently an ideal match, because from that point on, he rose rapidly in the ranks of the UW faculty, making assistant professor in 1918, associate in 1923, and—despite several year-long and semester-long leaves of absence to work in Spanish and European libraries and archives—full professor and chair of the Department of Spanish and Portuguese in 1930.[17] In addition, he also gave a series of lectures at the University of Chicago, Bryn Mawr College, and the University of Southern California during the academic year 1920–1921. Ortega enjoyed a distinguished career at Wisconsin, the pinnacle of which was perhaps the work he did with his colleague Antonio García Solalinde to found the Seminary of Medieval Spanish Studies (today known as the Hispanic Seminary of Medieval Studies), with support from numerous public and private sources.[18] During his time in Wisconsin, Ortega also spent several years as the official representative in the United States of the Spanish Ministry of Education. Looking back at past milestones in the evolution of the University of Wisconsin's College of Letters and Science, the 1949 *Badger Yearbook* noted Ortega's role in elevating the reputation of the university nationally: "It was during this time that many great teachers helped to make the University of Wisconsin one of the most outstanding schools in the country. Joaquin [sic] Ortega did a great deal to improve the Spanish Department."[19] If part of what made Wisconsin one of the premier public universities in the country was its "many great teachers," then Ortega was at the center of this success by bringing onto the faculty such world-renowned scholars as García Solalinde and the Spanish historian and literary critic Américo Castro.

As he set out for Albuquerque in May 1940 to teach in the UNM summer session, and of course not yet knowing that he would leave Wisconsin permanently the following year, Ortega wrote to the dean of the College of Letters and Science, George C. Sellery, extolling the virtues of New Mexico and inviting Sellery to visit the state with his wife: "They are having there this year an extraordinary program of pagaents [sic], Indian dances, and what not, in celebration of the Coronado Cuarto Centennial. Why don't you give me the pleasure of showing

FIGURE 11 "Joaquín Ortega [fifth from right, top row] at a University of Wisconsin Spanish & Portuguese Department 'Gay '90s Party,' 1938." Photo Collection (call no. 2019S01123, box 276, folder 11/1 Spanish). Courtesy of University of Wisconsin–Madison University Archives and Records Management.

you and Mrs. Sellery those beautiful spots I know so well? . . . If you have never been in New Mexico . . . [t]here is nothing in America more appealing. Landscape, architecture, people, merge into a perfect unit."[20] In one or another form, Ortega would make this claim about New Mexico time and again, and it goes a long way toward explaining the attraction that the new position held for him. In his idealized conception of the SIAA, its work would reinvigorate and help preserve the social dimensions of this "perfect unit" (see fig. 12).

"Reconcile Contradictions"

It will be recalled that two years earlier, when George Sánchez was communicating his interest in returning to New Mexico, Francis Kercheville had recommended him as the "logical" choice for director of the institute that he knew Zimmerman planned to establish at UNM when circumstances permitted. Others

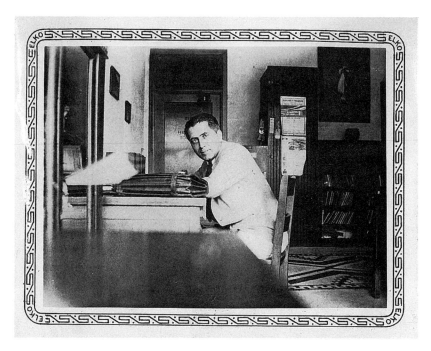

FIGURE 12 "Joaquín Ortega seated at a desk in the University of Southern California Library, 1933." Photo courtesy of Bruce Bolinger/Grass Valley, CA.

thought very highly of Sánchez as well and were confounded by the continuing animosity that blocked him from attaining an important executive position in his native state. Dennis Chávez exemplified this puzzlement when he wrote in a letter to Mauricio Miera that Sánchez was "good enough for the Rockefellers."[21] There is no evidence that Chávez was alluding specifically to the denial of a prospective role for Sánchez as director of the proposed UNM institute, but if that had been his implication, he would not have been wrong. Between Kercheville's late 1930s recommendation of Sánchez and the appointment of Ortega in 1941, the thinking seemed to have evolved (on the part of Zimmerman and a core group around him)—and we have unfortunately to rely on Kercheville as the sole authority on this matter because of the paucity of documentation—into the view that only an "outsider" could succeed as director. If that was the case, what were the "contradictions" that needed to be reconciled?

The deliberations among faculty and administration that preceded the founding of the SIAA revealed two fissures within the university. One concerned differing viewpoints about the mission and purpose of the school—what should be the relative emphasis on strictly academic versus community-oriented work, and where should those emphases be focused—on New Mexico, on Latin America, or on both? The other issue pertained to the question of leadership of the school and to alleged tensions and divisions that broke along ethnic lines. As the idea of the proposed school began to gel in late 1940, Kercheville wrote to Zimmerman in frank terms about the matter of finding a suitable director: "We ... should like to recommend that ... the administration bring to the University of New Mexico an outstanding Spaniard or Latin American scholar as all of us know the peculiar social and linguistic background of New Mexico makes it imperative that this be done. No Anglo-American, Mexican, or native New Mexican scholar would fit into this situation. . . . The peculiar setup in New Mexico with its social and historical prejudices indicate[s] the truth of the above statement."[22] Moreover, a memo sent by Kercheville to Zimmerman a few weeks earlier had said much the same, but in addition claimed that Zimmerman had often voiced a similar sentiment: "As you have repeatedly said and correctly so, no Anglo-American can fill this need in New Mexico. This is precisely why both Spanish and Anglo alike will listen with such respectful enthusiasm to a Spaniard like Ortega."[23]

It is not clear if Kercheville was simply using Ortega as an example here or if he was actively promoting him for the position. Very likely it was simply the former, since he reacted with great ambivalence when Zimmerman informed him of Ortega's appointment.[24] Kercheville's remark that neither an Anglo-American (and he most probably had himself in mind), nor Mexican, nor native New Mexican would "fit into this situation" is somewhat opaque, but it obviously implies the existence of separate blocs. Appointment of an Anglo or Nuevomexicano would bring historical mistrust and resentments to the surface and into the open, while a supposedly neutral "third party" would keep those tensions at bay. In this sense, the appointment of an outsider was a form of the accommodative balance adduced by Carolyn Zeleny and indirectly served the interests of the "rhetorical compromise" posited by Charles Montgomery. Also embedded in Kercheville's statement was another consideration. He had presumably been sincere in his earlier recommendation of George Sánchez as the logical choice to lead a future institute, but for many nativos, no native New Mexican would have been acceptable precisely because the memory of Sánchez, and the actions that he took while in state government, were still so fresh among Hispanic politicos. They did not necessarily trust Zimmerman to appoint a native New Mexican who would tally with their interests and allegiances.

It is difficult to know how much credence to put into Kercheville's allegations. Subsequent to learning of Ortega's appointment, Kercheville recalled, in a letter to Zimmerman, that as part of earlier discussions regarding the structure and leadership of the proposed school, only he—and not Hammond, Zimmerman, Brand, dean of Arts and Sciences Jay Knode, or anyone else—had expressed the opinion that whoever became the director would need to be from outside the university and preferably a Spaniard or Latin American. The rest of the group, Kercheville recalled, "countered by saying the men at the University were as able as anyone to handle the program. Apparently in the case of Ortega there has been a change of heart or opinion."[25] On this question, Kercheville may not be the most reliable source, particularly as his own self-interest was involved. First, he claimed that Zimmerman had "repeatedly" said that no Anglo-American (and presumably, no Nuevomexicano, either) could succeed as director; now he was claiming that Zimmerman took the opposite position. However we wish to take Kercheville's declarations, it seems clear that once Zimmerman and the core group of Latin Americanists learned of Ortega's willingness to accept the position, they united around his appointment, viewing it as a piece of good fortune for the university.

In recruiting faculty for UNM who had already earned important reputations, Zimmerman was always careful to be transparent and to be seen as not "poaching" them from other institutions. He did the same in Ortega's case, giving the Spaniard ample time to ruminate and discuss UNM's offer with administrators in Wisconsin. In 1941, Ortega was at the peak of his academic career and widely known for the successes he had achieved in Madison. His decision to leave there was seen as New Mexico's great gain and Wisconsin's considerable loss. As George Sellery, UW's dean of the College of Letters and Science, wrote to Zimmerman in August 1941:

> The acceptance of Professor Ortega's resignation was a painful experience for me. He has made our department of Spanish into one of the great departments of the University and of the country. He has been one of the half-dozen leading professors of the University; teacher, scholar, gentleman, and interesting man, full of ideas and graces, and utterly democratic and human. You have, I must say, assumed a heavy responsibility in taking him from us, and I can only congratulate you on your success.[26]

Why does this angle on Ortega's appointment—the fact of his being a non-Anglo and a non-Nuevomexicano who came from the outside—matter to the degree it does? It is worth pointing out because, whatever his own motives, Kercheville seems to have been giving an honest assessment of the environment in UNM. The tensions and divisions that characterized Anglo-Hispano social relations in the university and the feelings on the part of Hispanic students of being isolated and excluded had not diminished since the 1933 racial-attitude survey controversy. On the contrary, they appeared to remain just as strong. During the 1941 spring semester and summer session that Ortega spent at UNM, he observed this situation and advised that the university renew its efforts to break down barriers between Hispanic and Anglo students, one means of which was to have faculty promote their interaction more directly through student clubs and organizations. "Shortly after I arrived in Albuquerque," he informed Zimmerman, "three 'Hispano' boys came one evening to see me at the Zia Lodge and lamented the fact that as soon as they started any Club like the Coronado one, little by little the 'Anglo' boys withdrew, leaving them alone."[27] Using UNM's Pan-American Society as an example, he emphasized the positive role that faculty could play, and he also tied these conditions to what remained a charged and sensitive topic:

> I earnestly believe that this organization deserves the wholehearted support of the Faculty. It could render an invaluable service in bringing together on some common ground the "hispano" and "anglo" boys, and it could also represent a significant move in the whole setup of the New Mexico program in Inter-American Relations. If the members of the Faculty decide to take active part in their meetings, they could help very effectively in establishing a better harmony between the two groups in the Campus—one of the fundamental requisites for any Pan American program in the institution. For what would the distinguished Latin American scholars who might come in the future here think when they see the prevailing hostility between the two races.[28]

Ortega was only expressing in more reserved language what Zimmerman's more outspoken critics, such as Juan Clancy and Ernest García, had said more explicitly: that UNM's much-vaunted commitment to Pan-Americanism rang hollow in light of its nonobservance inside the university. Rightly or wrongly, this sense of the flaunting of a principle was seen to operate not just at the level of the student body but among the faculty as well. One instance of this perceived discrepancy occurred in 1941 when Francis Kercheville went on leave and the acting chairmanship of the Department of Modern Languages was given to a relatively new and untested faculty member, Robert Duncan. Someone identifying himself or herself only as "An Interested Observer of the Alumni Association" (but who in tone and substance sounded either like an insider or someone with access to inside information) wrote to Concha Ortiz y Pino criticizing Duncan's appointment as yet another example of how the university publicly proclaimed the Pan-American ideal but failed to implement it in practice. It was seen to fail in this particular case because, for Duncan's critic (and perhaps for others), the logical replacement for Kercheville would seem to have been Arthur L. Campa, a tenured, well-respected member of the department for more than a decade, Mexican by birth but a resident of New Mexico from an early age. The author of the letter did not mince words:

> Has this become another example of the usual practice of placing an incompetent Anglo above a competent Spanish-speaking person whenever there is such a choice? New Mexico lost George Sánchez, who was an able educational leader, because the University refused to offer him any advancement. Will New Mexico lose the few remaining Spanish educational leaders simply because such discrimination exists that they must seek advancement elsewhere? Pan-Americanism is a nice cover-up; it sounds like a good thing to flaunt for self-protection; but apparently there is no intention to show sincerity in a constructive way when the opportunity arises. Pretty speeches and shallow, insincere pretense seem to take the place of concrete advancement of the cultural unity and advancement of friendship with Latin American people.[29]

The letter makes at least one unfair accusation. There is no evidence that Robert Duncan was incompetent, but that is not the point. Rather, it is the perception, whether true or not, that Anglo faculty received preferential treatment. It is difficult to know whether this sentiment was widely shared or not. Yet that it existed at all tends to underscore why Kercheville might have stated that no Anglo, Mexican, or Nuevomexicano could "fit into this situation," and why Zimmerman might have thought it prudent to recruit a director for the SIAA from outside the university. Coincidentally or not, two of the most distinguished and productive members of the faculty, George Sánchez and Arthur Campa (Campa a few years later), did have to leave UNM to move up in the academic world.

The second "contradiction" that needed to be reconciled pertained to the matter of defining the scope and focus of the School of Inter-American Affairs. There were two main approaches, one championed by Kercheville, the other by Ortega. In the early 1930s, Kercheville had been an ardent proponent of the "cultural approach." He returned from his 1941 travels in Latin America, however, with a different perspective, believing now that UNM's inter-American affairs course offerings needed to emphasize the applied sciences, industrial arts, and practical subjects. In a preliminary report summarizing what he had learned about the educational side of Pan-Americanism, Kercheville stated, "there is tremendous interest in the more practical aspects—road building, automobile mechanics, and other phases of engineering in health programs, in the natural sciences, radio, commercial courses, and business, and in physical education (sports and games). . . . Any new program in Inter-American affairs . . . must be so arranged as to instruct young men and women for this more practical side of Pan-Americanism—often lost sight of in cultural programs of 'goodwill' and understanding."[30] In a separate communication, he also sharply criticized the preliminary report that Ortega had submitted in April 1941, at Zimmerman's behest, outlining the content and operations of a future SIAA, faulting it for "its over-emphasis on the general, the abstract, the philosophical, and on the addition and emphasis of courses and men in purely Hispanic phases of the program."[31] In effect, Kercheville was advocating that UNM create a kind of vocational school within the university to teach students with an interest in Latin America a range of practical skills that they could impart to people across the nations to the south.[32]

Zimmerman also saw the opening that UNM graduates (native Spanish speakers especially) would have in pursuing professional opportunities in Latin America if they focused their studies on that region. "With the Spanish language abilities of our students," he noted, "the University has a most favorable opportunity to cooperate in developing economic life in such fields as road construction, bridge building, oil geology, building refineries and pipe lines, or in operating banks and other business[es], and industrial purposes."[33] At the same time, however, he did not subscribe to the notion that the academic preparation of such students, so far as it focused on Latin America and US–Latin American relations, should be vocational in nature. For his part, Ortega did not dispute that there was room within a Latin American studies curriculum for courses that would prepare students for technical, commercial, and diplomatic work, but his orientation was fundamentally different. Distinct from the turn that Kercheville had taken, he believed that the core of the university's program in the Latin American/Inter-American field should entail a traditional curriculum that spanned the humanities, social studies, fine arts, and natural sciences. The idea that such a program was overly general, abstract, and philosophical—as Kercheville had characterized it—was silly and contrary to reason. A second difference between the two men's views was that Ortega wanted to strengthen the curriculum, bring it into line with the high academic standards of a research department such as he had known at the University of Wisconsin, so that it could support degree programs through the doctoral level, whereas Kercheville wanted the university to put almost all the emphasis, in a revamped Inter-American studies curriculum, on a program for undergraduates.

Moreover, there was a second strategic component to Ortega's plan that distinguished it importantly from Kercheville's: its call for the SIAA to develop community programs to serve underprivileged and historically disadvantaged segments of the New Mexican population. Ortega thus urged President Zimmerman to

> bend all departments of the university to solve the problems of the state—in Land Economics, in Education, in Social Adjustment, in Political Aptitude, in the Conservation and Study of its Archeology and History, in the strengthening of its characteristic features. . . . Such a thing is not "playing politics," but being of service to a state which needs so badly expert service in all directions. Let the University offer solutions. There is no need of any kind of lobbying. Those solutions, if they are realistic and intelligent, will have to be adopted sooner or later in spite of the peanut politics.[34]

On this score, Joaquín Ortega was unquestionably Dennis Chávez's man— here he was making the same case that Chávez had made to his brother, David, two years earlier. It was a message that also resonated with Zimmerman. When officially offering the SIAA directorship to Ortega, Zimmerman had addressed the same point: "I know that New Mexico and the University of New Mexico would profit greatly by your presence on our campus because of your sympathetic understanding of the many difficult human problems which we face and of your dynamic ability to seek a solution for those problems."[35] Zimmerman not only applauded Ortega's conviction that the university should play a lead role in helping lift New Mexican towns and villages out of poverty and deprivation, he also believed that Ortega—a Spaniard who had lived and worked in the United States for twenty-five years—was equally attuned to both the "Anglo" and "Hispanic" ways of viewing the world and thus capable of building bridges across the cultural divide: "It [the directorship] should provide an opportunity for you to make practical application of your knowledge and understanding of the psychology of the American and the Spanish-speaking populations in innumerable fields of cultural relations between our country and the countries to the south."[36] Furthermore, Ortega found a source of legitimacy and perhaps additional inspiration for this component of the SIAA in George Sánchez's *Forgotten People.* "It is my opinion," he informed Zimmerman, "that Dr. Sánchez's book does not invalidate my own plan—on the contrary, it helps it."[37]

Ortega was fully aware that not everyone on the UNM faculty wanted to march to the tune of Zimmerman's inter-American initiative. The opposition came from two camps: from those who objected to Ortega's design and plans for the SIAA, in particular the wide span of activities proposed for it; and from those with little enthusiasm for the premise that the greater Hispanic world and Latin American studies should be central to the identity and mission of UNM, with all of the resource allocations such a commitment necessarily entailed. Ortega's answer to critics in the second camp was to restate the argument made almost a decade earlier by Clyde Kluckhohn and one that Zimmerman, of course, had also made over the years: namely, that given the limited resources of the state and its late start in developing institutions of higher education, the university's best chance, its golden opportunity to achieve academic distinction was to build on the special advantages that its history and location gave it. On this matter, the sole difference between Ortega and Kluckhohn was that Ortega broadened Kluckhohn's focus from primarily the Southwest and Spanish Borderlands region to include Latin America. The principle was the same. In Ortega's words: "The University . . . needs to excel in some particular discipline to rise from anonymity to national recognition. History and destiny have combined to make this specialization logically be the Latin American field." A move in this direction, he argued, will "make a mark for the University and place it with distinctiveness on the academic map of America."[38] He also faulted these critics for their complacency. Theirs was a failure of imagination and ambition, a refusal to challenge themselves and "think big." They needed to be pulled along. Ortega firmly believed that the SIAA, to borrow A. E. Houseman's metaphor, was not a brook too broad for leaping. The task before UNM, he elaborated in the planning document that he prepared for Zimmerman in April 1941, was to

> foster a first-rate program in Inter-American Relations which will attract students from all parts of the nation and which will arrest the attention and enlist the financial support of all federal agencies and foundations interested in Pan-Americanicanism. In this program, New Mexico should ultimately vie with the best in the country—even if doing things in the small scale that its resources may permit. . . . Size is not quality. The academic world, for one thing, knows very well where

quality is and is quite ready to recognize it. . . . New Mexico will be a unique institution in this continent, offering from the educational point of view and from many other points of view things that nowhere else could be found.[39]

If there was a leading voice to the opposition from the first camp it was Donald Brand's. Brand was part of the inner circle of UNM Latin Americanists and for some time had advocated the expansion of student exchanges, scholarly conferences, publications, and other such conventional activities in the Latin American area. In his view, however, these could be accommodated within the existing organizational structure and did not require any planning and coordination beyond those of an interdepartmental committee. Brand was on leave in Mexico during the second half of 1941, and when he learned that the SIAA had actually been established, he wrote to Zimmerman, expressing the opinion that the university was overreaching itself. For Brand, the very name of the school was emblematic of this fact. "Dean Knode," he wrote, "mentioned Dr. Behrendt, a 'School of Inter-American Affairs'. . . [I] wish to say here that [the] title of [the] school seems too general or comprehensive—considering library facilities and faculty."[40]

While Brand may have genuinely believed that the SIAA was too ambitious for UNM in light of the university's underfunding and still limited infrastructure, there was both a personal side and an arbitrary narrowness to his skepticism as well. The Dr. Behrendt to whom he alluded in his letter was Richard Behrendt (of whom more to come), a Latin American specialist whose expertise crossed several fields. Brand had been informed by Dean Knode that Behrendt was going to teach a new course on the geography of Latin America and the West Indies. Brand already offered a course, through the anthropology department, on this subject, and even though Behrendt might approach it differently (leaning more toward economic than cultural geography), he bristled at the idea that someone else might invade his "territory."

Brand, in fact, wasted no time in trying to obstruct and whittle down plans for the SIAA. In a letter to George Sánchez, Arthur Campa described Brand's oppositional tactics that involved disallowing the offering of courses from faculty in inter-American affairs:

Our enrollment has fallen down considerably. We are around 400 short this year. [The effect of the impending US entry into World War II was beginning to be felt.] . . . No enthusiasm evident except by the new School. Brand and Donnelly

[Thomas Donnelly, at that time a professor of political science and government and future dean of the College of Arts and Sciences] refused to allow courses of the Inter-American School to be taught by the new men in their respective departments. . . . Those courses were outlawed at registration time. The new man, Dr. Behrendt, a Jewish refugee, is pretty much discouraged. Zimmerman is quite disturbed.[41]

Brand had set his opposition in motion. During the Ortega years, he affected a belittling, nay-saying attitude toward both the operations of the school and the consolidation of UNM's growing reputation as one of the country's leading academic centers for the interdisciplinary study of Latin America. Furthermore, he not only affected such an attitude but acted on the basis of it as well. While Brand had expanded departmental interests from the Southwest to Mexico, he was apparently unwilling to extend much coverage to the rest of Latin America. Thus, when Claude Lévi-Strauss (having taken refuge in the United States during the war) wrote to the department in 1943 inquiring about a possible position, he was informed by Brand (who had become head of the department in 1936 when Hewett was finally eased out) that South America "lay outside its field of interest."[42]

Even before Ortega relocated to New Mexico, UNM, as we have seen, was steadily making a name for itself in this field. Brand, however, wanted nothing more than to pour water on the parade. For example, during the 1942 spring semester—when the SIAA had barely gotten off the ground—he analyzed enrollments in the two courses in the anthropology department that theoretically should have attracted students with an interest in Latin America, regardless of their departmental major. On the basis of the quite low enrollment of such students, Brand drew several conclusions: that the anthropology department had little reason to concern itself with "academic interrelationships in the field of Latin American studies," that UNM students were provincial in outlook and lacked intellectual curiosity, and that there was little real interest in Latin American studies at UNM.[43] The interest, he implied, was artificially imposed from above. Needless to say, Brand's sweeping generalizations were not warranted by his very small sample. A number of mitigating factors could have explained the low enrollment figures. Brand had copied his memo to Zimmerman, the deans, several departmental chairmen, and Ortega, who as director of the SIAA had the status of a dean. Ortega reacted in a very nondefensive manner, stating that to some extent Brand may have been correct in his view, because "excessive departmentalization," as he put it, was unfortunately embedded in universities whose traditions often weighed against interdepartmental cooperation. Breaking down such insularity, Ortega added, would take time, but the process would likely accelerate—and he was correct in this prediction—after the war, when a greater emphasis would be placed on studying world areas (or on "area studies," as the field came to be known) as opposed to simply individual disciplines.[44]

Ortega's self-assured manner and professional demeanor enabled him (for the most part) to tolerate and deflect criticism, and to then move forward with his ideas. Indeed, the aforementioned George Sellery had portrayed Ortega as a fair-minded, empathetic, highly cultivated person who embodied the best virtues of the academy, and there is no reason to discount his description. One of Ortega's closest associates at UNM, Lyle Saunders, described him in very similar terms, as did former students and other colleagues of his at the University of Wisconsin.[45] But Ortega's personality was complex. He had not realized his ambitions by practicing a philosophy of quietism. On the contrary, he could be headstrong, generally quick to defend his point of view, and anything but humble. One has the impression that Ortega was a great listener and interlocutor and was glad to solicit the opinion of others, but well before the exchange of ideas was finished he knew exactly what he wanted to do and how it should be done. Arthur Campa provides an interesting perspective on Ortega's personality and leadership style, one not entirely consistent with Sellery's encomium about Ortega's "utterly democratic" ways of operating. Shortly after Ortega assumed the SIAA directorship, Campa let George Sánchez know that Ortega regretted his loss to UNM: "Ortega will be down to see you in Texas. . . . He still has hopes of bringing you to work in 'his School.' He definitely wants you to work *for* him. Should you be looking for a boss, you know where there is one" [emphasis added].[46]

As conceived by Zimmerman and Ortega, the SIAA thus had to confront a wave of opposition. Some objected to the priority given to this new initiative, some to its scope and institutional framework, and some—like Brand—to what they feared would be intrusion on their own teaching prerogatives. Yet all in all, it was a relatively minor wave. At bottom, the opposition, from whatever source it came, attested to the growth pains of a university. The arguments on behalf of the school were patently stronger than the arguments against it. Zimmerman had spent years preparing the ground, methodically cultivating the support of the regents, deans, and faculty, and now they rewarded him by lining up behind this new priority. Ortega would eventually lose control as the environment changed and priorities shifted, but for now he was fully in command and seen by almost all as the ideal choice to lead the School of Inter-American Affairs—someone who, by virtue of his origins, experience, farsightedness, and deep understanding of New Mexico could successfully weave the SIAA into the fabric of the university.

The Attainments of the SIAA, 1941–1948

The School of Inter-American Affairs, of course, did not emerge out of a vacuum. The half decade that preceded its opening had seen the university's instructional program in inter-American studies grow to quite respectable size. In his April 1941 survey of the program, Ortega found, in fact, that several UNM departments already had excellent "set-ups," as he put it, in the inter-American area, and that two—anthropology and history—could easily hold their own against the top-ranked programs in the country. At the same time, there were some prominent holes to fill, the most immediate of which—in Ortega's judgment—were in economics and the fine arts.[47] With both the additional funding provided by the legislature and the mandate for expansion now in place, the operations of the school got underway. The day-to-day business of the school was managed by Ortega and a small staff. Higher-level matters involving courses, programs, and student and extracurricular activities were managed by an interdepartmental committee composed of the SIAA director, ten faculty representatives from the university's three colleges, as well as representatives from the library, extension division, and summer session. The deans of the graduate school and the College of Arts and Sciences were ex officio members, as was the president of the university. Institutionally, the SIAA had the status of a college, inasmuch as it operated autonomously, with Ortega reporting directly to Zimmerman. As UNM's first integrated area-studies program (though it was not yet referred to as such) it administered and coordinated degree programs across many departments of the university, while also offering courses of its own.

With Zimmerman's approval, Ortega quickly moved to fill two professional positions within the School. Lyle Saunders, sociologist, was hired as a research associate, and Richard Behrendt as an assistant professor of inter-American affairs. Saunders, who became Ortega's indispensable right-hand man, was especially interested in the history of the Spanish-speaking people of the Southwest. He was strongly influenced by Sánchez's *Forgotten People*, several years later taking a leave of absence from UNM to work with Sánchez on the latter's "Study of the Spanish-Speaking People of Texas" project. The polyglot Behrendt, a German Jewish refugee, was an accomplished scholar and genuine "area studies" specialist, competent to teach in several departments. As Ortega wrote, in recommending him to Zimmerman, "with the excessive American departmental specialization, it is almost impossible to find in this country a man of such wide preparation."[48] Behrendt added three new courses to the curriculum: one through the anthropology department ("Geography of Latin America and the Caribbean"—the course to which Brand had so strongly objected), one in the Department of Economics and Business Administration ("Economics and Trade of Latin America"), and one in the sociology department ("Social Problems of Latin America"). Ortega himself taught a new course, offered through the SIAA, called "Ibero-American Civilization." Other new courses, such as "Ethnobiology of the New World" and "Latin American Crafts," were also added to the list of offerings in 1941–1942. The inter-American studies curriculum, which encompassed courses that focused solely on Latin America as well as on US–Latin American relations (the two terms—*Latin American* and *inter-American*—were sometimes used interchangeably), continued to be expanded throughout the 1940s.[49] All of the university's schools and colleges participated in this development, the benefits of which were considered to be national, not just regional or local. As the program grew in scope and size and became more sophisticated, the reputation of the university as a center for specialized studies on Latin America and US–Latin American relations was seen to be enhanced as well. A comment made in 1943 by John Donald Robb, the then acting dean of the College of Fine Arts, typifies this perception: "Particular attention is being paid to the assembly of an adequate library of Latin American music and records, a field in which institutions and individuals throughout the country rightfully look to us for leadership."[50] The same assertive sentiment could have been expressed by other deans and department chairmen.

Less than a year after the opening of the SIAA, one of Zimmerman's chief goals was achieved when the Graduate Committee of the Faculty Senate, in July 1942, approved Ortega's proposal for instituting a master's degree in inter-American affairs. As the program expanded, it continued to develop and offer new areas of concentration. In addition to the existing bachelor's degree in inter-American affairs (in which students had to specialize in one of four areas: "Historical and Cultural"; "Business Administration"; "Social, Economic, and Political Affairs"; or "Regional, The Hispanic Southwest"), the school coordinated a two-year certificate program for persons interested in clerical positions, or in work as interpreters, in a bilingual Spanish-English setting. Responding to Kercheville's challenge to equip technicians with background knowledge of Latin America, so they could train and work with counterparts in that region, it also offered a one-year postgraduate program in "Inter-American Relations for Majors in Science Departments and Graduates of Technical Schools." Finally, a combined curriculum in engineering and inter-American studies was also developed.

By any measure, the School of Inter-American Affairs had proven itself, and behind all of its activities was the tireless hand of Joaquín Ortega. Like all units of the university, the SIAA submitted statistical data and descriptive information for inclusion in the university's biennial reports. Ortega's submissions make for enlightening reading, conveying as they do the school's voluminous activities on the academic side during his seven-year tenure as director. For example, the report for 1943–1945 begins by noting that "despite war conditions," course enrollments were increasing from year to year, with fifty-seven inter-American affairs majors registered in November 1944.[51] It continues with sections on the scholarly activities and public service work of its staff; the scholarships it has awarded (through the Institute of International Education) to students from Latin America and the tuition scholarships given to other students (primarily from New Mexico but also from Massachusetts and Texas); the services rendered by it (which number in the dozens and extend to universities, agencies, organizations, and individuals over the whole of the United States) to the university's Research Bureau in the Social Sciences; the many student activities and contests it has sponsored; the work of its placement and advisory services (with many successful referrals and placements, especially to and in federal government agencies); a listing of thirty-five distinguished visitors it hosted from Latin America (e.g., Manuel Gamio, Osvaldo Guayasamín, Manuel Toussaint, Julio Jiménez Rueda), the nineteen public lectures it sponsored (some with other departments), covering topics in the politics, economics, public health, social geography, archaeology, art, and music of Latin America; the nine conferences it organized or co-organized (some held in Albuquerque, some elsewhere, dealing with similar themes affecting both the Southwest and Latin America); the seven art exhibits it mounted or sponsored; its numerous cooperative activities (extension of funds and services) with other university departments and units; the ten gifts and grants that it secured; and the thirteen publications it edited and brought out (including translations, bibliographies, short papers, miscellanea, and full-length monographs dealing with Latin America and cultural relations in the Southwest). The number of conferences, lectures, visiting scholars, and so on may have gone up or down in other years, but the SIAA's reports during the 1940s essentially duplicate the record for this two-year period. In short, the school more than lived up to its promise, maintaining a consistently high level of important activity throughout the decade.

Not contained in this report, because its activities occurred before and after the 1943–1945 biennium, was one of Ortega's most interesting academic projects, the Latin American Artist in Residence program, the idea for which he had brought with him from the University of Wisconsin. Although he believed that UNM's most pressing need in the Latin American area was in economics and political economy, he nonetheless accorded high importance to the arts and knew that the university, given the state's attraction for visual artists and its enviable standing in the art world, could be very competitive in this area. Furthermore, Ortega had a great source of support from persons in and connected to the arts community in New Mexico, who, no less than he did, saw how artistic endeavor could bridge ethnic divisions in the state and serve the aims of Pan-Americanism. Among the most enthusiastic partisans of that view was Ina Sizer Cassidy, then director of the WPA's Federal Writers' Project in New Mexico (and widow of Santa Fe painter Gerald Cassidy). She stressed this point to UNM professor George Emerson, who was in charge of the university's fine arts festival in 1941:

> Because of its unique background, New Mexico, the oldest Spanish community in America, and the University, founded as it was jointly by the Spanish-speaking people of the State and the Anglo-Americans, and supported as it is by them, should take the lead in forwarding the cultural relations of the Americas. Art . . . should prove to be one of the best means of inter-communication between the nations. Therefore I should like to see the Fine Arts Festival develop into a Pan American Fine Arts Festival with exhibits invited from all of our Central and South American neighbors.[52]

Able to strengthen his case with arguments like Sizer Cassidy's, Ortega moved swiftly and obtained a grant through the State Department's wartime Office of the Coordinator of Inter-American Affairs to fund the program.[53] Coincidentally or not, Ortega's proposal also underscored the university's interest in organizing its annual fine arts festival on a statewide basis and, as part of it, inviting the Latin American nations to send exhibits and performing artists. In accordance with these aims, the theme of the 1942 festival was "The Arts and Pan Americanism." In his application, Ortega referred to the visits to New Mexico, arranged by the US State Department, of distinguished Latin American scholars and public figures, dramatizing how "spell-bound" they were by the "kindred Spanish atmosphere" they found "in this land of Hispanic traditions. . . . What we propose is to open the heart of New Mexico to a creative artist who could appreciate our Indian and Hispanic life, lore, and customs . . . , who could interpret them." Striking a familiar note, he called up the omnipresent tricultural formulation, declaring that New Mexico, "by intrinsic right," is the "ideal human workshop for an artist wanting to capture the continental substance and give his creations American range. Only in this spot does one find the point of union, the natural triangle, of the three main racial components of the Americas."[54]

The first artist chosen to be in residence at UNM, during the summer of 1942 and the first semester of the 1942–1943 school year, was the Mexican painter, Jesús Guerrero Galván. Guerrero Galván, who was followed two years later by Guatemalan artist Alfredo Gálvez Suárez, taught a course in the College of Fine Arts, gave public lectures, established contacts with artists in the region, and—as a personal gift to the university—painted a fresco, the *Union of the Americas*, on a wall in the main administration building (see plate 2). In brief comments that he made at the unveiling of the fresco, Zimmerman celebrated the work as symbolizing the university's "ever widening, broadening and deepening interest in inter-American life and relations."[55] The artist-in-residence program also bore fruit in the music department, when Mexican musicologist and folklorist Vicente Mendoza accepted an appointment as Latin American musician in residence for the second semester of the 1945–1946 school year. As with Guerrero Galván, Mendoza's appointment also resulted in a "gift" to the university. During his stay, he developed a keen interest in New Mexican music and folklore and set about studying and classifying folkloric materials housed in the university library and elsewhere. His project resulted in a book of texts, musical transcriptions, and critical commentary, titled *Estudio y clasificación de la música tradicional hispánica de Nuevo México*, which he donated to UNM.[56]

These achievements, the great majority orchestrated by Ortega, were impressive, especially for a school that was only four years old, but no one could accuse them of breaking the academic mold; they were all traditional and uncontroversial scholarly pursuits. The SIAA, however, had a more innovative, creative side, one that Ortega came to call the "Community Program." It would take the school into new territory and—depending on one's view—to new heights but also lead, some years later, to the loss of faith in Ortega's leadership.

Reaching Beyond the Confines of the University

In the conclusion to his April 1941 report on the needs and opportunities confronting UNM's inter-American studies program, Ortega had stated that Sánchez's *Forgotten People* helped make the case for his own plan. It is not difficult to understand why he would draw that conclusion. He took Sánchez's description and diagnosis of the economic problems and sociocultural barriers faced by large segments of New Mexico's Spanish-speaking population—a model of academic research—as a call to action, in line with his advice to Zimmerman that he "bend all departments of the university to solve the problems of the state." And Zimmerman, as we have seen, would have been only too glad to receive such advice, since it not only accorded with his own thinking about the university's responsibilities to the state but also underscored his belief that Ortega—a man who moved comfortably between both the Anglo and Hispanic worlds—could "find solutions," as Zimmerman put it, to the "difficult human problems" faced by the university and the state.

While not every UNM faculty member may have welcomed it with the same degree of enthusiasm, the notion that the university should render service to the state, with particular attention paid to its less privileged citizens, was essentially a run-of-the-mill proposition, hardly the stuff of controversy. More problematically, however, why should such service originate in and be delivered through a school of inter-American affairs, whose mission and purpose were ostensibly to advance the study of Latin American history and culture, educate and train students to work in the Latin American nations, and further improve understanding and relations between the United States and its neighbors to the south? Why? The question was readily answered: because many aspects of inter-American affairs, and certainly many elements of Latin American history and society, found clear expression in New Mexico. The SIAA brought together and gave greater clarity to various ideas and impulses that had run through UNM since the early days of Zimmerman's presidency: the Pan-American ideal and concomitant belief that New Mexico provided the perfect setting to improve inter-American relations; the Boltonian orientation, centered on the belief in the fundamental unity of the two Americas; the transparent overlap of patterns of social and economic life of many rural and urban communities in Latin America with their counterparts in New Mexico, created by the shared history of centuries of Spanish colonial rule and administration (the latter's time as part of the United States notwithstanding); and—in its usual centerpiece role—the "three cultures" motif. Lyle Saunders expressed it thus:

In focusing much of its attention on the social and economic problems of New Mexico, the School has recognized that our state offers unique advantages for the development of techniques to facilitate cultural relations between the people of the United States and those of our hemisphere neighbors. For here in New Mexico the three great cultural groups of the Americas—the Indian, the Spanish-American, and the Anglo—meet and blend, each giving traits and characteristics to the others and each in turn borrowing elements from them. Here, if anywhere, is the ideal place to observe what happens when the cultures of the Americas meet: and here is the place to learn what can be done to facilitate the mutual adjustments that have to be made.[57]

So while to some the concentration on New Mexico may have needed explaining, the explanation, in Ortega's mind, was ready-made: if, as he planned, projects to assist communities were to be a vital part of the SIAA's mission, there was no compulsion to undertake them hundreds or thousands of miles to the south when the problems to be addressed existed on one's own doorstep. Doubtless some in the community traced a dotted line in this logic back to earlier criticisms of Zimmerman ("Pan Americanism should start in the very portals of Mr. Zimmerman's institution.")

In essence, Ortega endorsed Kercheville's view that the university needed to involve itself directly in practical affairs and provide vocational education, but he inverted the parameters. Instead of reorienting UNM's program in Latin American studies toward teaching technical knowledge and skills that graduates could take with them to succeed on work assignments in Latin America, as Kercheville advocated, the SIAA would utilize the existing knowledge gained from field studies (such as George Sánchez's), the capabilities of a diverse group of faculty, and the human and financial resources provided by local, state, and federal agencies, to develop and coordinate in-state projects. These projects would support and reinforce the work already being done by local Hispanic leaders to equip men and women in their communities with the education and skills they needed to lift themselves out of poverty and enter the market economy. In simplest terms, this was the reasoning that underlay the school's Community Program and why it seemed to make sense that the SIAA focus its outreach efforts on New Mexico, not Latin America.

In assessing the rationale for the program, though, and, more particularly, its focus on New Mexico, we should glance once more at Sánchez's *Forgotten People*, since Ortega was entirely correct in citing its helpfulness in marshalling evidence on behalf of the Community Program. In describing the chronic impoverishment of the largely rural, native-Spanish-speaking people of Taos County and their inability and failure to adapt to Anglo-American practices and life, Sánchez laid proper emphasis on the critical role played by land and its dispossession in the decades following the American annexation. Initially, disputes and claims over land were adjudicated by the office of the US surveyor general. It was a time of general lawlessness and unscrupulous land grabs, when Hispanic interests were forced to argue and defend their claims on Anglo terms. The system was inherently biased against them. The office of the surveyor general was replaced in the last decade of the nineteenth century by the Court of Private Land Claims. The process followed by this agency was more orderly, but accommodation to it still worked to the great disadvantage of the native population. Violent conflict was ended and replaced by the settlement (and often rejection) of claims to ownership on the part of Nuevomexicanos. "Disadvantageous land deals," as Carolyn Zeleny wrote, "began a process [of loss] which cultural factors rapidly made more disastrous."[58] Hispanic village and community life had been organized around the farming and grazing of communal lands; when those were broken up and dispersed or sold off as a last measure to cancel debts, the way of life they had supported was in turn fractured and weakened. *Forgotten People* captured this loss, which extended beyond land to education, language, and economic power and privilege. Ortega's Community Program sought to address the unfortunate legacy of this process, which had left the Hispanic population in a subordinate position within the "social and economic structure of the new society in New Mexico."[59]

Just as the academic side of the SIAA could at times involve the participation of civic and community leaders, so, too, did its extracurricular activities and work sometimes incorporate a scholarly dimension. The two sides of the school were never entirely divorced from each other. One of the best examples of how they came together to their mutual benefit was a five-day instructional conference, called the "School for the Rio Grande Valley," planned and organized by Ortega and Carl Taeusch, then head of the Division of Program Study and Discussion at the Bureau of Agricultural Economics in the US Department of Agriculture. The theme of the conference, held on the UNM campus between April 27 and May 1, 1942, was "The War and Cultural Relations in the Rio Grande Valley," and to judge from the program, the School for the Rio Grande Valley had three main purposes: to enlighten attendees (and a special point was made of inviting participation by the public) about the "difficult human problems," as Zimmerman phrased it, faced primarily by the Spanish-speaking and Native American populations of the valley; to promote better relations among the different ethnic and racial groups who lived in the valley; and to strike a blow for hemispheric goodwill and solidarity in the context of the war.[60] While this latter purpose could have struck some as being more about public relations than policy-directed and as benefiting the federal government's diplomatic initiatives more than the needs of people living in the valley, the poor state, alone, of intercultural relations that existed on the UNM campus demonstrated its relevance to meeting a major local and regional challenge. As another of Joaquín Ortega's contacts, Charles Bunn, a US State Department official, wrote to Ortega a few months before the conference: "I spent last evening with a man in the Department of Agriculture who has exactly the same idea that you have, namely that the acid text [*sic*] of the good neighbor policy is in the Rio Grande Valley in New Mexico. . . . The man in question is Carl Fritz Taeusch."[61]

The conference was presided over by President Zimmerman, and its speakers included a mix of academics, the majority drawn from UNM; federal government officials, representing such agencies as the US Forest Service, the US Indian Service, the US Soil Conservation Service, and the Farm Security Administration; representatives of state and local agencies, such as the New Mexico Department of Public Health, New Mexico Department of Public Welfare, United Pueblos Agency, and the Bosque Farms Resettlement Project; regional agencies, such as the Southwest Inter-Mountain Committee on Post-War Planning; private foundation officers; and prominent members of the community, for example, Erna Fergusson, Gilberto Espinosa, and John Simms (Albuquerque businessman and attorney and New Mexico Supreme Court justice [1929–1930]). The themes of the five topical sessions were: "The Rio Grande People: Characteristics and Cultural Contributions," "The Broader Settings of the Question in Wartime," "Education," "Health and Economy Problems," and "The Spanish-Speaking American." Panelists focused on such topics as "Government Action in the Valley: Accomplishments and Possibilities," "A New Concept of Adult Education in Rural Areas," "Health Problems of the Valley," and "Agricultural Problems of the Valley." At the end of each panel, considerable time was allotted for discussion sessions that were led by a similar mix of faculty, public officials, and private citizens. One of the scholars invited to speak at the conference was George Sánchez. Sánchez made two presentations, the first titled "Bilingual Education" and a second titled "The Spanish-Speaking American: Helping Him to Help Himself." As Lyle Saunders pointed out, that phrase perhaps summed up better than any other the central motivating idea behind the various community-based projects supported and carried out by the SIAA.[62] The approach taken by the school was to cooperate with and lend support—financial, technical, administrative, or a combination thereof—as nonpaternalistically as possible to grassroots development projects. It often acted as both a go-between and direct participant, passing through and also helping administer and carry out grants made at the federal level to community-based entities and projects.

A classic example of such cooperative action, putting into practice ideas articulated at conferences such as the School for the Rio Grande Valley, was a program entered into jointly by the SIAA and the Albuquerque councils of the League of United Latin American Citizens to train young Spanish-speaking men and women for community leadership and social service, "a field," as the cosponsors noted, "in which there is a notable lack of native Hispanic personnel in this region."[63] Analogous in some ways to the Taos County Adult Education Project, the program had been started in January 1942 and was based in the Barelas Community Center. Its focus was eminently practical, with an emphasis given to on-the-job training. Under the supervision of center staff as well as volunteers from UNM and state and federal government agencies, trainees helped run the day-to-day operations of the center, guiding activities tied to home training and citizenship, classes in first aid and knitting; home nursing; prenatal and well-baby clinics; nutrition and physical fitness, and 4-H clubs. They likewise received instruction in the theory of community leadership and organization, social welfare work, and family, child, and group casework.

Eager to expand the program, which had made a successful start, the SIAA and the LULAC submitted a proposal for additional funding, on a matching basis, to the Office of the Coordinator of Inter-American Affairs. The monies requested (in the amount of $25,000) were to be used for personnel, capital outlay, operating expenses, and scholarships and travel costs for nonresident students from the Southwest and Latin America. This last component of the program was instructive. Why would the Barelas Community Center, serving a population of some six thousand residents living on the fringe of Albuquerque, approximately 85 percent of whom were Spanish-speaking, stray from its core mission and possibly dilute its effectiveness by bringing students up from Latin America? The immediate answer was the backdrop of war. The desire on the part of the US government and its agencies to strengthen relations between North and South America made the expenditure of funds on non-nationals politically palatable. The SIAA and LULAC couched the community service program, on one level, as a demonstration project that could lead to the creation of similar centers and programs in other Spanish-speaking communities of New Mexico, the Southwest, and Latin America. The year spent in the Barelas Community Center by Latin American trainees would equip them to render more effective service as community leaders and organizers in their own countries. Moreover, the aims of the Good Neighbor Policy would be well served, since "the contacts ... created during the training periods" would provide "an effective link of understanding and appreciation between young leaders of the Hispanic Southwest and those of the republics represented."[64]

There was another answer as well, however, one that played directly into the rationale for the SIAA's Community Program and helped legitimate it. As the proposal pointed out, the community of Barelas was the ideal choice for the program because "here, as nearly as can be found anywhere in the United States, is a duplication of conditions, trends, and problems found throughout Latin America and southwestern United States. Population composition is similar to that of Latin American communities, the cultural level is about the same, and the stage in transition from rural to urban life conditions [i.e., from a traditionally pastoral and agricultural existence to a wage economy] is likewise comparable. New Mexico, in which Barelas is strategically located, may be characterized as a 'little Latin America.'" [65] Looked at through a very broad lens, Ortega's perception and characterization of New Mexico as a "little Latin America" was not unfounded. Similar claims by others who studied the region lent credence to the idea. The statement by Ortega's rough contemporary, the sociologist John H. Burma, that "New Mexico is, in many respects, an extension of Latin America into United States territory," typified that view.[66] Still, in claiming a transparent duplication of "conditions, trends, and problems," was Ortega taking the analogy too far? How equivalent were New Mexico and Latin America at that time, or even in preceding centuries? Historically, New Mexico was always at the very margins of Spanish colonial and, later, Mexican state authority. It was poor by Spanish American standards and marginal to the core economies and societies of New Spain and, later, Mexico. And while Latin America, in Ortega's day, was generally poorer and less economically developed than the United States, much of Latin America by that time was far removed from the isolation and poverty of rural New Mexico.[67] In his eagerness to equate New Mexico with Latin America, in part because it allowed him to treat the state as a microcosm of inter-American relations, Ortega either failed to see these differences or chose to gloss over them.

In language and tone reminiscent of George Sánchez's biting criticism of the hollowness of the Good Neighbor Policy, the Barelas Community Center proposal concluded by reiterating the benefits it would bring to the government's interest in this area:

> It is an obvious weakness of our Good Neighbor Policy as a nation, that the native peoples of New Mexico have lived for a hundred years as citizens of the United States without any real or planned effort having been made to alleviate distressing social and economic conditions prevailing among them. By contrast, it would greatly strengthen our inter-American program if we could point with pride to accomplishments within our own borders; accomplishments brought about through the initiative and efforts of the Spanish-speaking people themselves, but with the active encouragement and aid of the dominant culture group.[68]

In stating the case so forthrightly and by invoking expressions such as "dominant culture group," Ortega (who, given the proposal's style and phrasing and some of its boilerplate content, was clearly its author) was treading on sensitive ground. The Office of the Coordinator of Inter-American Affairs, however, was not bothered by the language and its political undercurrent. The proposal met with approval and was funded. When notifying Zimmerman of the success of the application, Ortega gave full credit to three other members of the UNM community: Paul Walter Jr. (see fig. 13), who had been instrumental in the original design of the project; Francis Kercheville, for strengthening the university's connections to LULAC; and Tom Popejoy, who provided useful practical advice and had earlier guided the construction of the Barelas Community Center. Ironically, Popejoy would soon suppress another proposal by Ortega because he found it too inflammatory, too disposed toward breaching the "conspiracy of silence."

Zimmerman had called upon the university to help solve some of the state's most enduring problems, and he tasked Ortega and the School of Inter-American Affairs with taking the lead in this regard. Over the next several years, the school enthusiastically obliged, mounting a series of projects that targeted deficiencies in education, home economics, and nutrition in particular. Material and financial support for these projects came from a variety of local, state, and federal agencies as well as from private donations. The Barelas project exemplified the SIAA's basic modus operandi—that of cooperating with other agencies and organizations that sought to implement social and economic reform and to provide assistance to marginalized groups. In 1943, moreover, funded by a new grant from the Office of the Coordinator of Inter-American Affairs, the school was able to fine-tune and extend its Community Program by offering direct technical and financial

FIGURE 13 Paul Walter Jr. A protégé of Edgar Lee Hewett and the son of Santa Fe newspaperman and civic figure Paul A. F. Walter, Walter Jr. had a multifaceted career. In 1930, he became the first director of the University of New Mexico Press, moving on some years later (after graduate study at Stanford University) to become the founding chairman of UNM's Department of Sociology. His ethnographic research focused on the Spanish-speaking villages of New Mexico, and his interests— broadly speaking—aligned closely with those of George Sánchez, Lloyd Tireman, and Joaquín Ortega. Faculty Files Collection (UNMA 152, box 29, folder: Paul Walter Jr.), Center for Southwest Research, University Libraries, University of New Mexico. Courtesy of CSWR.

assistance to rural villages and communities around the state.[69] The underlying purpose of this new venture, in addition to the compulsory "help in the war effort" element, was to "stimulate community initiative" and, through grass-roots action, develop in people the understanding of how they might mobilize collectively to improve their lives. The mechanics of the program involved visits to communities, "no matter how small or how remote," by the school's two field representatives, Lyle Saunders and Marie Pope Wallis, as well as by Ortega himself (see plate 3). According to a summary of program activities, their duties were (1) "to listen, to ascertain the needs of the community and to stimulate an expression of those needs by the persons feeling them"; (2) "to mix with all groups in the population and to obtain first-hand information as to the situation, facilities or lack of them, attitudes, material and human resources available, and other factors bearing on local problems"; (3) "to encourage the formation of an active group of Anglos and Hispanos interested in local problems and willing to devote their time and effort towards finding solutions"; and (4) "to propose the lending of support, within the limited scope of the grant, to worthwhile projects for remedial action which the communities may start" [underlining in original].[70] No outright grants were to be given; communities either needed to match the cash outlay of the grant or provide a roughly equivalent amount in volunteer services. Assistance under the grants was provided in amounts ranging from as little as fifteen dollars to as much as a thousand dollars, for projects in public health, recreation and community centers, improvement of agricultural techniques, youth activities, and radio listening centers.

This last aspect of the program was perhaps its most original contribution. The SIAA designed a series of radio programs to be broadcast regularly around the state and for transmission throughout the region and Latin America, under the title *The Voice of the Southwest*. As described (and hosted) by Ortega, these broadcasts (people gathered in "listening centers" to hear them) were to consist of "good musical and dramatic talent, biographical sketches of leading personalities, accounts of worth-while deeds by Southwesterners, brief talks in Spanish and English on inter-American relations given by Latin American residents and visitors and by Anglos and Hispanos of our region, dramatizations of outstanding achievements on the war and home fronts, and similar features."[71] The radio broadcasts complemented a second major component of the program—the organization and mounting of a comprehensive "exhibit" designed to bring "useful information, educational values, and enjoyment" to every community in the state. The exhibit had several parts, including a motion-picture projection unit, a radio-phonograph, records, books, posters, pamphlets, and the like, with all texts in both Spanish and English. It was divided into sections called "Latin America," "The Southwest and its Significance in Inter-American Relations," "War Information," "School Materials," and "Governmental Community Services."

Wallis, Saunders, and Ortega traveled literally thousands of miles throughout the state to identify and coordinate projects. In 1943–1944 alone Wallis logged 12,144 miles and Saunders, 4,000, with Saunders stopping to visit sixty-three communities.[72] In all these initiatives and activities, the SIAA sought to coordinate with and enlist the active cooperation of local political officials; county, state, and federal agents; churches; chambers of commerce, service clubs, lodges, and other civic organizations. To be sure, cooperation was also needed inside the university, for a program of this scope could not have been planned without the involvement and support of many, most importantly UNM's Committee on Inter-American Activities in New Mexico. As the Community Program took shape, university officials formed this new committee (as distinct from the interdepartmental, university-wide committee that coordinated the school's academic program) to help plan and guide its activities. Although the committee's work was a collaborative affair, it was Ortega—on the basis of his extensive contacts with local, state, and federal government officials and his own ideas and alertness to new possibilities (often after prior counsel with Zimmerman)—who brought most of the proposed projects to the table. Along with Ortega, its members included Donald Brand, Robert Duncan, George Hammond, Victor Kleven (of the government and political science department), Jay Knode, Lloyd Tireman, and Paul Walter Jr. Policies and procedures developed by the committee were then passed on to the SIAA for execution, which in practice meant follow-up by three persons—Ortega, Saunders, and Wallis.

Not only was Ortega the committee's prime mover, but in no other part of the Community Program was he so fired by an idealistic spirit of grassroots activism, suffused, as it were, by the idea of democracy functioning in something close to its purest form. In his words, "Through a bona fide cooperative arrangement of this nature . . . we may bring the government closer to the people and make the people more aware of their duties and rights and more capable of making those decisions which are the backbone of active democratic citizenship."[73] Nonetheless, his idealism was tempered by the realization that progress would at best be slow and piecemeal. Ingrained attitudes and practices could not be quickly overturned. Although Ortega kept expectations about this program within narrow bounds, he still saw it as a key component of the SIAA and held out hope that positive responses in a few communities could lay the foundation for expanding it in the future. In this wish, as it turned out, he was sorely mistaken. For the time being, however, the country's massive war effort, the residual spirit and energies of the New Deal, and the emphasis that both of those placed in states with large Spanish-speaking populations on projects for social and economic rehabilitation (with New Mexico viewed as the cutting edge) masked important changes to come. With his customary élan and as an adjunct to the issues raised by the Community Program, Ortega also turned his attention to questions about language and ethnic identity and how these defined and affected the place of Nuevomexicanos within American society as a whole.

CHAPTER FOUR

≡

Ortega on Language
and Ethnic Identity

In 1941, while spending the spring semester as a visiting professor at the University of New Mexico, Joaquín Ortega authored a slim tract titled *The Compulsory Teaching of Spanish in the Grade Schools of New Mexico: An Expression of Opinion*. Ortega's pamphlet, and the arguments it made about whether or not the teaching of Spanish should be mandatory in the public schools, reflected the resurgence of an issue that had divided citizens, educators, and politicians in New Mexico since before the territory became a state. The issue was complicated and fraught with emotion, because it intertwined with struggles over questions of ethnic loyalty and identity and the preservation of cultural heritage. To some, furthermore, the language one learned and used was the main yardstick by which to measure and test not only degrees of integration into Anglo-American life and society, but—at the extreme—whether one was even eligible to be called "American" and to thereby receive and participate in the benefits conferred by such status and identity.

As noted earlier, public education was slow in coming to New Mexico. Prior to 1846, the Borderlands region lacked schools, public or private, and illiteracy was pervasive. During the territorial period, limited financial resources and resistance to paying taxes for public education continued to thwart its development, as did a persistent fear on the part of Hispanic leaders that submergence in an Anglo-dominated system would undercut and erode their own language and culture.[1] It was easier to delay progress in this area than to face "the inevitable conflicts which a common school system would entail."[2] When a public school system was finally established through an act of the territorial legislature in 1891, the political power of Hispanos enabled them to safeguard the use of Spanish in the schools for a period of time. Out of the 342 public schools that began operating in the territory, 106 were taught entirely in Spanish, while 93 were bilingual and 143 taught purely in English.[3] Thus, in New Mexico 58 percent of public schools provided some instruction in Spanish in the late 1800s. This situation gradually changed during the next twenty years, however, as Hispanic state-school superintendents were replaced by Anglos, who favored bringing policy and practice in New Mexico into alignment with the general US policy that enshrined English as the sole and necessary language of instruction. Moreover, as New Mexico moved toward gaining statehood, the belief that the "English only" policy should apply with particular force to New Mexico gained greater currency among the national media and US congressmen, given that more than 50 percent of the territory's population still spoke what they branded (without any sense of irony) a "foreign" language.[4]

Still, the substantial representation that Hispanos continued to have in the legislature and the disposition of various Anglo politicians to court their vote ensured that some protections would remain for Spanish, although these were to prove weaker in the public schools than in the arena of government service. A watershed for the partial survival of Spanish came in 1912, in deliberations over a proposed state constitution. Hispanic civic and political leaders, who would later divide over the language issue, united in opposition to a potential article in the constitution that would have required state government officials and legislators to be able to read, write, and speak English without the aid of an interpreter. This article was struck out, replaced by one (scheduled to sunset in twenty years but twice renewed for ten-year periods) that mandated the publication of all legal notices in both languages. In addition, all bills, resolutions, and other business of the state legislature were still to be heard in both Spanish and English. All public election notices, pollbooks, ballots, and the like had to be printed in the two languages. The right to vote, hold office, or sit upon juries could not be denied due to a lack of knowledge of English.

As set down in the state constitution, however, the fate of Spanish in the public schools did not fare as well. On the one hand, in keeping with what the US Congress had demanded as a condition for statehood, the document stipulated that school instruction should always be conducted in English. Since Spanish was an ancestral language for many Nuevomexicanos and a living language in every sense, the language of "the home, the church, the playground, the community,"[5] it was seen as a direct barrier to the goal of "Americanization." Thus, to this way of thinking, English could be the only legitimate language of instruction. On the other hand, seemingly loathe to blot out every vestige of official protection for ancestral-language rights, legislators inserted a clause in the constitution that implied that Spanish could in fact be used to teach students in Spanish-speaking communities. To this end, unlikely as the plan was to work in practice, aspiring teachers attending the Spanish-American Normal School in El Rito were to be trained so they were proficient in both languages.

The language issue took on a new coloration with the 1915 opening of the Panama Canal. The expectation of increased business and commercial opportunities as well as a wider field of political and diplomatic activity in the Latin American republics gave some interest to teaching Spanish in the schools and universities. As we have seen, during his tenure as UNM president (1909–1912), Edward Gray cited these growing initiatives as justifying the need for a Spanish American college. But Gray also emphasized the state's moral obligation to acknowledge and recognize the inherent right of Nuevomexicanos to retain and use their own language. On the latter point, however, and in his advocacy of bilingualism, Gray's was a voice in the wilderness, or at least one not shared by the great majority of his Anglo compatriots, who drew a clear line between recognizing the utilitarian value of teaching Spanish versus commending and sanctioning native-language rights in and of themselves. Hispanos clearly saw that they faced a Hobson's choice—if they demanded equality for Spanish, they would appear to be, or could leave themselves open to, the accusation of being, "un-American." The ultranationalist feelings unleashed by World War I served to intensify the Americanizing, English-only ethos. Under the glare of this spotlight, many Nuevomexicanos preferred to compromise, opting not for bilingualism per se but for the "bilingual method," that is, for utilizing Spanish as the means to teach English.[6]

The issue was tamped down for a few years but came back to life upon the election of Octaviano Larrazolo to the New Mexico governorship (1919–1920). Although he promoted both the Hispano Cause and bilingualism and believed that New Mexico's Spanish-speaking *nativos* possessed the right to retain and use their ancestral language, the Mexican-born Larrazolo was also a political realist and understood the pitfalls of forcefully advocating that position. Instead, citing the documented failure of relying exclusively on English to teach children who either did not know the language or barely understood it, he endorsed the bilingual method and urged the adoption of a law requiring that teachers in largely rural Spanish-speaking communities be able to speak, read, and write in both languages. In 1919, the legislature passed just such a bill, with the added provision that Spanish-language textbooks be those commonly used in Spanish schools. Assailed by partisans of the "one country, one flag, one language" ideology and by some in the national media who accused him of trying "to create a Spanish-speaking State on the border of Mexico," Larrazolo found a powerful defender in the person of Bronson Cutting.[7]

Outside the legislature, however, the path was somewhat rockier. The New Mexico State Board of Education parted company with the governor and the legislature, stressing its commitment to the overriding goal of Americanization, the avenue to which, it insisted, began in and ran through the public schools. Although Larrazolo and his faction initially prevailed, they had their opponents within the Hispanic community, one of whom was Dennis Chávez, then studying at Georgetown University Law Center and working as a clerk in the US Senate. Chávez (who would later endorse the opposite view) roundly criticized the pro-Spanish teaching camp, arguing that its members hampered the ability of Hispanic youth to integrate into American society. For that goal to be achieved, instruction in English had to be the priority. With victory in the struggle to win statehood a mere seven years in the past, Chávez "equated 'American' with the English language."[8] Hammering away and making common cause with the English-only faction, he and others who shared this viewpoint ultimately succeeded in defeating the campaign for native-language rights. Against all logic, Spanish was deemed a foreign language and, as such, was to be excluded as a language of basic instruction. As the debate slowly waned, the earlier resolve to give Spanish some official standing in public education evaporated, and Larrazolo's bilingual law was repealed in 1923. In the public sphere, the issue lay more or less dormant until it was resuscitated in 1940–1941, on the eve of Joaquín Ortega's spring-summer move to Albuquerque.

In a more indirect, less politically charged way, however, the University of New Mexico had already entered into the argument. Zimmerman's belief that UNM's opportunity to separate itself from the general run of universities and achieve national distinction lay in exploiting the state's particular history and heritage was reinforced by the Santa Fe–based Spanish revival and its defense and promotion of the Spanish language and Hispanic culture. Moreover, the division within the Hispanic community notwithstanding, Zimmerman would have found broad support for his ideas among its members, since their split concerned the place of Spanish in the public schools, not its vital role in helping preserve their customs and traditions. By the time of Zimmerman's 1927 inauguration, Nuevomexicanos, as John Nieto-Phillips wrote, "had begun to look to Spanish history and language as symbols and living expressions of their identity."[9]

The centrality of Spanish to the academic mission and program of UNM was therefore not in question. All agreed that Spanish was at the heart of the enterprise, properly identified as a core field of study. Reference to its use on campus, however, whether in the classroom or in more informal settings, traversed the gap between rhetoric and reality. Official statements by the university tended to present a rosy picture, claiming or implying that a good many students and faculty were at least semibilingual. A university bulletin from 1932, for example, proclaimed, "the Spanish House has now become a permanent feature of the University of New Mexico Summer Session.... New Mexico is the greatest natural laboratory in the United States for the study of Spanish. A large percentage of the students, as well as most of the teachers, are Spanish-speaking."[10] Spanish-speaking, yes, but with what degree of fluency, understanding, and grammatical accuracy? Did more than a handful of Anglo students really know enough of the language to exchange ideas and carry on full conversations, not just utter a few bland, well-known phrases and pleasantries? Similarly for English-speaking faculty, outside of the Southwest–Latin Americanist group, how truly comfortable were they when faced with using the other language? And for Hispanic students who came from Spanish-speaking homes and communities, but who had been subjected to English-only instruction, how freely did they speak and write English, and how capable were they at these tasks in their native tongue? Some insight into this latter question was provided by Carolyn Zeleny, who in her time on the UNM campus was given to understand that

> the degree to which the language handicap impairs academic achievement is clearly shown at the University of New Mexico. Here many of the Spanish-American students appear bewildered by their classwork and reading materials. Their writing and speech evidences a very imperfect knowledge of English, and their thought processes are clearly still controlled by the old mother tongue. The difficulty experienced by Spanish-speaking students has led to a dual system of marking, according to a tacit understanding of faculty members at the University, since this group of students cannot measure up to standards demanded of the English-speaking students."[11]

This assessment, however, bore an undertone of ethnocentrism, since it necessarily raised the question Whose standards were being applied? As with her statements regarding the ethnic tensions and hostile social environment for Hispanos at UNM, these claims made by Zeleny about language were based on the interviews she conducted while gathering data and material for her dissertation. It seems safe to consider them valid, since others—Ortega prominent among them—observed the same conditions. Consequently, if it is true that university officials had reason to be hopeful about the future state of Spanish on the campus and elsewhere—after all, given its quantity of native Spanish speakers, New Mexico still held the promise, in 1930, of bilingualism—it is also true that they had reason to be discouraged about the current state of the language.

A long memorandum submitted in early 1938 by Francis Kercheville, laying out long-range goals and objectives for the Department of Modern Languages, called attention to the slow, measurable decline of the Spanish language across the state. The weight of the English-only movement, the devaluation of languages other than English, and the active discouragement by the federal government, during the territorial and early statehood periods, of the continued use of Spanish in civic and public life had unfortunately taken their toll. As we have noted, Kercheville had his weak points, but a passion for Spanish and for seeing it flourish once again was not one of them. He elaborated a thirteen-point plan for expanding and improving the UNM Spanish program and for revitalizing the language in New Mexico, the foundation of which would be the renewal of instruction in Spanish in the grade schools, moving up from there to more advanced levels.[12] The warning note he sounded about saving the language was straightforward and devoid of sentimentality: "It is an indisputable fact that if we are to accomplish the work we should with Spanish in New Mexico, if the language is to continue and to serve a purpose, we must restore it to a position of respect and esteem in the eyes of all our people. They must not be ashamed to speak it. We believe that this can be done, and that it must be done in this present generation if it is done. In another generation or two it will be too late."[13] Restoring respect and esteem for the Spanish language "in the eyes of all our people," as Kercheville advocated, was certainly a laudable goal, but the prospects for realizing it were hardly encouraging. If the public schools were the obvious place to begin, they were also a graveyard of the cause, with many teachers continuing to oppose anything that smacked remotely of bilingualism. On this point, and citing Joaquín Ortega as his source, Carey McWilliams reported that "Anglo teachers have actually changed the names of Spanish students, on the first day of school, to some English equivalent by way of emphasizing the 'terrible handicap' that Spanish speech is supposed to be. In other cases, Hispanic teachers in rural schools made up of Spanish speaking children would resort to using Spanish surreptitiously for fear of being called on the carpet by some irate Anglo administrator."[14]

The decline of Spanish noted by Kercheville did not negate that it was still the home language of thousands of New Mexican youth or that English was a still a foreign tongue in many New Mexico counties. Others delivered a slightly different message and verdict, noting that the presence of two languages in New Mexico indeed opened up possibilities but, if not treated or exploited properly, also had the potential to create problems. On this score, the university's Post-War Planning Committee emphasized that "Great opportunities will probably exist in the future for students who read, write, and speak well the two languages of this state. But because this is a bi-lingual area, very often neither of the two languages is spoken naturally in pure or correct form, and the need for corrective work is great."[15] The difficulties manifested by students in handling the spoken language, be it English or Spanish or both, were undoubtedly a cause for concern, and the committee was perhaps correct in finding some relationship between this problem and the exposure that students had in New Mexico, during the course of their schooling and general upbringing, to hearing two languages being spoken, often imperfectly. The mistake that the committee made, however, was seemingly to conflate such exposure—the semblance of a "bi-lingual area"—with actual bilingualism. By and large, and certainly among almost all of the Anglo population, that ability did not exist in New Mexico. Nevertheless, it was not altogether unrealistic to think that it could, because the basic elements were present. Its failure to take root reflected a lack of political will and the necessary educational and cultural supports and disposition. In the piece that he wrote for *The New Mexico Quarterly*, underscoring the wisdom of Zimmerman's strategic vision and plan for the university, Clyde Kluckhohn had pointed to Quebec as an example of why New Mexico, if it adopted liberal-minded policies and practices, could acquire a truly bilingual character.[16] Furthermore, he found it "inexcusable" that teachers were permitted to graduate from UNM's College of Education into primarily Spanish-speaking communities with no real knowledge of Spanish.[17] The implications of Kluckhohn's criticism were spelled out in Sánchez's *Forgotten People*. The state's failure to honor the provision in its constitution requiring that teachers be trained to deal with the problems presented by Spanish-speaking children meant that in communities like Taos, where the great majority of children in the district's public schools came from Spanish-speaking homes, instructional programs had virtually no hope of succeeding.

Reemergence of the Public Debate

As soon as Ortega reached New Mexico in early February 1941, or perhaps even before he crossed into the state, he had become aware that the legislature was once again immersed in a contentious debate over the question of whether or not the public schools should be required to teach Spanish. One of the legislators who wrote to him about this matter and who was also a strong proponent of mandating Spanish-language instruction in the public schools, was Concha Ortiz y Pino (see fig. 14). They had formed a friendship some years before, during one of Ortega's previous UNM engagements. Now she wrote to him about the new legislative initiative to write such a mandate into law, seeking his support on its behalf and his counsel about how a bill could best be advanced. Ortega's heart inclined him to favor such legislation—all of his natural sympathies lay in this direction—but his head argued otherwise. For the moment, however, he was circumspect, conveniently (and quite understandably) citing his status as a temporary resident of the state and visiting professor in the university to avoid taking any position publicly. In reply to Ortiz y Pino he wrote, "Through the press and through friends I have learned of the divergencies of opinion in regard to the proposed legislation for the teaching of Spanish in the elementary grades. As an outsider and guest of the state, I am reluctant to stick out my neck in the controversy. However, I have some workable ideas on the subject, which I believe might satisfy both sides and bring harmony to the *familia hispana*. That is, as you very well know, my only interest" [underlining in original].[18]

As Ortega's letter makes clear, the language issue had once again flared up and exposed clear divisions within the Hispanic community, and for much the same reason as it had on prior occasions. If the arguments pro and con, however, sounded familiar, where people chose to line up relative to them might well be different. A case in point was Dennis Chávez, now serving as a member of the US Senate. Hoping to rally him to her side, Ortiz y Pino wrote to Chávez, seeking his opinion on the matter. Chávez replied that he strongly favored passage of a bill requiring that Spanish be taught in the public schools (in fifth through eighth grades). Conveniently sidestepping his own earlier opposition to such a measure, he expressed regret that there were those in New Mexico who were now fighting the initiative, when even national leaders supported its premise.[19] "It is sad," he wrote, "that Vice-President Wallace and Nelson Rockefeller, Coordinator of our commercial and cultural relations with Latin America, and the Pan American Union realize and appreciate the necessity of learning Spanish for the benefit of

FIGURE 14 "Concha Ortiz y Pino de Kleven with James F. Zimmerman [at right] in back seat of car driving in front of the Alvarado Hotel in downtown Albuquerque during Homecoming, 1940." As a member of the New Mexico House of Representatives between 1936 and 1942, Concha Ortiz y Pino played a key role in building legislative support and funding for two of President Zimmerman's strategic initiatives: the acquisition of a valuable collection of Mexicana, the nine-thousand-volume library of Paul Van de Velde and the creation of UNM's pioneering School of Inter-American Affairs. A friend and ally of Joaquín Ortega, she worked with him to advance the Good Neighbor Policy "at home," and the Hispano Cause generally. University of New Mexico Alumni Association Records (UNMA 128, ACC 128 004 010), Center for Southwest Research, University Libraries, University of New Mexico. Courtesy of CSWR.

our country, and in New Mexico there are some who would retard our progress in this regard."[20] Chávez grounded his support in both practical and political considerations. Persons proficient in both English and Spanish would have stronger career opportunities, and the proposal, if enacted into law, would promote Pan-Americanism and Roosevelt's Good Neighbor Policy, initiatives important in themselves but all the more so in a time of war.[21] Ortiz y Pino understood the utility of Chávez's way of framing his support and couched her arguments in quite similar terms. Responding to the criticism of the proposal as offered by a local LULAC council, she stated, "Why should any of us, as Spanish people, discourage this step to make New Mexico, as it should be, a focal point for the betterment of Pan-American relations?"[22] No less than their Anglo counterparts, Hispanic students needed to acquire expertise in the Spanish language as it "applies to commercial as well as cultural relations. . . . These [commercial and culturally grounded usage and terminology] are essential if the Spanish people are to be trained as good-will ambassadors to the nations to the south, and it is equally necessary for any others who may wish to take advantage of this opportunity to cement relations among the Americas."[23] Others in Ortiz y Pino's camp used the same argument but also broadened it, maintaining that introducing the compulsory teaching of Spanish was needed to restore the integrity of the language, which the dominance of English had steadily corrupted. The effects of this trend were everywhere apparent and painful to witness. "Even pupils of Spanish extraction," lamented Leo Amador, supervisor of the Rio Arriba County Schools and president of the Central New Mexico Educational Association, "normally spoke only 'the Anglicized, incorrect, and New Mexico Spanish.'"[24] If the decline of the native language was noticeable in Rio Arriba County, in which people of "Spanish" descent represented 93 percent of the population in 1938, how much more evident was it likely to be in counties where the ethnic distribution of the population was more even?[25]

For Ortega, whose offer from Zimmerman to become the first director of the university's School of Inter-American Affairs was still some two months away, the need to highlight the role of the Spanish language in New Mexico—past, present, and future—and to avoid allowing the issue to drive a damaging wedge between Nuevomexicanos, were both of paramount importance. Thus, after settling into his UNM teaching assignment, Ortega made a trip to Santa Fe to get a firsthand briefing from Concha Ortiz y Pino and to outline for her the nature of his "workable ideas" on the subject. One day later, on April 9, 1941, he sent her the draft of a revised version of the bill, predicting—in characteristically bold fashion—that it would "represent a tremendous gain for the Spanish language in the State . . . and will create a great deal of good feeling among the anglos and hispanos. With my proposal the maximum could be accomplished with a minimum of political loss for the hispanos."[26] The need to ensure that result and to avoid political bloodletting in general was uppermost in Ortega's mind. He believed that under his plan the Democratic Party floor leader in the New Mexico House of Representatives might make a plea for "State solidarity above party lines, in view of the fact that New Mexico is the only Anglo-Spanish commonwealth in this continent." Ortega attached a copy of the bill, as rewritten, to his letter, advising Ortiz y Pino that if it met with her approval she was at liberty to adopt it as her own and to amend it in whatever way she saw fit. Section 1 of Ortega's proposed bill was a generic statement, asserting, "the Spanish language shall occupy an important position in the educational program of all public schools of the State of New Mexico." But its key provision, the one that Ortega thought would placate all factions, was in Section 2, which called for a canvass to be made each year, under the direction of county school superintendents, of the students enrolled in each school as well as of the next year's prospective enrollment, "to ascertain the number of students who wish to take Spanish during the next school term." In brief, if that number were 25 percent or higher in any school it would then "be mandatory upon the State Board of Education to establish the teaching of Spanish in such school."[27]

Although this letter from Ortega to Concha Ortiz y Pino raised critical points, it only touched the surface of his full understanding and analysis of the debate over the Spanish language in New Mexico and why it created such controversy and unease among Hispanos. Ortega's sense of the issue was comprehensive. He grasped all of its dimensions, all of its subtleties and contradictions, and now proceeded to lay them out in the form of his pamphlet.[28] He began by noting that "anglos" and "hispanos" alike have sought his opinion on New Mexico Senate Bill 3, introduced by Ralph Gallegos and Joseph Montoya, which—if passed and signed—would require the teaching of Spanish from the fifth through the eighth grade in New Mexico's public schools.[29] He indicated that he had found almost total opposition to the idea among "Anglos" and a "sharp division among the Hispanos." He found the lack of unity among Hispanos highly disturbing, because he believed it would weaken "the efficacy of their action in the life of the state." What accounted for Hispanic opposition? He construed it, at least in part, as evidence of a tradition of cozying up for personal gain, whereby some will unfortunately "trade their solidarity and future of their kin for the small pittance of an office." In other cases, the motivation may be more class-related or derive from the quest for social status. Once they have gained a foothold, a "little power" as Ortega put it, and out of their desire to curry favor with and win acceptance from Anglo society, there are Hispanos who will "separate themselves," in place of standing with the mass of their people and "raising their level." This practice, as we have seen, was portrayed in Otis's *Fire in the Night* through the strivings and divided loyalties of the declassed aristocrat, Lorenzo de Baca.[30] Moreover, Ortega viewed this trait and pattern as being very Spanish, although in reality it smacks of an age-old game. In this version, Hispanos played into the hands of the Anglos, many of whom were only too glad to exploit divisions or, in Ortega's words, "book" one "hispano" against another and thus "sap their total voting strength in a sterile fight." Alternatively, following Zeleny's interpretive line, the opposition of some Hispanos could possibly have stemmed from their wish to avoid the conflict that reconsideration of the language issue would inevitably bring. On this reading, a repeat of the debate meant overstepping the bounds of decorum and violating the pact of "silence."

Concha Ortiz y Pino had invited Ortega to testify before the New Mexico House legislative committee that was considering the bill, but conscious of his "outsider" status and afraid that he would be too outspoken, he declined to do so. Nevertheless, he felt duty bound to satisfy the numerous requests he had received from both Hispanos and Anglos to give his views on the subject. Hence, he decided to follow the more judicious course of putting them in writing. In a sense, Ortega's ten-year association with New Mexico and the friendships he had formed with so many New Mexicans of all political stripes made him an outsider with "insider" status. Just as Francis Kercheville had claimed "No Anglo-American, Mexican, or native New Mexican" could fill the directorship of the SIAA, whereas Ortega could, so on the language issue he could divorce himself from the grip of local rivalry and politics.

Ortega then moved on to consider another element in the drama, the rejection of the proposed bill voiced by the League of United Latin American Citizens. This group's stand against the bill might at first glance seem paradoxical to some, but it was not. Rather, as Ortega pointed out, it reflected the aspiration of those of "Spanish extraction," to "free themselves from the taint of foreignism, and to enter fully into the life of the country which adopted them." On this point, the soon-to-be SIAA director detoured for a moment to elucidate the problem (and ironies) of "Americanization," as it related to Hispanos in New Mexico. The process was different for them than it was for other foreign groups who came into the fold after the nation was founded, since the Hispanos (or many of them) were already established in New Mexico, as "true Americans," with a much longer ancestry in the land than the intruders who took control.[31] In this vein, he went on to note (in line with the observations made by Zeleny at roughly the same time) that "there has hardly been any real attempt at assimilation in New Mexico. Even the external social relationship between the two groups is not normally American. Consider the systematic exclusion of 'hispanos' (only very few and very exceptional individuals have been anointed) in college fraternities, service clubs, etc." Again, the literary analogue to the prejudice that operated here arose from the kind of ignorance alluded to by Lorenzo de Baca, when—responding to Clair Mosely's description of him as "a Spaniard"—he replies, "No, I'm a Mexican." As we shall see, Ortega entered into a fuller discussion of the problem of ethnic identity and labeling in a later pamphlet.

Returning to the question of LULAC's opposition, he viewed it as a defense mechanism employed against the discrimination experienced by Hispanos. It represented an expression of their desire for acceptance into the mainstream of American life. In keeping with this wish, they rejected asserting a privilege for their own language, because it seemed to run contrary to the desire to receive the "full privileges of common social life and economic opportunity from other American citizens." Mario García has underlined and provided further context to Ortega's interpretation. LULAC, as García has written, was spearheading concerted efforts at defeating the educational segregation of Mexican American children in so-called "Mexican schools" in the Southwest. At the time Ortega addressed the language issue, the organization was mobilizing for civil rights and full integration into the American system. Thus for LULAC, the bill supported by Ortiz y Pino, Montoya, Gallegos and others highlighted separateness when the league was trying to stress the opposite.[32]

While Ortega appreciated the reasons behind LULAC's opposition, he still thought it a miscalculation, because he believed (and this was his ever-higher aim and vision) that the development in New Mexico of a bilingual "truly Pan American commonwealth" would be the "most original contribution" the state could make. The league's members, he conceded, need not favor the compulsory teaching of Spanish in the public schools, but they should recognize that they are the "human bridge between two concepts of life that need to harmonize" if the continent is to achieve solidarity. We can see here that Ortega used his analysis of the language issue to tie together a number of familiar themes, such as Pan-Americanism, the unique opportunities that the state's history and tricultural heritage gave it, and New Mexico's Spanish-speaking communities as "little Latin America."

After celebrating the virtues and possibilities of the continent's only "Anglo-Spanish commonwealth," however, Ortega felt obliged to balance the scales, noting—even more strongly than Kercheville—that the Spanish language had become seriously degraded in New Mexico. Hispanos were losing the language and, with that loss, the ability to make it an effective tool with which to exploit the career opportunities that the "Pan American era is opening." Worse still, they will lose the ability to preserve and carry on their cultural heritage, "today well nigh stagnant." For a moment, this invariably optimistic man yielded to stark pessimism, decrying, "Spanish in New Mexico is naturally on the defensive, giving ground all the time. . . . the odds are against it, and it will keep on deteriorating and eventually disappear. Its disappearance may be a patriotic solution welcome by some. I, for one, [and on this point we again hear echoes of Edward Gray] will consider such happening a heavy loss in the national assets of New Mexico."

If the Spanish language among Hispanos had fallen into such a sad state, the question naturally arises: Why would Ortega be against the proposed bill? Why did he find it ill-timed and "fraught with dangers for Hispanos?" He listed several reasons: (1) the principle of compulsion was un-American, especially in the West, with its frontier ethos (subjects like English and civics are made compulsory, but this was different—Spanish could hardly be classified as foundational in the same sense); (2) the moment was inopportune to make the study of Spanish obligatory; a war psychology was building in the country, so introducing issues involving "foreignisms" was provocative and might spark a jingoistic backlash; (3) New Mexico had a certain type of Protestant who would bitterly resent his children having to learn the language of a chiefly Catholic group that he disliked on religious grounds; this factor, too, could provoke a discriminatory backlash— loss of jobs, and "the hispanos, unfortunately, do not have too many jobs they can afford to lose"; "the 'hispanos,' weary of discrimination, may be courting more discrimination still with this bill"; (4) the state lacked the resources to implement the policy or to enforce it properly; it lacked the number of teachers needed to make it effective, and the low salaries paid to teachers in the state would make it very difficult to recruit bilingual teachers from the outside (objections also raised by many educators and administrators, including Zimmerman); and (5) given all these drawbacks, the cause—so worthy in itself—would be harmed. Were the experiment to fail, it would be a major setback.

What, then, was the solution? What would tip the balance back in the other direction? The answer, he wanted us to believe, rested in looking ahead and beyond, to the expanding era of Pan-Americanism, when bilingualism would be valued for the economic benefits it brought. Ortega, however, was not quite ready to step back onto optimistic ground. New Mexico and the Southwest, he argued, could be a stellar example of how democracy and equality work. Yet, under existing conditions, "the Spanish-speaking population of the Southwest represents a living example of disorientation, of American political and social failure as a colonizing metropolis—an ugly sore in the flesh of Pan America." On this score, Ortega sounded exactly like George Sánchez; and, like Sánchez, too (as well as Zimmerman's critics), he questioned UNM's uplifting rhetoric about Pan-Americanism in light of its own failure to practice the policy. Of what use was it to talk of democracy, to expound the Good Neighbor Policy across borders, "if we have made within our own borders a mess of the relatively simple problems of dealing with an Hispanic group?" The state's political leaders, he maintained, had evaded the issue and made no effort to realize the promise of the "Anglo-Spanish commonwealth." It was therefore time for the federal government, through its multiple agencies and departments, to enter the picture and "remedy the situation." Here, in this pamphlet on the language issue, we see the background to the aggressive courting of late New Deal and wartime funding. "Washington," Ortega asserted, "can do many things to guide the 'hispanos' into a fuller American life," channeling its support to such areas as education, social and economic rehabilitation, resettlement programs, agricultural and community organization, and the promotion of civic responsibility. Moreover, it could serve the goal of bilingualism within all of these efforts. Needless to say, the SIAA would be Ortega's platform from which to launch UNM's initiatives on behalf of the "commonwealth."

Much of Ortega's critique vis-à-vis the state of the Spanish language and the hollowness of the call for implementing Pan-Americanism and the Good Neighbor Policy rang true, as did his prescription for remediation of the state's social and economic ills. He left pessimism altogether behind, however, in the conclusion to his pamphlet on the language issue. "Bilingualism," he idealistically claimed, "will come in spite of all obstacles when New Mexico builds leaders—there are some already—with statesmanship and imagination. And when bilingualism is a reality, the University of New Mexico will be the most original institution in this continent, a unique Pan American university . . . where the voice of all the Americas . . . will be heard in its halls." He finished by offering a number of practical suggestions for how to move, step-by-step, toward this goal, starting within the public school system.

Ortega was nothing if not a man of action, and the same could be said for George Sánchez. Together, the two tried to advance the cause of bilingualism by organizing a major national conference on the subject. The idea originated with Sánchez, who shared it with Ortega. Collaborating with Lloyd Tireman, who had not only researched the problem for years but as director of the San José Experimental School had wrestled with it empirically, Ortega then developed Sánchez's rough ideas into a formal proposal. The timing of this initiative thrust it directly into the headwinds of the legislative debate over the proposed bill requiring that Spanish be taught in the public schools. That alone ensured that it would not escape notice. In preparing the proposal, Ortega—following his usual practice—reached out for political and community support. In particular, he sought and received the backing of Concha Ortiz y Pino and Judge David Chávez. Initially, it was hoped that the state might underwrite the costs of holding the conference, or at least a portion of them, and Ortiz y Pino agreed to lobby Governor John Miles for this purpose. Miles, however, did little more than string her along, making vague promises about calling a meeting, but his priorities, and his commitments as to where state money should be directed, lay elsewhere. Zimmerman, kept informed by Ortega about progress on the proposal, had in fact predicted that the "meeting" would never take place. In a memo to the president that he sent in early May, Ortega confirmed as much, stating, "You were right. For you warned me that the meeting will never be held." Miles, he added, "was in a fix because of the political dynamite" over the possibility that he might divert state monies for the conference.[33] Ortega still held out some hope of a token contribution by the state and, toward the end of May, appealed to Ortiz y Pino to not give up entirely. "Somewhere," he wrote to her, "we must find a sense of realities and a real concern for the welfare of the state."[34] Despite his guarded hope, however, even token support from Santa Fe proved to be a dead end. Since the UNM budget was already strained to the limit, Ortega looked to the outside.

From a colleague in the College of Education at Ohio State University, James Tharp, Ortega had learned that the American Council on Education (ACE), through its Committee on Modern Languages (on which Tharp sat), might be willing to entertain a proposal for a conference devoted to the problem of teaching students whose native language was not English. Tharp had apparently shown considerable interest in Ortega's ideas on bilingualism and wrote to Ortega that he planned to bring "the educational problem of New Mexico" before the ACE.[35] Tharp, however, may have been a lone voice on this ACE committee, because according to Ortega, not only was its chairman, Robert H. Fife, personally an advocate of the "English-only" viewpoint, but the ACE itself wanted to deemphasize bilingualism in favor of English. In September 1941, in a memo to Zimmerman, Ortega wrote, relative to the problem of teaching Spanish to a mixed school population: "the facts of bilingualism here in our Southwest . . . are that the pupils do not learn either. Dr. Fife seems to take the point of view of the 'Americanizer,' far from mine. It is not a question of Americanizing anybody. (That is the wrong approach in the Southwest and in Puerto Rico), but of teaching properly both languages."³⁶ Misled by Tharp's encouragement, UNM had sent Ortega's proposal to the ACE. Not surprisingly, he came up empty-handed. Ortega's next recourse—the last as it turned out—was to send the proposal (over Zimmerman's signature) for the bilingual conference to the US Office of Education.

The proposal, which Ortega wrote during his spring 1941 visiting professorship, incorporated many of the bedrock ideas that anchored the projects he would soon coordinate as director of the SIAA, among them the following: that an initiative of this type would be timely, in that the federal government was making a great effort to bring about a better understanding between the peoples of "this continent"; that the Hispanic Southwest, and in particular New Mexico with its high percentage of Spanish-speaking people and its tricultural heritage, was the ideal experimental ground for Pan-Americanism and for understanding processes of cultural adaptation; and that the current push for hemispheric solidarity would be strengthened through the example of "putting our own house in order." Cutting a little closer to the bone, Ortega asserted, "The bilingual problem of the Southwest ... with the delicate racial adjustments implied, should be in the vanguard of our educational front for national defense. The Southwestern states are at present breeders of misunderstanding when they are meant by political destiny to be focuses of understanding."³⁷ The application outlined a tentative agenda for the conference, emphasizing, in the context of teaching English to a bilingual population, the administrative and organizational challenges faced by school systems; the general and special instructional and methodological problems that teachers confronted; and the social and psychological dimensions and implications of a dual-language situation. In addition, it also stressed the value of establishing a university in the Southwest with a bilingual student body. Such a university—UNM was identified as the probable choice—could "serve as 'headquarters' of the cultural approximation between the Americas" and "act as a clearinghouse for educators and students from Latin America, furnishing them all types of information and making judicious arrangements for their best possible contacts with other American universities."³⁸ The proposal identified the national, regional, and state-level organizations that might be expected to participate, described the preliminary planning and organizational work that had been done, provided a budget, and explained why the University of New Mexico would be the logical venue for the conference. In only one respect—his claim that "the legislatures of New Mexico and Texas are now deeply concerned with the problem of bilingualism, and are trying to place the teaching of Spanish on

PLATE 1 "Mela Sedillo at her home," ca. 1960. Part of the core group of Latin Americanist and Southwest Hispanic studies faculty hired by James Zimmerman early in his term as UNM president, Sedillo taught a range of courses in the university's College of Fine Arts from 1931 until 1952. She was also a central figure in promoting the revival of Hispanic arts and crafts in New Mexico, worked on various literary and arts-related WPA projects in the state, and helped champion the defense of Hispanic rights during the 1930s and 1940s. Mela Sedillo Pictorial Collection (box 1, folder 7, PICT 2000–021), Center for Southwest Research, University Libraries, University of New Mexico. Courtesy of Mela's nietos. Courtesy of CSWR.

PLATE 2 Jesús Guerrero Galván, Union of the Americas, fresco painted by Guerrero Galván during his time as artist-in-residence at the University of New Mexico, 1942–1943. Main floor of Scholes Hall, University of New Mexico. Photo by Harrison Cook.

PLATE 3 "Joaquín Ortega with shepherds on El Mogote Mountain, near the town of El Rito, New Mexico." Ortega traveled to villages and towns across the state during the mid-1940s, to help advance the SIAA's Community Program. It is likely, however, that on this occasion he was accompanying John Donald Robb on one of Robb's numerous field trips to record the Hispanic folk songs of New Mexico. John Donald Robb Photograph Collection (box 1, folder 5, PICT 000–497), Center for Southwest Research, University Libraries, University of New Mexico. Courtesy of CSWR.

PLATE 4 Painting of Joaquín Ortega, oil on canvas (date and artist unknown).
Department of Spanish and Portuguese, Ortega Hall, University of New Mexico.
Courtesy of the Department of Spanish and Portuguese. Photo by Harrison Cook.

PLATE 5 First panel of the Three Peoples mural. Facilities Planning Department Digital Collection (UNMA 028), Center for Southwest Research, University Libraries, University of New Mexico. Photo by Karen Mazur. Courtesy of CSWR.

PLATE 6 Second panel of the Three Peoples mural. Facilities Planning Department Digital Collection (UNMA 028), Center for Southwest Research, University Libraries, University of New Mexico. Photo by Karen Mazur. Courtesy of CSWR.

PLATE 7 Third panel of the Three Peoples mural. Facilities Planning Department Digital Collection (UNMA 028), Center for Southwest Research, University Libraries, University of New Mexico. Photo by Karen Mazur. Courtesy of CSWR.

PLATE 8 Fourth panel of the Three Peoples mural. Facilities Planning Department Digital Collection (UNMA 028), Center for Southwest Research, University Libraries, University of New Mexico. Photo by Karen Mazur. Courtesy of CSWR.

a pre-eminent position in the public school curriculum"—did Ortega possibly sugarcoat or gloss over the volatile local politics of the issue and downplay its divisiveness.[39]

The proposal was fundamentally sound and made a seemingly strong case, but whether the US Office of Education found it compelling is another matter. In any event, it was not approved. Without a funding source, Ortega and Sánchez were forced to drop the idea of the conference. The language issue, however, and Ortega's concern for how it intertwined with other SIAA projects and priorities, would not disappear so long as he remained at the University of New Mexico. To his way of thinking, English was the dominant language of the land and, as such, should be learned first. At the same time, however, Spanish also needed to be emphasized and retained by Nuevomexicanos, as the language of their ancestors and their collective past. To reject it was to embrace a form of colonialization. His position on this question echoed that of the early cultural pluralists.

Ethnic Identity and Cultural Pluralism

Reflecting on the current state and future of the Spanish language in New Mexico, Arthur Campa astutely observed that bilingualism connotes, in effect, biculturalism. It is very difficult for people to become bilingual if they live in a unicultural society.[40] Did the inverse hold true for the state's Spanish-speaking Nuevomexicano community? Could their own culture remain authentic and vibrant if the language that encased and expressed it was under threat and diminishing in quality? The question was not quite as simple as it sounded, because within it or behind it were competing narratives about the nature and origins of their "own culture." Everyone could agree that Native Americans, Hispanos, and Anglos formed New Mexico's three main population groups. Beyond that truism, however, controversy and disagreement broke out. How blended or separate were they, biologically and culturally, after centuries or decades of intermixing and exchange? How "Spanish" was Nuevomexicano culture, how "Mexican," how "indigenous"? To what degree had it absorbed traits and characteristics from Native American culture, or from what Ortega referred to as "the motley crowd ineptly called Anglos"?[41] The position one took on these questions was conditioned or dictated by a variety of interests—political, social, economic, ethnic, racial—not all of which aligned in a consistent way. In a few words, cultural identity itself became a zone of contestation.

Ortega was not only intrigued by the problem, he knew that it deeply affected

the strategic role of both the university and the School of Inter-American Affairs.
Just as he had with the language issue, he plunged right into the middle of it,
publishing two tracts that explained his ideas about the relationship among the
dominant cultures of the Southwest, their individual and collective characters,
and how the SIAA could chart a cultural "road map" for the region, the country,
and the hemisphere. The first of these two publications, *New Mexico's Opportunity: A Message to My Fellow New Mexicans*, appeared in 1942; the second, *The
Intangible Resources of New Mexico*, in 1945. Ortega's ideas can stand on their own,
but they take on greater meaning if one remembers that New Mexico was still a
young state, just nineteen years removed from joining the union, when Ortega
first visited it. In the debates that led up to statehood, the tricultural formulation came increasingly into play. In this context, however, the Native American
population functioned more as a prop. Since it was treated as an isolated group,
coming under federal tutelage and control and consigned to life on tribal lands,
it figured only marginally in the discourse around statehood. The Hispanic
population, in contrast, posed a problem, since so many Anglos believed it too
alien, too dark of skin, to qualify for admission into the union. Faced with the
need to cultivate the support of an Anglo majority in the United States to attain
statehood, many Hispanos began to identify themselves as "Spanish Americans,"
in effect "whitening" and "Europeanizing" their racial and cultural heritage,
respectively.[42] The elite families of the territory, prominent Hispanos, sought
to distinguish themselves from the "Mexican" Southwest; they carved out a
separate "Spanish" Upper Rio Grande, a delineation that could operate because
Mexican immigrants were fairly scarce in this area. In addition, the persistence
of many traditions of rural and village life, dating to colonial times, helped but-
tress the distinction. As Charles Montgomery writes, "By 1900 the vitality of
New Mexico's *paisano* culture—expressed in a particular Spanish dialect, in
lore, art, and Catholic custom—lent support to the claim that Spanish colonial
tradition was alive and well on the upper Rio Grande."[43] The move to embrace
an unblemished Spanish heritage was accompanied by the new use, on the part
of the Spanish-speaking population of the region, of the term *Hispano-Americano* to describe itself, in place of the terms that had long been used: *nativo,
Mexicano, Nuevomexicano*, and *Neomexicano*.[44] In the political realm, the *rico*
landowners and sheep ranchers who might legitimately claim Spanish "blood"
had joined with the ascendant Anglo business and commercial class to form a
partisan bloc. Together, as noted earlier, they worked out mutually acceptable
ways of referring to each other that barred any overt discussion of ethnic or

racial discrimination (ushering in Carolyn Zeleny's "conspiracy of silence.") This Anglo-Hispano accommodation was challenged by the more pluralist-minded faction and upholders of the Hispano Cause, led by Octaviano Larrazolo, which asserted ancestral-language rights and the need to preserve distinctive attributes of Hispanic culture and ethnic identity inside of American citizenship.

The relatively small Hispanic elite who self-identified as "Spanish" or "Spanish Americans" had a distorting influence that considerably exceeded their numbers.[45] Within their own communities, on an everyday level and in middle-brow and popular culture, Nuevomexicanos generally identified as Mexican (i.e., mestizo) and did not link themselves directly to Spain or to a European (i.e., white) background. Tellingly, the effect of socioeconomic class on declarations of identity in New Mexico was on full display with the introduction of the Selective Service System during World War II. Army personnel dealing with inductees "learned that the Spanish speaking New Mexican called himself a Mexican. He did not mean [by this] that he had been born in Mexico, but he used the word to let the outside world know that he came from another culture and spoke another language."[46]

The fungible terminology and labeling of racial and ethnic heritage and identity in New Mexico sowed long-lasting debate and confusion. One of the more insightful attempts to explain and sort out the muddle was provided by Arthur Campa (see fig. 15). From a cultural standpoint, Campa contended, the difference between Mexicans and New Mexicans were "regional distinctions that occur within a similar culture." To drive home this point, he reached for concrete, colloquial examples:

> The substitution of the name "Spanish" for everything in New Mexico does not change the substance of traits that are indisputably Mexican. The "Spanish" suppers given by clubs and church societies are in reality Mexican dishes to which no truly Spanish palate is accustomed. The "Spanish" songs sung by school children and by radio performers in New Mexico are as Mexican as *tortillas de maiz*, *chicharrones de puerco*, *chile con carne*, and the *sopaipillas* at Christmas time. The real cultural difference between the region north of the Rio Grande and that below are those which the New Mexican has acquired by close contact with the American life. In a sense, it is his dehispanization, his falling away from the Spanish, that stamps him as a different individual. The Mexican is different in that he preserves his Spanish language, literature, and menu. The New Mexican is educated in English and naturally acquires traits and habits that are American.[47]

FIGURE 15 Arthur L. Campa. Hired onto its faculty after graduating from UNM in the late 1920s, Campa soon became part of the core group Zimmerman assembled around him to build a program focusing on Southwestern and inter-American studies. He did groundbreaking work on both Hispanic folklore in New Mexico and elements of Mexican American culture in the Southwest. Campa also actively supported President Zimmerman's community-based initiatives. Unfulfilled, however, in his ambition to rise higher in the academic and administrative ranks of the university, he left UNM in 1946 to take up a position at the University of Denver. Faculty Files Collection (UNMA 152, box 4, folder: Arthur L. Campa, March 29, 1960), Center for Southwest Research, University Libraries, University of New Mexico. Courtesy of CSWR.

The conclusion that Campa drew was that Spanish-speaking New Mexico needed to locate its identity in the land of its birth. Its members had a distinct regional identity. Some Spanish cultural traits still existed, but they had been transmuted, by virtue of centuries of relative isolation, from being embedded within a specific land, and thus had evolved into something particular to their place. The transculturation of Spanish and Native American cultural elements had created a distinctly mestizo culture, largely Mexican in character. The "Americanization" of that culture would necessarily modify or change it, but not dissolve it. It was constantly being refreshed by cross-border population moves and waves of Mexican immigration.

Elsewhere, Campa had directly attacked one of the core ideas supporting the claim of an untainted "Spanish" heritage—that of the supposed *limpieza de sangre* (purity of blood, and therefore of lineage) of the descendants of the early Spanish settlers of New Mexico. That notion, he argued, was absurd on its face, since "none of the great leaders had brought a wife or family with him."[48] It was a belief, as Nancie Gonzalez put it, "based upon some truth and much fiction."[49] Furthermore, the conditions that colonists faced from the earliest days of settlement—the essential abandonment of the territory to its own devices by the viceregal capital and its isolation since the late sixteenth century—provided a "context for genetic blends."[50] Thus *mestizaje* (race mixture) took place from the very start. Campa, of course, did not sway everyone to his point of view. The notion of purity of blood may have been easily refuted, but not so the idea of a distinctively Spanish character in the present-day heritage of New Mexico. The debate over the elements of Nuevomexicano identity, as reflected in different segments of the Hispanic population, remained alive and has persisted down to the present.[51]

In the decade prior to the founding of the SIAA, the tricultural formulation—the idea of New Mexico as the land, primarily, of three distinct peoples—Native American, Hispanic, and Anglo—living side by side, separately but in harmony, with each maintaining its own customs, histories, and kinship patterns—continued serving as another cultural reference point for the state's intelligentsia. Some, after questioning the idea, essentially upheld it; others saw it as distracting from a more basic reality and cast it aside; and still others (like Ortega), subscribed to it in broad terms, partly out of conviction and partly for pragmatic reasons.

An interesting voice in the first camp was that of folklorist and UNM professor of English Thomas M. Pearce. In 1931, Pearce published an article in *The New Mexico Quarterly*, titled "Southwestern Culture: An Artificial or a Natural Growth?" As a starting point for examining the issue, Pearce quoted a question posed in a symposium conducted by *Southwest Review*: "Do you think the Southwestern landscape and common traditions can (or should) develop a culture recognizable as unique, and more satisfying and profound than our present imported culture and art?"[52] In response, Pearce asked, "Have the Spanish and Indian groups in this region a common tradition? And likewise, from whose viewpoint is the culture imported, from whose viewpoint are the traditions common?"[53] Pearce was driving at the question, How much of Southwestern and New Mexican culture is really native and how do the groups that express it interrelate? Although of greater antiquity, the Spanish tradition is just as imported as the Anglo. As he stated, "our 'common' Southwestern tradition . . . has been a community of differences. One has but to recall the attitude of the Pueblos toward imported culture in 1680 to see part of the common tradition in an historical light."[54] He pointed to similar situations and attitudes during the late Mexican period, remarking, "culturally, the English [i.e., Anglos] remain 'outdwellers' in New Mexico." With respect to the suggestion of a common tradition, Pearce expressed his skepticism metaphorically: "The strands of Southwestern material, Indian, Spanish, English, are beside the loom. A little of the material is on the frame and has begun the weaving of a fabric. The colors appear in the cloth, but the pattern is not yet distinct."[55]

As the accomplished folklorist that he was, Pearce thought that the "story of a race and region will be told in its language." What, then, did the language of the Southwest and New Mexico tell about its culture? All three cultures, obviously, were represented in names—place names, landmarks, villages, and the like. In dress, food and cookery, and in everyday slang, the two (English and Spanish) had borrowed more or less equally from each other. Pearce concluded: "[W]hen any one of the three idioms becomes truly dominant then perhaps the regional claim to a unique and common culture will become an authentic one." The persistence of different spoken languages underscored the persistence of different cultures or cultural traditions. None, surely, were pure, but at the same time, each was fundamentally different and stood apart. While Pearce may not have agreed with the part of the tricultural trope that had the three groups living in harmony, he seemed otherwise to have found it an accurate representation.

In his brief article titled "A Mosaic, not a Synthesis," critic and essayist Albert Guérard provided a second perspective. Guérard argued that the Southwest no longer possessed a "separate culture," whatever that culture might have entailed or however it might have been defined. By the 1930s, under the impact of radio, airplanes, highways, and other modern influences, its isolation had broken down. Certain elements (like language) could possibly be revived and others preserved. In the main, however, his judgment was unswerving: "Apart from the historical factor, there is no such thing as the Southwest [i.e., as a separate culture area]. It is a mosaic, not a synthesis, of many elements."[56] That it constituted a mosaic, that its elements were implanted, one next to the other, without interweaving or combining, would not have negated the tricultural formulation per se. What invalidated that idea, in terms of Guérard's argument, was the practice of extending it beyond its natural orbit, to make the claim that there was something uniquely different about Southwestern culture. The proponents of the tricultural formulation, the "heroic triad," were making something more out of it than it naturally meant. Transformed by them into the beating heart of New Mexican culture, it ran the risk of becoming a cliché, a fetishized construct. Genuine culture developed organically. It could not be fabricated. As Guérard wrote, "if you live it, if you make it your own . . . it will take root."[57] The message he delivered was, let the region express itself, in all spheres of culture, without fitting such expression into pre-marked-off boundaries and categories.

In his two pamphlets, Ortega—the transplanted Spaniard who felt he had come home spiritually when he stepped onto New Mexican soil—addressed all of these themes: the preservation of ethnic identity and of local and regional cultural heritage, the Anglo assumptions about Americanization, and the special character given to the state by virtue of its history and evolution as the meeting ground of three distinct cultures and population groups. He had a deep interest in all of these matters, but his greatest concern was to explain their implications for the mission and work of the School of Inter-American Affairs. This was precisely the aim of his 1942 pamphlet, *New Mexico's Opportunity*. Originating as a paper read by President Zimmerman at the inaugural session of the SIAA, it identified the betterment of the less fortunate citizens of New Mexico as one of the school's central purposes: "I hope that this School will bring forth sharply the needs of the entirely too numerous impoverished citizens of the state—Anglo, Hispano, and Indian. Many students of the situation believe that more resources . . . should be devoted to a realistic action program in health and nutrition, housing, education, and economic rehabilitation."[58]

The SIAA was particularly well suited to confront these problems and devise a program of action because it understood that to a considerable degree they were rooted in the unique history of the region, in its living connections to the wider Hispanic world, and to those cultural and socioeconomic factors that caused many communities in New Mexico to resemble a "little Latin America." Ortega often expressed this belief in reports and project proposals, and when he did, he almost invariably accompanied it with some version of the tricultural formulation. The meeting-ground image was never far from his mind. Moreover, as he explained in the pamphlet, it was at the heart of New Mexico's "opportunity." "With its three cultures," he wrote, "Indian, Hispanic, and Anglo-Saxon—developing in parallel lines and yet united in interest and allegiances, there is no place in this hemisphere better equipped than New Mexico to become a synthesis of the Americas."[59] The synthesis to which he referred was that of New Mexico as a microcosm of the Americas. Elsewhere, it shaded toward a blending of the three cultures. Guérard had objected to the word *synthesis* in reference to Southwestern culture, but Ortega was employing it in a way that is compatible with Guérard's argument. A synthesis of the Americas was what New Mexico could *become*. It was conditional upon following a certain course. Ortega was not entirely consistent in the language that he used to describe the optimal relationship of the three cultures—how they would be interdependent yet stay apart—but whatever terms he chose to use, he was resolutely anti-assimilationist.[60] His synthesis was anything but a Southwestern melting pot. In his words, "Those who speak of 'Americanizing' this region . . . want to impose upon us a stupid uniformity that many educators here and elsewhere repudiate." On this

point, Ortega cited George Sánchez's criticism of how "experts" from outside
the region wanted to import methods devised for East Coast and Middle West
schools to teach Spanish-speaking children in New Mexico, where the challenge
clearly required a different approach, and he again expressed great admiration
for *Forgotten People* ("He brought his people forcibly to our memory, and the
book is of lasting merit").

Moving from the theme of the three cultures and the hoped-for synthesis,
Ortega addressed the issue of acculturation with respect to the territory's Spanish-speaking population after the US annexation. Simply put, Hispanos were
given no choice in the matter; they were forced to adjust to the alien way of life
of a colonizing power and its capitalist economy. It was either that—accept the
new reality—or perish. But the more insistent issue now was "to determine how
far the Hispanos must go in adapting themselves to modern industrial conditions
without losing their personality."[61] Toward the end of the pamphlet, Ortega
turned to the issue of prejudice and discrimination. He contrasted New Mexico
and Wisconsin, writing that for many of his twenty-five years in the latter he was
a "little Spanish colony" all by himself, in a "Nordic town." Yet he was understood
and honored for who he was. He claimed to have found a tolerance of difference
there—racial and ethnic—that was lacking in New Mexico. The implication
was that Hispanos in New Mexico were neither understood nor honored for
who they were. In this telling, of course, Ortega neglected to point out that as a
Spaniard in Wisconsin he was undoubtedly perceived as being European. Had
he been seen as being "Mexican" he might have been treated differently.

Ortega's 1945 pamphlet, *The Intangible Resources of New Mexico*, repeated
several of the same themes but did so in a more reflective, at times rather elegiac
mood. He began by devoting several pages to a poetic evocation of the physical
beauty of the land, the "contrast and harmony" that he found in nature and also
in "men and things." But he soon moved to more familiar ground, drawing on
the three-cultures motif and the diverse ways of life it represented. There was
New Mexico as the "receptacle of a civilization"—that of the United States,
with its superior numbers and drive for uniformity. But there was also New
Mexico as "the repository of strong cultures, and these cultures refuse to give
in totally. They are willing to blend, but not to disappear."[62] To explain what he
meant by "blending," Ortega resorted to the potential synthesis that lay in wait,
ready to be molded and take shape: "New Mexico could become the synthesis
of the Americas, for it contains, living side by side, autonomous in their ways
of life, yet forged together into common allegiance to our flag and our destiny,

the three main ethnic groups that carved out a future in the New World."[63] He saw the three (conspicuously absent, as in the earlier-quoted passage from Lyle Saunders, is the fourth main group that "carved out a future in the New World," the African American and Afro–Latin American) as "imperceptibly" merging, creating something unique, something purely New Mexican, an original contribution, in the spiritual sense or realm, to the "total pattern" of the nation. The idea is a trifle mystical, but that quality explains why he used the word *intangible* to describe New Mexico's resources.[64] Interestingly, Arthur Campa expressed similar sentiments regarding New Mexico's possibilities in this sphere. The state could be the birthplace, the seedbed, of a "new civilization." It was the place where two (Campa omitted the third) civilizations met and could, in that meeting, give rise to an authentic New World culture, "an American culture in the fullest sense of the word."[65]

Having elucidated the special character of the state and its people, Ortega shifted into a somewhat more practical mode, calling on New Mexico (as he had done for UNM) to make of itself something original, not imitative, "for if we only imitate, with our meager resources, we can hope only to be second rate."[66] The road forward, the road that would lead to this brighter future, had been charted by the SIAA and especially by its community program, in working at the grassroots level to address the social and economic ills of Hispanic and Native American communities, instill new life into their native arts and crafts, and, through these actions, help preserve distinct ways of life. Reduced to their essentials, New Mexico's intangible resources were there to promote fairness and justice and to bring about, to borrow Mario García's words, "integration with a pluralist, or in today's terms, a multi-cultural face," a society that respected ethnic and cultural diversity but also afforded equal opportunity for all, equal access to health care, nutrition, education, housing, and jobs.[67]

A last question remains to be asked: Was Ortega guilty, like some, of using the meeting ground and the three-distinct-cultures motifs in a naïve, simpleminded way? An entire cottage industry had grown up around them, much of it directed toward serving the interests of tourism and business. A line fomented in the late nineteenth century by the territorial Bureau of Immigration, that only in New Mexico could one—as Ortega often phrased it—"witness the confluence of three distinct living peoples," was certainly a favorite of his and made good copy: "A recurring subtext of tourist propaganda depicted New Mexico as a three-tiered society wherein Indians possessed the most pristine and least developed civilization; Nuevomexicanos had conserved medieval traditions and chivalry, and Americans were the bearers of the industry, science, or progress."⁶⁸ Clearly, this was a one-dimensional, static, and ahistorical image created for tourists and commercial purposes. As Chris Wilson has noted: "Civic leaders have employed the tricultural formulation throughout the twentieth century."⁶⁹

Did the more simplistic rendering of this formulation creep into Ortega's use of it? Wilson has observed that in Ortega's first pamphlet, *New Mexico's Opportunity*, it seems to, at the point when Ortega describes New Mexico's "three cultures—Indian, Hispanic, and Anglo-Saxon—developing in parallel lines," *parallel lines* taken to mean, in effect, the rigid three-tiered society referenced earlier. But Wilson then provides a corrective, noting that "a knowledgeable scholar such as Ortega would admit elsewhere [and here he quotes from the second pamphlet, *The Intangible Resources*] that 'biologically these groups are mixed already in a considerable degree.'"⁷⁰ It is safe to say that the second quote more accurately reflected Ortega's understanding of the formulation. Although he loved to find traces of old, undiluted Spain in New Mexico (as in his romanticized depiction of Carlos Vierra [Santa Fe art colony member and early proponent of the Pueblo Revival style] as the quintessential embodiment of Old World Spanish values and culture), he was well aware of how the process of mestizaje had come to shape a large percentage of the population of New Mexico. Ortega never commodified the meeting-ground confluence-of-three-living-peoples trope (a sole exception may have been his eagerness to participate in the 1940 Coronado Cuarto Centennial) in the way the tourist industry did, but he leveraged it to advance the programs of the SIAA. Ortega, as we have seen, saw the state for what it was. He disparaged the cheap touristic exploitation of New Mexico and the image(s) such exploitation promoted. "Let us," he wrote in *The Intangible Resources*, "without cheap sentimentalism, free from the superficially picturesque, poses, and cults—the escapist cult of the native, of the past, and other clichés—amass sober sentiment around New Mexico." He understood that such sentiment demanded a realistic grasp of the tricultural formulation, one that did not disguise or downplay the conflicts—ethnic, cultural, religious, and economic—that separated New Mexicans: "It is obvious," he wrote (in a brief article examining the workings of factionalism in the state), "that the Hispano and Indian have outlooks on life quite different from that of the Anglo. Values that seem paramount to one group are marginal for the other."⁷¹ Ortega had a different temperament from that of George Sánchez, but they shared a common vision for addressing the historical ills of the state and the ways in which the US annexation had worsened conditions for the majority of Hispanos.

CHAPTER FIVE

⟆⟆⟆

Ortega

Reorientation and Decline

Although founded only a few years earlier, the School of Inter-American Affairs was already a well-established part of the University of New Mexico by the mid-1940s, coordinating one of the largest and most comprehensive programs in the country devoted to the Latin American field. Few institutions, and certainly none of comparable size, could match its range of course offerings and related series of conferences, lectures, institutes, fine arts festivals, artists in residence, and publications. It managed to reach this plateau, in a university frequently plagued by funding shortages, because of Joaquín Ortega's success in attracting support from state and federal agencies, private foundations, and—on occasion—individual donors. The school's outreach effort, revolving around the Community Program, added a regional dimension and was pursued with equal vigor. One measure of the school's impact was the level of student interest. Enrollments in its different programs grew steadily throughout the decade, with the greatest increase recorded during the immediate postwar period, when (driven by the influx of men and women returning to school) the SIAA registration multiplied threefold in the two years between 1945 and 1947. In the academic year 1946–1947, twenty-two students graduated with a degree in inter-American affairs, an impressive total for the time.[1] Indicative of the growing reputation and prestige of the school, many of the graduates were accepted for advanced study in the top rank of universities, such as Harvard, Georgetown, Columbia, and the University of Wisconsin.[2] Growth on the undergraduate level was matched by that in the graduate school. In 1948–1949, for example, there were ten students pursuing a master's degree in inter-American affairs, exclusive of students in other departments whose work and interests intersected with Latin America or the Spanish Borderlands region. Moreover, the ten graduate students in the inter-American affairs master's program exceeded their counterpart numbers in several well-established departments, including psychology, sociology, economics, engineering, government, and art.[3]

Despite all its successes, however (and, to the more small-minded, perhaps because of them) the SIAA was still viewed suspiciously and resented by certain elements in the university. To its critics, it was expanding too rapidly, commanding too much attention, and draining off too many resources. Some, as noted earlier, were opposed to the more innovative side of the school—the idea that it should work aggressively to help solve the problems of the state, which—if one understood them in the proper historical light (i.e., accepted the central tenets of the SIAA)—were simply the problems of "inter-America" on a smaller scale. The grumbling seems to have been largely covert (it would become more vocal in the late 1940s) since one encounters almost no mention of it in the relevant university records, but it did occasionally find expression in memoranda and correspondence. For example, in helping lay the groundwork for a trip that President Zimmerman made in the fall 1942 to Washington, DC, to meet with officials in the Office of the Coordinator of Inter-American Affairs, Joaquín Ortega referred to the opposition toward this wider definition of the school's mission, describing its critics, somewhat allusively, as "weak sisters" whose objections were ill-founded, the product of a fearful complacency or territorialism: "I know that in spite of the 'weak sisters' who because of pusillanimity or other personal and therefore minor reasons—the ilk is common in academic families—bewail the extent of our activities, you are in sympathy with them. We must animate things and plunge headlong if we want to go places."[4]

The opposition was sometimes expressed through a reluctance or refusal to approve new courses when there was seemingly no basis for such resistance. In 1946, Donald Brand (the most outspoken territorial-minded "weak sister") requested approval of a temporary, one-semester course in Quechua linguistics, to be taught by a visiting Ecuadorian scholar with impeccable credentials to teach the language, Silvio Luis Haro Alvear. Brand provided a strong justification for the request, including the fact that nine students were prepared to take the course. "It is an unusual opportunity for our students," he wrote, "to obtain instruction in the most important Indian language in the world."[5] Nonetheless, the Curricula Committee denied his request. In 1945, Miguel Jorrín proposed a new interdisciplinary course called "Man and Society in Latin America." Although it was designed as a basic introductory course needed to help fill out the span of the inter-American affairs degree program, Jorrín had to fight tooth and nail to get it approved, submitting request after request to the committee.[6] Jorrín, who in the early months of 1948 would replace Ortega as director of the SIAA, was an excellent teacher and first-rate scholar, but the circumstances of his appointment in 1944 illustrated another avenue through which resistance to Ortega and the SIAA was channeled. In 1943, the linchpin of the school's academic program, Richard Behrendt, decided to leave the university and return to Panama. Behrendt, as noted earlier, was an areas-studies specialist par excellence, qualified—without any inflation of his credentials—to teach in several departments (and, had it been necessary, in several languages). He had an enviable publications record. Against all the evidence, however (or at least what seemed on the surface to be all the evidence), the faculty committee charged with considering promotions recommended against Behrendt. Zimmerman was dismayed. Afraid that this action would lead Behrendt to turn his back on UNM, he wrote to Ortega, beseeching him to "do all you possibly can to keep Dr. Behrendt."[7] Behrendt, however, was in no mood to dally any further, and he left. The loss of Behrendt was followed later that year by a decision to eliminate the instructional component and function of the SIAA. Its courses were transferred to the departments of sociology, economics, and government. When he came in as Behrendt's replacement, Jorrín was attached to the modern-languages department.

"Dangerous and Unwise"

Still another means by which opposition to the school was voiced involved setting strict limits on its activism. The school itself did not come under fire, only those initiatives that were deemed too provocative or radical, a classic example of which was a proposal that Ortega submitted in 1944 for a new SIAA-sponsored journal, to be called *Inter-Americana*. His idea for the journal grew out of a talk that he gave on the radio in April of that year as part of the USO Pan-American Day program.[8] His broad theme was the standard appeal to Pan-Americanism and the need to unite and stand fast against the totalitarian threat emanating from Nazi and fascist Europe. But more directly than he had ever done before, Ortega criticized the "big stick" diplomacy of the United States and portrayed the inter-American ideal as attainable only when relations between the peoples and countries of the hemisphere were characterized by true equality of rights and obligations. The work of diplomats and high-level officials was important, as were exchange programs of students and professors, but full progress, he insisted, would not be made without the exchange of farmers, industrial workers, and plain citizens promoting communication and understanding between "our brothers here" and "their brothers there." Sounding like Francis Kercheville after his return in 1941 from Latin America, Ortega argued for going beyond political and cultural ties to "the economic and social ones, which are of capital importance in the construction of a lasting edifice of Inter-Americanism." He went well past Kercheville, however, in delivering a clear anti-imperialist, anti-mercantilist message: "Let us be neither exploiters nor exploited, but a large family of free men working out their free destiny with guaranties of a decent return for their efforts. We must forget the type of colonial economy which feeds on the principle of keeping cheap producers of raw materials in subordinate nations and expensive producers of manufactured products in the privileged ones." Social and cultural relations would stagnate, he warned, until we relinquished our pretensions to superiority. "Anglo-Saxon America must come down from its self-erected pedestal and treat the peoples of the other Americas as equals, for otherwise the whole fabric of Pan Americanism is flimsy." Ortega's prescription for the future?: "We must work together for raising the social conditions of man in the Americas; for providing him with minimum standards of education, sanitation, housing, and nutrition, so that he can find full outlets for his personality and usefulness." In that sentence, Ortega had merely to substitute "many Spanish-speaking communities in New Mexico" for "the Americas" to carry his directive over to the mission and work of the SIAA's Community Program.

Ortega's radio broadcast was the springboard for his journal proposal, and when he submitted the proposal to President Zimmerman he attached a transcription of the USO Pan-American Day talk. *Inter-Americana*, as he envisioned it, would be a quarterly review casting light on the social and economic conditions and problems of the Spanish-speaking population of the Southwest. Later, if judged desirable, its geographic coverage could be extended to include "the Spanish-speaking colonies of Detroit, Chicago, and other eastern cities and the agricultural and railway workers of the West and Midwest." There was a critical need for such a journal, because the attention paid to the problems of the country's Hispanic population—despite its numbering some three million, the majority of whom lived in the Southwest—was at best scattered and piecemeal. *Inter-Americana* would also include reviews of books and bibliographies pertinent to the topic, articles on folklore and linguistics, summaries of events affecting the Spanish-speaking people, and "progress reports of significant projects or experiments concerned with improving conditions among the Spanish-speaking Americans." Because the University of New Mexico was "strategically located" in the state with the largest percentage of Spanish-speaking people nationwide, it was, Ortega argued, the logical place for a publication of this type.

Zimmerman sent the proposal to Tom Popejoy (see fig. 16)—at that time comptroller of the university as well as Zimmerman's executive assistant—perhaps because he wanted to get his opinion about Ortega's cost estimates, perhaps to elicit his reaction to the idea itself, or perhaps for both reasons. Popejoy's reaction was entirely negative. He returned the proposal, with the radio-talk transcription attached, scribbling in the top right-hand margin: "Dr. Zimmerman. I think this is dangerous and unwise."[9] Although he did not explain his thinking, it is not difficult to understand why Popejoy might have reacted as he did, in describing the proposal as "dangerous." For someone who believed in the power of conciliation and, very likely, preferred to take middle-of-the-road positions (as befitted a future president of the university), Ortega's proposal was too radical and his language too extreme, too populist in tone ("our brothers here . . . their brothers there"; "exploiters" and "exploited"). If the review were faithful to its purpose to lay bare the "social and economic problems" of the Spanish-speaking population, it would necessarily have to cover Anglo-Hispano relations and a range of associated topics, such as prejudice and discrimination, cultural displacement, land appropriation, and economic exploitation. As we have seen, open discussion of some of these topics was at least seriously frowned upon if not proscribed outright. It offended Hispanic ethnic sensibilities and pride. Like Richard Page's racial attitudes questionnaire, Ortega's magazine might transgress the acceptable limits of such discourse and violate the pact of "silence." Popejoy, surely, saw these possibilities and the chance that the publication would foster a sense of grievance among Hispanos and bring old resentments to the surface, accentuating differences and worsening relations between the two groups. In short, if viewed from this angle, a UNM journal along the lines proposed by Ortega would serve little or no constructive purpose and might well light the flame of ethnic discord. Exactly how Zimmerman reacted to Popejoy's opinion is not clear, since he apparently chose not to put anything down on paper. It will be recalled, however, that only a few years before it was Zimmerman himself who, in the context of the Coronado Cuarto Centennial celebrations, had argued for holding a conference to consider the very issues and problems that Ortega wanted the proposed journal to cover. Zimmerman may have decided, for strategic reasons, to draw back from his earlier position, or he may have welcomed Ortega's idea but thought the timing wrong, or he may have been distracted by his own health problems (see the following section). Whatever the reason, the journal proposal was not pursued.

FIGURE 16 Tom Popejoy. Popejoy wore many hats at UNM, beginning in the 1920s and culminating in his service as the university's president from 1948 until 1968. While he played a lead role in President Zimmerman's efforts to extend services to New Mexico's Hispanic community, Popejoy was always cautious about supporting projects that he thought too radical, and in the early 1940s he thwarted Joaquín Ortega's proposal that UNM publish a journal, *Inter-Americana*, dealing with the social and economic problems facing the Spanish-speaking population of the Southwest. Faculty Files Collection (UNMA 152, box 22), Center for Southwest Research, University Libraries, University of New Mexico. Courtesy of CSWR.

A Series of Blows

1944 had started out as a very good year for Joaquín Ortega and the SIAA, but it did not end that way. In October 1944, Zimmerman, whose health had been in decline, suffered a fatal heart attack, dying at the relatively young age of fifty-seven. The loss was keenly felt by the entire UNM community and by Ortega in particular. The two men, although very different in temperament and disposition, had nevertheless formed a close bond. They relied on each other; Zimmerman on Ortega for his ideas and creative energy and his dedication to building UNM's program in Latin American and Southwest Hispanic studies into a model for the nation; and Ortega on Zimmerman for articulating the vision of what the program could be and doing all in his power to implement it. The degree of any person's pain is ultimately a private matter and thus difficult to ascertain, but it seems unlikely that very many in the university could have born Zimmerman's death with a heavier heart than Ortega. Zimmerman was his backstop and defender, a confidante who had come to his rescue and restored his spirits in moments of doubt. Furthermore, his support had been the keystone to the expansionist role and regional focus of the SIAA; or as Ortega expressed it to Zimmerman, employing a different metaphor, "somehow or other I consider you the anchor of my work here."[10] Now he would have to sail alone through sometimes choppy waters.

Zimmerman's death marked the end of an era and was followed only a little more than a year later by the resignation, in 1946, of three of the core Latin Americanist–Southwest studies faculty: Donald Brand, Arthur Campa, and George Hammond. Each, of course, had his own reasons for leaving, but in all three cases these were tied to what Campa said had motivated him: "better professional opportunities and considerable advancement."[11] In Campa's case, appointment as chair of the modern-languages department at the University of Denver at the rank of full professor; in Brand's, appointment as professor of geography at the University of Michigan at a significantly higher salary with the assurance of substantial research funds; and in Hammond's, appointment both as professor of history at the University of California–Berkeley and director of UC's Bancroft Library. The prospect of the university having to move forward without Zimmerman's leadership may also have weighed in their thinking. They were all part of the inner circle of the inter-American affairs teaching and research complex, so their loss would be felt strongly, that of Hammond in particular. The new president of the university, John Phillip Wernette, tried to induce the "famed historian" (as he was referred to by numerous New Mexico newspapers that covered the story of his resignation) to remain at UNM, but to no avail.[12] Wernette does not appear to have written in the same vein to either Brand or Campa.

It was not the loss of faculty, however, that posed the real challenge to the high reputation and continued primacy of the university's inter-American studies program or to Ortega's ability to maintain the full scope of SIAA activities. Faculty—even those generally recognized as among the best in their field— could be replaced by equally prominent scholars. Hammond himself was a case in point. Very soon after he had left France Scholes accepted an offer to return to the University of New Mexico. UNM departments as highly regarded nationally as history, anthropology, and modern languages (its Spanish-language and -literature components in the case of the latter) would have little trouble recruiting top-flight faculty. Rather, the challenge sprang from the reshaping of the postwar environment, both inside and outside the university. After 1945, UNM—no different than other state universities—saw its enrollments swell, but as President Wernette explained to Lloyd Tireman (who was then on leave as a technical adviser to the Bolivian Ministry of Education), the percentage rise at the University of New Mexico seems to have placed it at the forefront of that trend: "[T]he enormous increase in our enrollment places us first, I believe, among state universities in percentage increase above the pre-war peak."[13]

Wernette, as the statistics cited earlier bear out, was scarcely exaggerating. In just one academic year, 1945–1946, UNM's student population quadrupled, increasing from 924 to 3,662.[14] The face of the university necessarily had to change, given the great number of students streaming in and the inevitable need they created to broaden the curriculum. It was a logical end point for the singular focus that Zimmerman had put, since 1927, on building up the inter-American program. The program was not abandoned or even adjusted downward. It was simply that the ground had shifted, and it now had to compete with the hunger for growth and expansion in other areas.[15] A memo sent in April 1951, by a member of the Faculty Senate Curricula Committee, Charles Judah, to two fellow committee members (and copied to France Scholes and Miguel Jorrín) provides a clear indication of how these pressures were building. Judah had compiled a list of the courses offered in the Latin American field versus those concentrating on Asia. The results, he believed, showed that some rebalancing of interests was needed. "Perhaps it is not significant," he wrote in classic understatement, "but I find it interesting in terms of emphasis and the state of the world that the University offers 34 courses dealing entirely or chiefly with Latin America and one (Philosophy 185) dealing entirely or chiefly with Asiatic civilization."[16]

The postwar changes were felt in Washington, DC, as well as when the federal government began redefining national priorities, dismantling many of the New Deal–era and emergency wartime programs launched in the interest of Pan-Americanism and of bolstering hemispheric solidarity. The idealism that had inspired government policy and practice during the Roosevelt years began to dissipate. Agencies such as the Office of the Coordinator of Inter-American Affairs (OCIAA), which had supported local development projects (like the Barelas Community Center) partly as domestic extensions of the Pan-American initiative, were either eliminated or restructured to serve other needs. The closing of the OIAA at the end of 1945 dealt a serious blow to the School of Inter-American Affairs, since the majority of its community-based projects in New Mexico had been funded through grants from this agency. Faced with the cessation of a generally reliable source of external funding, Ortega mobilized support among a small but key group (which included Tom Popejoy, dean of Arts and Sciences Jay Knode, and Lloyd Tireman) to ring-fence the Community Program and see to its continuation. Initially, his move succeeded. In 1946 the university took steps to ensure its permanency as a "regular function" of the institution, with responsibility for its activities now to be shared between the SIAA and the Department of Sociology. As it turned out, however, the permanency was extremely short-lived. Only a year after it was designated a stable feature of the institution, the program was summarily closed down.

In 1941, during the legislative debate over the issue of making Spanish-language instruction obligatory in the public schools, Ortega had written to Concha Ortiz y Pino (in reference to the proposed bilingual conference): "I am an inveterate optimist and keep hammering for things close to my heart—and this is one of them—until I reach my goal."[17] Nothing was closer to Ortega's heart than the Community Program, but some goals proved out of reach, and for Ortega, fending off the demise of this program was one of them. What had happened between the university's action in support of the program in 1946 and its decision just a year later to terminate it altogether? The immediate cause was a growing belief among many of the SIAA students that the school had wandered off track and, to an increasing degree, was emphasizing local and statewide outreach projects at the expense of its academic mission. In a sense, the very success of the Community Program was its undoing. A sort of minirevolt took place, leading to a memorandum and report to Ortega sent in April 1947 by the four members (one Hispano, three Anglos) of one of the SIAA's student committees, the Committee on Employment and Advanced Study, objecting to the "obvious and campus-wide known reorientation of the School de facto from its original understood goals and principles" [underlining in original].[18] After further asserting that "New Mexican and not Inter-American affairs are now the major concern of the School," the report claimed that the SIAA's outstanding national and international reputation—systematically built up since its inception—was being placed in jeopardy by this shift in emphasis: "It seems to us," the disenchanted students complained, "that the School is resting upon its past victories, is basking in the reflected glories of other days, that while privies and water tanks are rising as solid little monuments to its in-state program, the price of this local lustre must inevitably be the tarnishing and eventual general deterioration of its larger reputation and status as a professional center of Inter-American studies."[19] The report continued in this vein for several more paragraphs, reiterating the message that the focus of the "executive organ" (a thinly veiled euphemism for Joaquín Ortega) of the school was more and more devoted to New Mexico at the expense of Latin America and inter-American affairs. If this trend continued, the "New Mexico Development Program," as the Community Program was also called, would end up swallowing an ever-greater share of the school's resources. The students who authored the report had taken care to formulate their position and lodge their complaint only after canvasing other students and faculty.

It soon became clear that the willingness of the small group that Ortega had assembled to ensure the survival of the Community Program was not to be found among the university community at large. The report was circulated only to the Club de las Américas and to Miguel Jorrín, who, since replacing Richard Behrendt in 1944, had taken on a lead role in the inter-American affairs program. Nonetheless, it was bound to leak out, and it did. It quickly emerged that the students had tapped into and articulated a sentiment shared by others in the university, including high-ranking administrators. Even if Zimmerman were still president and chose to use his authority as a buffer, it is quite possible that he would have found it prudent to accommodate this unrest to some extent and trim the Community Program. The university, however, was under new leadership that faced a set of new challenges and budgetary demands. Operating within a changed environment, Wernette felt no compunction to honor and preserve every commitment that had been made under differing circumstances by a previous administration. Viewed from one angle (although the interpretation may be too cynical), the students' "manifesto" gave cover to the administration to institute changes that it welcomed and may have been contemplating in any case, while clipping Ortega's wings into the bargain. Ortega's reaction to the report is not known, but coming so soon after Zimmerman's death and given his resolute belief in the rightness of the Community Program, it must have been a bitter pill to swallow and bruising to his ego. Once the report had become public knowledge, university officials—especially Thomas C. Donnelly (who had become dean of Arts and Sciences upon the retirement of Jay Knode)— held a series of discussions with Ortega regarding the structure of the school and its future direction. Subsequently, in August 1947, Donnelly announced that effective immediately the Community Program would be terminated and that "the emphasis . . . in the School of Inter-American Affairs will be placed on inter-American affairs per se."[20]

Some of the SIAA's more unsparing critics proposed folding it into a new school of international affairs, but Donnelly rejected this idea, arguing—in line with the strategic vision laid out by Zimmerman—that UNM's most advantageous course would be to continue to specialize in the Latin American and inter-American fields. Indeed, far from representing a move away from that vision, the elimination of the SIAA's Community Program reaffirmed the commitment to maintaining inter-American studies as a major priority of the university, one that its top-level administrators often cited and used as a wedge in recruiting new faculty. In 1949, for example, Tim MacCurdy, about to join the Department of Modern Languages and begin a long career at UNM, noted in a letter to Francis Kercheville, "Also satisfying is the enlightened view of Dean Donnelly, Vice-President Scholes, and President Popejoy that the University of New Mexico should naturally assume leadership in the Hispanic field because of the state's cultural heritage."[21] When Popejoy succeeded Wernette (in 1948) as president, he stressed the same point in his inaugural address, invoking—like so many before him and others after him—the tricultural formulation: "The School of Inter-American Affairs . . . is especially favored by the unique combination of ethnic groups which New Mexico affords."[22]

The redesign of the SIAA included some other changes aimed at concentrating its focus on instruction and the pursuit of purely academic interests. The school's extensive publications program (which had helped elevate its profile nationwide) was turned over to the University of New Mexico Press and the curriculum was reorganized.[23] In addition, Miguel Jorrín's non–Latin American teaching duties were assigned to other members of the government department so that he could devote himself full-time to expanding the number of Latin American–related courses coordinated through the SIAA. In swift measure, then, and apparently with no outward expression of dissent by Ortega, the integrative approach, flowing out of the idea that New Mexico was a "little Latin America" and that the regional and the hemispheric therefore went together, was jettisoned, and along with it the parallel belief, which Zimmerman had shared and supported, that the SIAA should be an arm of service to the state.

In retrospect, it seems clear that the reform of the SIAA was unavoidable, given the broad changes underway in the postwar environment. Had Ortega examined these with a view to their practical implications, he might have anticipated the challenge that was brewing and partially deflected it by instituting some rebalancing of SIAA priorities himself. Perhaps to his own credit, however, but certainly to his own misfortune, he was too deeply invested in the model that he and Zimmerman had devised to do that. There is no evidence that Ortega tried to mount a defense of the SIAA's orientation toward local community projects, but if he did, he would probably have found himself with few staunch allies. In 1941, his Spanish origins and status as an "outsider" had been a major factor in his appointment as director of the new school. The position gave him high visibility and brought him into frequent contact with faculty in various departments, but in many ways he seems to have retained the outsider persona, positioning himself on the margins, relatively isolated in his own bailiwick and seemingly disinclined or too preoccupied otherwise to participate in ground-level governance of the university. For example, only once across the entire decade of 1941–1951 do the minutes of Faculty Senate meetings indicate that he raised his hand to say anything, and on that one occasion it was simply to inform fellow faculty of an upcoming talk by a visiting Latin American dignitary.[24] Otherwise, if he was a presence, then he was a silent presence. In all these years, he was not nominated even once to serve on any key Faculty Senate committees to which members were elected, and he was never an officer of that senate. For a few years, he did serve on the Library and Publications Committees. The only committee of any great consequence on which Ortega served was a committee that Zimmerman formed in December 1943, the "Post-War Planning Committee," and this happened only because the president personally appointed four of its eleven members and made Ortega one of his appointees. Consequently, he never became a leader among the faculty, and perhaps that was partly by choice, rather than an indicator of "outsider" status, and resulted from the desire on his part not to be encumbered with burdensome committee work that would take away time and drain energy from his numerous off-campus activities. He paid a price, however, for this apparent lack of involvement in university affairs, outside of those that pertained to his own area. When he most needed them, his defenders among the faculty leadership were few and far between. At bottom, Ortega was Zimmerman's man, or at least that is how many viewed him, advancing Zimmerman's inter-American initiative and program. Those who opposed the program's broad scope now had the upper hand.

In addition to the students' complaint about the SIAA's strong emphasis on local community-based projects, a second crisis occurred—at almost exactly the same moment—that brought Ortega more adverse publicity and was likely a source of discouragement to him. In late April 1947, he was enveloped in a controversy that both in broad outline and in many particulars—although accompanied by a much less vitriolic public protest—became a virtual carbon copy of the 1933 racial-attitude-survey affair. The controversy arose when two Anglo students decided, as a project for a sociology class, to examine the attitudes of fellow UNM students toward Spanish Americans. Like Richard Page fourteen years earlier, they elected to use the Thurstone scale as their survey instrument, adapting it for their purposes by substituting the term *Spanish Americans* for *Negro*. Once Hispanic students learned of the survey and realized that it was being circulated (about two hundred copies had been filled out), they approached Joaquín Ortega to protest its "discriminatory" wording and to insist that he intercede to stop its circulation. Word, of course, soon got out to the press and the wider community. Two Santa Fe councils of the League of United Latin American Citizens and the Hispanic Club of Albuquerque demanded that the two students be expelled from the university. Moreover, Ortega was caught in the crosshairs of the controversy, when the president of the Catholic Teachers College of Albuquerque, Rev. Edward T. McCarthy, not only accused the university of trying to "whitewash the whole dirty business" but also charged Ortega, personally, with having moved to "hush up the whole affair when a number of students protested."[25] No credible evidence existed to uphold this allegation, and a group of forty-two students immediately rallied behind Ortega. Their defense read in part, "We sincerely believe that he has done, and is doing, his utmost to promote true democratic ideals which will make our country more united and stronger."[26] Wernette took steps to contain the situation and limit the damage, clarifying that the two students had acted entirely on their own and expressing regret "that such a questionnaire should have been prepared since the subject matter obviously is offensive to us all in New Mexico."[27] Wernette also appointed a committee of three faculty members—Paul Walter Jr., Miguel Jorrín, and Joaquín Ortega—to investigate the matter and report its findings to the University Administrative Council. The committee conducted a hearing, attended by some thirty individuals, at which the two students reiterated that they had acted alone, had been motivated solely by the desire to produce a report based on an impartial, scientific study, and were "very sorry it has been misconstrued." Based on all the information gathered and all the testimony heard, the committee ruled that the two students had to drop their class without credit. The university administration accepted the committee's decision, and the students in turn issued an apology "to the university, the Sociology Department, Prof. Lyle Saunders, Dr. Joaquín Ortega, and the people of Spanish descent of New Mexico."[28]

Certain elements, however, did not believe this punishment was sufficient. The LULAC councils and the Hispanic Club of Albuquerque continued to call for the students' expulsion, although the Hispanic Club, it should be noted, voted unanimously to express confidence in Ortega.[29] At this point, Senator Dennis Chávez weighed in on the affair, defending the honesty and integrity of the two students, while also underscoring that racial prejudice and discrimination still hampered and dragged down the university. "The two students who circulated the questionnaire," he wrote, "have been condemned too much . . ." adding, "the only thing for which they might be condemned is that they had the nerve and intestinal fortitude to bring out in black and white what anyone with any degree of intelligence knows is a condition that exists at the university."[30] Consistent with this observation, Chávez also supported those who believed that the incident called for further investigation, to determine, he said, "whether or not regents and others in authority are carrying out the purposes and ideals for which the university was created."[31] By this time, as Phillip Gonzales has noted, the controversy had the makings of another affair like the 1933 Richard Page debacle, but instead of gaining more impetus, it began to dissipate. According to Gonzales, "the scope and intensity of Hispano protest identity ... was lower than in the period leading up to the thirties."[32] This changed dynamic did not mean that Hispanos, collectively, were no longer discontented with UNM "in relation to their ethnicity," only that they did not sense the same degree of vulnerability to Anglo power or the same level of threat to their own cultural identity.

His sterling reputation with the Hispanic community still intact, but with the span of his SIAA activities now considerably reduced, Ortega soldiered on, expanding his teaching load and devoting more time to small research topics that interested him. Still, he could not reconcile himself to turning away, permanently, from the regional focus. Since maintaining it was no longer possible within the new SIAA structure, he had to look for an opportunity elsewhere, and one would soon open up with *The New Mexico Quarterly*. Ortega had long taken an interest in the journal, both as a member of the Faculty Senate Publications Committee, which oversaw its production, and as a contributor himself. His first pieces appeared in 1941–1942, in the form of a four-part series titled "Insects on a Pin," consisting of epigrams he had written, and a brief but substantive article, "Remarks on Modern Mexican Art," worked up from an address he had given to the Art League of New Mexico in conjunction with the installation at UNM of the landmark MOMA exhibition (or at least the sections of it that had traveled) "Twenty Centuries of Modern Art."[33] In this article, Ortega's interest was to examine the relationship between art and propaganda or the role of art as a vehicle for social and political expression, and he posed the critical question, Does the work of art, relieved of its message, stand on its own? He applied this test to the Mexican artists represented, in particular to the work of "*los tres grandes*" (Diego Rivera, José Clemente Orozco, and David Alfaro Siqueiros), and found that in their case it was easily passed. This article is a good example of Ortega's protean interests and wide range of knowledge. He demonstrated his supple grasp of art historical theory in relation to other forms of creative expression, such as poetry and philosophy, both of which were interwoven into his presentation. With the additional time his new duties afforded him, Ortega published several articles in the journal during 1947–1948, along with a short piece titled "Factionalism in New Mexico," in the periodical *Rio Grande Writer*. "Revisiting Cervantes" was another example of his intellectual breadth, covering as it did the full sweep of European literature from the renaissance on.[34] "Doctor Chimera. Story," was a rather fantastical tale in which he seemed to be satirizing the pomposity, pseudo-sophistication, and arid emptiness of much academic writing.[35] Another piece, "The Professor and the University" (of which more to come), was, among other things, a concise statement of his beliefs regarding the higher purposes of a university.[36]

Through his years of service on the Publications Committee, his review of potential articles on topics related to Latin America or the Hispanic Southwest, and his own contributions, Ortega had demonstrated a sustained interest in *The New Mexico Quarterly*. In 1947, its longtime editor, Dudley Wynn, decided to leave the position, and so the committee began looking for his replacement. The process turned out to be rather tortuous. At a July 1947 meeting, Ortega moved that historian and novelist of the Southwest Paul Horgan be "placed first on the list of candidates to be recommended."[37] The motion carried. Wynn finished all work for the summer issue and also gave time to preparing the fall issue as well. Horgan, however, seesawed back and forth about taking the editorship and ultimately withdrew altogether. In the meanwhile, with uncertainty clouding the picture, the responsibility for editing *The Quarterly* was handed on an acting basis first to Ada Rutledge, a staff member, and then to Charles Allen, director of the UNM Press. The issue dragged on through all of 1947, with Ortega at one point nominating a Miss Simon of the UNM English department for the position. The committee endorsed Ortega's nomination, and it seemed as though she would inherit the editorship. President Wernette, however, was apparently not of like mind, and so the search continued. At this juncture, the last month or two of 1947, with the committee unable to identify a replacement, Ortega began seriously to think of himself as filling the role. With that possibility in mind, he composed a document several pages in length, spelling out his own thoughts about the future of *The Quarterly*, and sent it to the other members of the committee and to dean of Arts and Sciences Tom Donnelly. There were other sidelines to the story, but in March 1948, with all of the obstacles having finally been cleared and the committee having unanimously recommended Ortega to be the next editor of the review, Wernette confirmed him in the post. Thomas M. Pearce, who had cofounded the review with Dudley Wynn and helped edit it for many years, strongly supported the appointment of Ortega. "He is widely known in the state," Pearce wrote, "and has been very successful in the undertakings he has worked with since he came here. I . . . agree with Dr. Ortega that the magazine will thrive best with a regional emphasis."[38] To alleviate the fears of some that he was taking on too much work and of others that he might be telegraphing too great an ambition, he gave up the directorship of the School of Inter-American Affairs, passing that responsibility to Miguel Jorrín.

We do not really need a clue to know why Ortega should have been drawn to the prospect of editing *The New Mexico Quarterly*, but if we did, Pearce's endorsement contained it, and it lay, naturally, in the word *regional*. *The New Mexico Quarterly* provided Ortega with the platform from which he could redirect his energies back to regional concerns and again promote—though in a more diffuse way—the idea of New Mexico as the meeting ground. He had been rebuffed in his proposal for starting a new journal, *Inter-Americana*, that would focus on the social and economic realities of contemporary Hispanic life in New Mexico and the Southwest. Although primarily a cultural and literary review, *The Quarterly* nonetheless offered Ortega the possibility of circling back, albeit in a narrower way and minus the emphasis on a single ethnic group, to cover some of the themes he had intended for *Inter-Americana*.

The autumn 1948 issue of *The Quarterly* carried a note from acting editor Charles Allen explaining that Joaquín Ortega had been appointed the new editor and would assume his full duties with the winter 1948 issue (see plate 4). He added that a reorganization plan for the review, entailing new policies and features, would be outlined by Ortega in the winter issue and implemented as of spring 1949. In an "editorial statement" appearing in the winter issue, Ortega paid due respect to Pearce and Wynn for having launched the review and having subsequently brought it to a "position of regional-literary leadership."[39] He then noted, however, that since change is a constant in life, there would be some modifications in emphasis. First and foremost, the personality of the review would reflect "the meaning of the Southwest in general and of New Mexico in particular: the historical tradition, the spirit, the interests, the forms, the values, the needs, and the significance of all these as they cast their influences upon the national cultural pattern." When he first presented his ideas for *The Quarterly* to the Publications Committee, Ortega had given notice that he would put a strong emphasis on delineating the special characteristics of New Mexico and the region, those that stamped it as different. "A region," he wrote, "and ours more than others, is a world in miniature; and the Review should reflect it—past, present, and aspirations for the future."[40] Now, in his editorial statement, he defined more specifically what that meant: "Here in New Mexico is a blending unique in the Americas—the aboriginal population and the two main conquering peoples." It was a variation on the familiar theme and announced that regional matters would be linked to inter-American affairs.

He also made clear in a more direct way that the review would not focus inordinately on the region, for the region was part of a greater whole. *The Quarterly's* outlook needed to be cosmopolitan: "It is in its global significance that the region realizes its larger meaning. . . . It is those regional values that have a national and a universal application that we wish to emphasize—not the provincial, the picturesque, and banal." These ideas, too, were a carryover of the principles upon which the School of Inter-American Affairs had been founded. Ortega's ambition was to produce a literary-cultural review that offered not just sentimental "impressions" of the region but original work of real substance that would engage the reader's interest and attention. The content would embrace numerous genres: fiction, poetry, biography, literature, history, folklore, anthropology, and language. There would be articles on art and arts and crafts, music, architecture, photography, aspects of Native American, Spanish American, and Anglo-American life, with business, politics, agriculture, and the sciences also to be covered. In addition, Ortega wanted to enliven the physical appearance with graphic material—line drawings, vignettes, and similar devices, created by a regional artist for each issue.

The first issue over which Ortega had full editorship and could implement some of the new features was the spring 1949 issue. The novelties included a new column, "The Editor's Corner," a redesign of the review's typography and lettering, and—one of his best innovations—an "art series" feature, with drawings and a cover ornamentation done expressly for individual issues by an accomplished artist, accompanied by a critical essay on that artist's body of work. The first artist featured was Ernest L. Blumenschein; others included John Sloan, Howard Cook, Kenneth Adams, Gustave Baumann, and Raymond Jonson. Ortega's "Editor's Corner" also offered notes—veritable articles in themselves—on the contributors to each issue. His commitment to having a stimulating mix of content, focused both on the region and beyond, was also fulfilled. Contributors, some already prominent, some with reputations yet to be made, were talented and set a high mark for a regional review. They included Shirley Jackson, Stanley Edgar Hyman, Alfred Kazin, Ramón Sender, and Kenneth Patchen.

Ortega had found a new calling with *The New Mexico Quarterly* and, true to form, threw himself into it wholeheartedly. Yet his time with the review was destined to be short. He edited all of the 1949 and 1950 volumes (including volume 20, number 4, which covered winter 1950–51)—or eight issues in all—too few to have molded the review along new lines or to have left a distinctive stamp. Concerns over his health had initially checked his willingness to assume the editorship. Like Zimmerman, Ortega had a heart condition (and other serious ailments), and his strength and stamina had been slowly ebbing for several years. By February 1951, his health had declined sharply, such that he felt obliged to withdraw from the editorship of the review. The move to *The Quarterly* had given Ortega a new lease on life; now that was gone, so it was a low time for him, as Lyle Saunders indicated in a letter to George Sánchez: "Keen has resigned the Quarterly editorship and is off to the mountains for a rest. He's been looking like a ghost lately . . . [;] this time it was a real sickness, although I think much more spiritual than physical."[41]

Saunders seems to have underestimated the physical side of Ortega's malaise. France Scholes, UNM's vice president, reluctantly accepted his resignation and, on Ortega's recommendation, elevated George Arms from associate editor to editor. After a period of rest and recuperation, Ortega planned to resume his teaching duties at the start of the 1951–1952 academic year and, as time permitted, also begin work (in a collaboration with Lyle Saunders and possibly Sabine Ulibarrí) on an extensive study of Hispanic New Mexico. His teaching schedule was to include two new courses: the first (to be taught over two semesters) would be devoted to Cervantes's life and works, his literary relationships, and his influence in the cultural history of the Western World; the second was split into three courses (to be taught in a three-semester sequence), each covering a period in the evolution of Spanish realism, from the late Middle Ages through the nineteenth century. Even for a man in good health, the plan was ambitious. For one in poor health it would have been a very tall order. Ortega had the will to carry it out but not the physical strength; and as his body failed him, he became increasingly dispirited, the old fervent sense of mission deserting him. As the fall semester got underway, he found himself too weak to go on, and so on October 31, 1951 he wrote to university authorities informing them of his unconditional resignation from the university. Ortega was fifty-nine years old at the time. He had composed his letter in a state of mental depression and in some haste, without proper consideration for how his abrupt resignation might affect his retirement benefits. France Scholes acted quickly to protect Ortega and his family in this regard, writing (with Tom Donnelly and the chair of the Department of Modern Languages Robert Duncan) to President Popejoy to alert him to this situation, outlining two scenarios that would ensure Ortega's benefits. Ortega held out some hope that a prolonged rest might restore him to sufficient health so that he could resume his research on Hispanic life and culture in New Mexico. As a note in the *Alumnus*, covering his retirement, optimistically put it: "A continuous stream of manuscripts is expected to emanate from the book-crammed garage which he uses as his study."[42] His decline, however, was irreversible. His health continued to deteriorate, and in the winter of 1954 Ortega returned to Spain, traveling to Ronda to settle his personal affairs. The end was near. In a postscript to a letter to George Sánchez, dated March 23, 1955, Lyle Saunders wrote, "Sad news from Spain—Joaquín Ortega has had his second leg amputation. Blood clots. He is [in] really bad shape and nothing seems to help."[43] On August 23, 1955, Joaquín Ortega died.

CHAPTER SIX

Conclusion

Joaquín Ortega's public face, his sociability, busy life, and active engagement in civic and political affairs, which brought him into regular contact with a wide circle of people, can lead one to the wrong conclusion. He was at bottom a private person, with a small circle of close friends and associates, thus making it difficult to get a true sense of the inner man. Fortunately, however, Ortega did reveal himself in some of his writings. His brief article "The Professor and the University," which appeared in the autumn 1948 issue of *The New Mexico Quarterly Review*, is especially useful in this regard. The piece had been written by him a year earlier on the occasion of the retirement of Max Otto, a longtime professor of philosophy and a colleague of Ortega's at the University of Wisconsin. Otto assumed the stature of a heroic figure for Ortega, the Socratic embodiment of all that was best in universities and the academic life. When attacked for encouraging discussion of ideas that many Wisconsinites considered blasphemous or subversive, Otto stood up for free inquiry and the untrammeled pursuit of knowledge and for the preservation of the university as a "center of conflict," the definition and role assigned to it by the University of Wisconsin's president, Charles R. Van Hise, who ardently defended Otto. Ortega also greatly admired Van Hise, many of whose values and qualities and dedication to service he also saw in James Zimmerman. Indeed, apart from its Spanish heritage and the promise it offered of the "fusion of the best there is in three great cultures which have molded the pattern of the Americas,"[1] New Mexico held the draw that it did for Ortega because of James Zimmerman. In his estimation, Zimmerman, like Van Hise, was part of a rapidly disappearing breed—university presidents who were not primarily administrators but "men of learning."

Of Max Otto and himself, Ortega wrote (giving us the measure of his own sensibilities and worldview), "He is essentially the *raisonneur* and I am essentially the mystic."[2] At heart, Ortega conceived of himself as following in the footsteps of Spanish philosopher, educator, and essayist Miguel de Unamuno. Furthermore, Otto was also the practical man. "He wants knowledge to be translated into action,"[3] but only after all sides of a question or issue have been examined. Despite his self-declared mystical bent, Ortega—as we know—shared a belief in the virtue of applying knowledge to the problems of everyday life. Like Otto, he was a great admirer of John Dewey and Dewey's pragmatism. As such, he fit snugly into the mold of the so-called "service intellectual"—the New Deal–era university professor who answered Franklin D. Roosevelt's call to action because he believed that his role dictated active service to society.[4] Joaquín Ortega's Community Program was a classic example of this type of academic activism, as was the University of New Mexico's Taos County Adult Education Project, from which Ortega drew both inspiration and factual data.

No one explained Ortega's convictions better than France Scholes, one of his few close friends on the UNM faculty. In a tribute to Ortega that he wrote after the Spaniard's death, Scholes described him in much the same terms as Ortega had lauded Otto, that is, as a great defender of the timeless purposes of a university and its tradition of humane learning, but to this description he added, "he also believed that the teacher and the university have inescapable obligations to community life and culture. As Director of the School of Inter-American Affairs at UNM, he was not content to administer a purely teaching program. Under his leadership the School actively sponsored community projects for the amelioration of the social and economic status of the Spanish-speaking people in the State."[5]

The postwar environment fundamentally altered the equation, sweeping away the idealism that had helped inspire and validate Ortega's approach. Because it was deprived of that pillar of support, his pragmatism no longer had a ready outlet. Although he failed to anticipate the implications of the changed environment, Ortega's contribution to the university was nonetheless exceptional and lived on. There were many faculty members and administrators who distinguished themselves in establishing the University of New Mexico as a national leader in the Latin American and inter-American fields, but apart from James Zimmerman, none played a more vital role in solidifying that strength than Joaquín Ortega. What Zimmerman had said in 1929 at a memorial service eulogizing a longtime UNM staff member, Josephine Parsons, could also be applied to Ortega—that the university above all needed "more people who are willing to lose themselves in service to this institution."[6]

During the years that he spent in New Mexico, first as a visitor (1931–1941) and then as a full-time resident (1941–1954), a number of contentious issues that divided the Anglo and Hispanic populations and, at times, created divisions within the Hispanic community alone had risen to the fore: preservation of language and cultural heritage, historical patterns of prejudice and discrimination, the drive for "Americanization" versus a more pluralist-minded view that honored ethnic diversity, and the challenge to make Pan-Americanism a reality, not merely a slogan, in New Mexico. Not surprisingly, given its visibility, its importance as a state institution funded primarily by public monies, and its role in funneling young men and women into successful careers, the university became a site on which these issues played out, at times overtly, at times more quietly. Never one to shy away from controversial topics, Ortega injected himself into the thick of this discussion. Like George Sánchez, another prominent figure and spokesman for the Hispano Cause, Ortega struck a non-"accomodationist" line. He did not believe that Hispanos in New Mexico needed to assimilate fully to Anglo-American culture. Indeed, he was opposed to that idea. The ethnic identities of the two groups (and, of course, of Native Americans as well) were different. They might blend to a certain degree, but each group found expression according to its own lights. In a way, because of his great fondness for New Mexico and its people, Ortega, it seems only fitting, should have served as a kind of prism through which most of the issues affecting Hispano-Anglo relations at UNM in this period were refracted. Ortega's way of resolving them, outside of the call for simple justice and equality, was to take the tricultural formulation and transpose it into his "synthesis of the Americas"—New Mexico as the meeting ground on which Sánchez's "forgotten people" would defend and reclaim their heritage and through which the promise and goals of Pan-Americanism could eventually be realized. It was a hope and a possibility that he summed up, almost aphoristically, in a simple sentence: "New Mexico is the shortest route to Mexican goodwill, and to the goodwill of all Latin America."[7]

Although on the national level he was known primarily within academic, philanthropic, and government circles, Ortega did gain some recognition outside of them. One such instance came through the work of the journalist and public intellectual Carey McWilliams. In his book *North from Mexico*, published in 1948, McWilliams acknowledged Joaquín Ortega for the actions he had taken to improve Hispano-Anglo relations in the Southwest. Universities, McWilliams noted, were at the forefront of such efforts, and he cited Ortega as a prime leader in this sphere. The University of New Mexico was also credited by McWilliams for playing "a prominent part" in stressing the importance of utilizing the Native American and Spanish-speaking people of the Southwest as a bridge in forging more productive relationships with Indo- and Latin America.[8] In doing so, McWilliams was necessarily crediting Ortega by default.

Today, the name Joaquín Ortega is little recognized by those who pass through the halls of the building that bears his name. It stands as silent testimony to one of UNM's pioneering figures. Otherwise, the traces of his presence are largely gone. At the time of his resignation, Ortega had informed Tom Popejoy that he planned to devote the coming months to the organization and disposal of "my personal papers and books."[9] On the following day, he informed France Scholes that if certain conditions were met, he intended to leave his extensive personal library to the university, and if the university library agreed to house his books together, in a dedicated space, he would accompany them with a donation of paintings, art objects, etchings, and the like. Either the conditions were not met to his satisfaction, or something caused Ortega to change his mind, or perhaps after his death his family made other plans, because an *Albuquerque Tribune* article of November 26, 1958, reported that his library, consisting of more than two thousand titles, had been bequeathed to the College of St. Joseph on the Rio Grande.[10] This article also noted that the probate filing of Ortega's will reported that Lyle Saunders, who had moved on to the University of Colorado–Boulder, be designated to supervise the disposition of Ortega's personal papers and manuscripts.[11] Whether that ever happened, whether his personal papers still exist, and, if so, where they currently repose, are questions that still hang in the air.

In his own time, however, Joaquín Ortega was well remembered and duly honored. In 1957, two years after his death, a campus dining hall was converted for the use of the modern-and-classical-languages department and renamed Joaquín Ortega Hall. When the repurposed building was officially dedicated in mid-June 1958, three of his closest associates at UNM—France Scholes, Miguel Jorrín, and President Popejoy—spoke about Ortega, his attachment to New Mexico and its people, and the deep impact he had left on the university.[12] Thirteen years later, when the department took up residence in a new building facing Smith Plaza, the department chair, Robert Duncan, recommended (as the consensus wish of the department's faculty) transferring the name Joaquín Ortega Hall to this building. A year and half later, in December 1973, a ceremony was held to dedicate the new Ortega Hall, at which two members of the Spanish faculty, William Roberts and the aforementioned Duncan, spoke, along with UNM President Ferrel Heady. Roberts had studied under Ortega at the University of Wisconsin and focused his remarks on Ortega's career there, emphasizing his openness and broadmindedness ("there was in D. Joaquín no parochialism") and his fairness, urbanity, and dedication to excellence ("As chairman, D. Joaquín had very high standards and was absolutely honest; to these prime attributes he added style and tact"). These were the same qualities and characteristics, it will be recalled, that UW's dean of Arts and Sciences, George Sellery, had noted in his 1941 letter to James Zimmerman.[13] Duncan, Ortega's colleague at UNM, emphasized not just New Mexico's attraction for Ortega but the sense of service that the Spaniard brought with him from Wisconsin—the "Wisconsin idea . . . that the state university should devote itself to the needs of the entire State." His acceptance of the editorship of *The New Mexico Quarterly*, Duncan noted, allowed Ortega to concentrate his energies on what had become his greatest concern: "to bring New Mexico to a point where the people of Spanish heritage would play an increasingly important role in national and international affairs." Duncan went on to conclude, "I think if he could have forseen [sic] the increased participation of the New Mexican of Spanish descent in all phases of our life today his Hispanic pride would have glowed unusually bright, not only because of his interest in the people but also because he made a significant contribution to that end." The 1973 dedication ceremony represented the high-water mark in the remembrance and appreciation of Joaquín Ortega by the University of New Mexico. After this gesture, followed by the gradual departure of faculty and staff who had known and worked with him, the fading memory of Ortega began to set in. Still, the official recognition granted him by the university's Latin American and Iberian Institute, as having been its founder, provides some assurance that it will not disappear entirely.

If there is a final word on Joaquín Ortega, a statement that sums up his deepest character, it is perhaps best supplied by the man himself. For him, as he explained in his pamphlet *The Intangible Resources of New Mexico*, what mattered most in human experience was the intensity and quality of one's life, not its length: "The heroic philosophy [as opposed to the bourgeois] measures life in action, accomplishment, meaning, and the heroic man is always willing to die to live a few moments more intensely. Life is an amount of vitality that can be lived in instants or in years, or that can be not lived at all if we inhibit ourselves from its highest imperatives."[14]

Epilogue

It will be recalled from my introduction that in the late 1950s, not long after Joaquín Ortega's retirement from the University of New Mexico and his return to Spain, New Mexico senator Dennis Chávez and the civic figure Ezequiel Durán were caught up in an argument over Chávez's use of the terms *Mexican, Spanish American*, and *Anglo-American*. That argument (which Ortega, had he still been alive and living in New Mexico, would likely have followed with keen interest) had involved only two of the state's main population groups—Anglos and Hispanos. In 2016, however, all three groups became embroiled in a controversy over the official seal of the university (see fig. 17), and in this case it was the Native American community that played the lead role. Objections to the iconography on the seal were not new. They had first been raised in the early 1990s, but now they were more pointed and unsparing. Through the Kiva Club, a Native American student organization, and supported by Red Nation, an indigenous-rights advocacy group, Native American students began a campaign to replace the existing seal, arguing that it was essentially a racist symbol because it represented them as an inferior people while glorifying the systematic violence that had been committed against them, first under the Spanish conquest and colonization and subsequently through the Anglo invasion and recolonization. They also argued that the current seal, adopted in 1969, was emblematic of deeper-seated racism and exclusionary practice in the university.[1]

One would be hard-pressed not to accept the charge that, at the very least, the imagery on the seal reduced the indigenous heritage to a lower status. With their backs to one another, the seal depicts a white frontiersman holding a rifle and a Spanish conquistador (the Mexican component is noticeably absent) holding a sword close to his side; while above them, according to one critic, "the forlorn native is depicted, as a [diminutive] stylized parrot,"[2] or, according to a second critic, as "a Zia symbol of the roadrunner."[3] The Kiva Club–Red Nation alliance was explicit in its condemnation of this image: "The two men, agents of conquest, the conquistador and the frontiersman, stand as armed colonial gatekeepers . . . [;] while violence and conquest are thought of as things of the

FIGURE 17 The university seal. Vertical Files (UNMA 006, drawer 6, folder title: University Seal, folder 1), Center for Southwest Research, University Libraries, University of New Mexico. Photo by Marla Brose. © Albuquerque Journal. Reprinted with permission.

past, they inform present inequalities at UNM and do not deserve celebration."[4] The president of the university's Board of Regents, Rob Doughty, appeared to be supportive of the Native American position, writing, "A seal should be a core reflection of the university's identity, and . . . an accurate reflection of who we are now . . . [;] this seal seems to fail that test.[5] Opinion, however, both on the board and elsewhere, was not uniform. Another regent "claimed that he was not aware of the feelings of discrimination against Native Americans or issues regarding the seal, despite previous in-depth research and other information being presented to him at other meetings,"[6] a claim that the vice president of the Kiva Club likened to "a classic predicament of the oppressed having to explain to their oppressor [that] what they're doing is wrong."[7]

The reaction of the Hispanic community to criticism of the seal was divided. Some saw a valid cry for justice on the part of Native Americans and an opportunity to address the history of violence between the two communities.[8] Others saw it as tipping the historical scales too far in the opposite direction, maintaining that a redesigned seal might be acceptable but removing the conquistador from it was not. To more traditionalist-minded Hispanos, that would be equivalent to denying the role that the Spanish played in colonizing New Mexico. Following numerous forums and meetings dedicated to resolving the issue, the current seal was retained. Despite a recommendation for equity and inclusion, by the university's vice president, whose office had overseen the process of holding meetings and soliciting opinion, that new imagery on the seal was needed, the Board of Regents took only two minor actions: forming a committee to study how a redesign might be executed and commissioning a cost analysis of the same. In effect, the board put off the matter for another day, causing the vice president of the Kiva Club, Jennifer Marley, to declare, "it is time to challenge the tri-cultural myth."⁹ Two years later, in 2018, Marley's challenge bore fruit, when the university announced that a task force would be assembled to propose a new seal and that the old seal had been officially "suspended."¹⁰

The second running controversy has a somewhat longer history and entails a similar critique of the tricultural formulation. The controversy involves a four-panel mural attached to one of the walls of the historic West Wing of the university's central library. In 1938, President Zimmerman commissioned Kenneth Adams, a member of the Taos Society of Artists, to paint a mural depicting the Native American, Hispanic, and Anglo cultures in New Mexico and their respective contributions to the region. The visual language of Adams's mural, dubbed the *Three Peoples*, reflected the cultural and ethnoracial stereotypes embedded in the general early twentieth-century Anglo perception of Southwestern history and society. Native Americans and Hispanos are represented as close to the land and nature, the former portrayed "as primitive peoples engaging in pre-industrial forms of work and art"¹¹ (see plate 5). Hispanos are shown as agriculturalists, ploughing the fields by hand as their ancestors had, or as artisans plastering and finishing adobe walls (see plate 6). Anglos, on the other hand, are associated with the advances of the industrial age, depicted as the agents of modern medicine and science (see plate 7). As subsequent interpretation emphasized, Adams's fourth panel broadcast a contradictory message. It evoked a spirit of tricultural brotherhood while also enshrining past (and existing) racial hierarchy. At the center of the panel is a blond, blue-eyed Anglo male, his open gaze directed straight ahead, as if looking into the future. Standing sideways to his left and right, shrouded in a semidarkness and faced toward him but eyeless, are his Hispanic and Native American counterparts. The Anglo male has grasped their hands and, from his central, forward-looking position, appears to be leading them into the light (see plate 8).

Protests against the stereotyped imagery of the mural and how it seemed to consign Native American and Hispanic peoples to more passive roles dependent on Anglo dynamism and technology, started to be heard in the 1970s, given voice by the militant actions of recently formed Chicano/a, Native American, and African American student movements.¹² On two occasions (1970, 1974) in that decade, the fourth panel was defaced with paint, requiring extensive restoration work.¹³ Objections to the mural continued to be raised during the 1980s. In the mid-1990s, however, they again flared into organized protest when several student organizations formed a "Mural Coalition," with the goal of either pressuring the university to remove Adams's artwork or, short of this, mounting "some sort of marker recognizing its racist content."[14] The university at this juncture acknowledged the validity of the students' concerns and accepted the need for some change, with its Board of Regents offering two solutions: first, that a plaque be installed next to the four panels to place and explain their symbolism and content in "the context of their time and ours," and, second, that further consideration be given to commissioning a new mural to reflect current understanding and interpretation of the three-cultures motif. Although the regents, in March 1995, unanimously approved installation of the plaque and other actions proposed by the Mural Coalition,[15] their decisions evidently got lost in the bureaucratic maze and were not carried out, so in the end nothing was done. The failure to take action was bound to cause a new round of protest, and eventually, in 2016, it did. On this occasion it was a group of staff and faculty who work in the library that condemned the mural, their objections resting on the same arguments as previous protests: "By perpetuating stereotypes and not accurately depicting the true diversity of New Mexico's peoples and cultures," the group asserted, "the mural stands both as a distortion of history and a dubious projection of the University of New Mexico's character and mission."[16] Amid the latest controversy, and against the background of other institutions similarly grappling with contentious issues about public art,[17] the university acted more forcefully. It formed a planning group (representing a wide spectrum of interests and viewpoints) that had two principle objectives: (1) to develop a proposal "to transform the West Wing mural space" in a way that both acknowledged UNM's "problematic racial and colonial history," and also served the requirements of historic preservation (the building is on the National Register of Historic Places, and Adams's artwork features prominently in that designation); and (2) to help organize an interdisciplinary course, to be taught in the spring 2018 semester, that would examine and study the Adams mural and its charged history from multiple perspectives and offer recommendations to the university on how the controversy might be resolved.[18] Although both objectives were realized, the issue remains unsettled. The solutions offered ranged from removing the four panels and locating them elsewhere, to keeping them in place but covering them, to simply leaving them as they are. In virtually all cases, however, the recommendation was to contextualize Adams's mural with new artwork and interpretive text. Members of the Board of Regents Historic Preservation Committee would take all commentary into account and make their recommendation, and the full

Board would ultimately reach a decision (which would also be reviewed by the state's Historic Preservation Division). The university's central administration deliberated the matter for nearly a year before announcing, in September 2019, that two proposed solutions were under review, both of which entail covering the *Three Peoples* mural, but in a way that also allows them to be viewed on particular occasions or upon appropriate request.[19]

Appendix

El Panamericanismo Comienza En Casa

Aún los descendientes de los españoles de tiempo de la colonia, que han convivido aquí por tres siglos o más; son "gente que nunca ha sido tomado en cuenta." La palabra "Mexicano," se ha vuelto un término de oprobio que se aplica indistintamente a los ciudadanos ó extranjeros y está asociado con la discriminatoria práctica en la tarifa de sueldos y procedimientos de trabajo, en la educación, en el ejercicio de derechos civiles y demás. En efecto, estas personas han vivido y todavía viven en un verdadero campo de concentración. Aún los fondos federales, destinados al bienestar público, han sido algunas veces usados para aumentar su aislamiento y ostracismo, para acentuar desigualdades y su posición sin privilegios.

México y las otras repúblicas Latino-Americanas ven el suroeste y en Puerto Rico la prueba de nuestras sugestiones para un orden hemisférico.

. . . La situación que enfrentan muchos de los habitantes urbanos de este grupo de la población, es análoga a aquella del agricultor. Las escuelas segregadas, el ostracismo social, la diferencia económica y prácticas cívicas, han sido la suerte de miles de ambos, urbanos y agricultores "Mexicanos." Afecta tanto a ciudadanos Americanos como extranjeros.

Pan-Americanism Begins at Home

Even the descendants of Spaniards dating from colonial times, who have lived here together for three centuries or more, are "people who have never been taken into account." The word *Mexican* has become a term of opprobrium that is applied indiscriminately to citizens or to those from outside the country and is associated with discriminatory practices in setting wages and work procedures, in education, and in the exercise of civil rights and more. In effect, these people have lived and still live in a veritable concentration camp. Even federal monies meant for the public good have sometimes been used to further their isolation and ostracism, [and] to worsen inequalities and their underprivileged position.

Mexico and the other Latin American republics see the Southwest and Puerto Rico as the test of our overtures on behalf of hemispheric solidarity.

... The situation faced by many of the urban dwellers within this population group is analogous to that of the farmer. The fate for thousands of "Mexicans," urban and rural alike, has been segregated schools, social ostracism, [and] different treatment in economic life and civic affairs. The effect is felt both by those foreign to the country and by those who are American citizens.

These extracts come from "El Panamericanismo comienza en casa," a Spanish-language version of George Sánchez's article "Good Neighbors—at Home." The full piece may have been delivered as an address by Sánchez in Mexico and appeared, as a press release, from Worldover Press, ca. 1940, issued in Cuernavaca, Mexico. See GISP, Series II, Correspondence and Subject Files, box 71, folder 16.

Abbreviations

CCCC   Coronado Cuarto Centennial Commission, Center for Southwest Research/Special Collections, University Libraries, University of New Mexico.

CSWR   Center for Southwest Research/Special Collections, University Libraries, University of New Mexico.

GHP   George P. Hammond Papers, 1896–1993, The Bancroft Library, University of California–Berkeley.

GISP   George I. Sánchez Papers, 1892–1972, Benson Latin American Collection, University of Texas at Austin.

JFZP   James Fulton Zimmerman Papers, 1920–1960, Center for Southwest Research and Special Collections, University Libraries, University of New Mexico.

MWHUNM   "The History of the University of New Mexico," unpublished manuscript, Michael Welsh Manuscript Collection, 1987–1988, UNMA 169, Center for Southwest Research and Special Collections, University Libraries, University of New Mexico.

UNMA   University of New Mexico University Archives and Administrative Records, Center for Southwest Research and Special Collections, University Libraries, University of New Mexico.

UNMBRR   University of New Mexico Board of Regents Records, Center for Southwest Research and Special Collections, University Libraries, University of New Mexico.

UNMFSR   University of New Mexico Faculty Senate Records, Center for Southwest Research and Special Collections, University Libraries, University of New Mexico.

UNMR   University of New Mexico Records, 1889–1927, Center for Southwest Research and Special Collections, University Libraries, University of New Mexico.

UWUA   University of Wisconsin Archives and Records Management, Steenbock Library, University of Wisconsin–Madison.

Notes

Introduction

1. Burma, *Spanish-Speaking Groups*, 4.
2. Barker, *Caballeros*, 307.
3. Exemplifying this intensified focus are the studies by Montgomery, *Spanish Redemption*; Nieto-Phillips, *Language of Blood*; Mitchell, *Coyote Nation*; Mora, *Border Dilemmas*; Noel, *Debating American Identity*; and Phillip B. Gonzales's introduction to the anthology he edited, *Expressing New Mexico*. For a concise synthesis of the major schools of thought underlying opposed interpretations of the "true" ethnic heritage of New Mexico, see Phillip B. Gonzales, "Whither the Nuevomexicanos," 273–86.
4. Phillip B. Gonzales, *Forced Sacrifice as Ethnic Protest*.
5. Nancie Gonzalez, *Spanish-Americans*, xi.
6. As quoted in McWilliams, *North from Mexico*, 63.
7. Fergusson, *Our Southwest*, 3.
8. Gonzales-Berry and Maciel, *Contested Homeland*.
9. The term is borrowed from Nieto-Phillips, *Language of Blood*, 171–72.
10. For a detailed exposition of the assimilationist position and specific examples of it, see Noel, *Debating American Identity*, 32–39, 111–14.
11. Noel, *Debating American Identity*, 43.
12. Gonzales-Berry and Maciel, *Contested Homeland*, 17.
13. See United States Department of Commerce, Bureau of the Census, *Sixteenth Census of the United States: 1940 Population. Characteristics of the Nonwhite Population by Race*, p. 5. accessible at https://babel.hathitrust.org/cgi/pt?id=mdp.39015081224480&view=1up&seq=5. The rights and experiences of New Mexico's black and mulatto populations are addressed at length in Laura E. Gómez's *Manifest Destinies: The Making of the Mexican American Race* (New York: New York University Press, 2007; 2nd. ed. 2018).
14. For an incisive analysis of the tricultural image, its psychological, cultural, and political underpinnings, and why the mestizo, or Mexican, was absent from it, see Fairbrother, "Mexicans in New Mexico."
15. McWilliams, *North from Mexico*, 297.
16. Otis, *Fire in the Night*. The quotes that follow are from pp. 18–19 and 133,

respectively. During the last ten years of his life (1928–1938), Otis lived in Santa Fe and was on close terms with other members of the city's arts and literary colonies. He was a keen observer of local society, up and down the social scale, and of how relations between and among the main population groups played out.

17. Interestingly, however, the Spanish-speaking portion of the population, whose residence or origins in New Mexico dated to colonial times, did not self-identify as Mexicans during the twenty-five-year period of Mexican rule. Thus a strong "Mexicano" identity did not take hold. See Nieto-Phillips, *Language of Blood*, 38.

18. This parallelism is described in a manuscript by Mills, "Origins of Latin American Programs," 52–53, 70–71.

19. It is difficult to overstate the importance of George I. Sánchez's research and writings either to any full understanding of the conditions of Hispanic life in New Mexico during his time or to the development of Mexican American scholarship generally during this same period. In the estimation of Carlos Kevin Blanton, "George I. Sánchez . . . is the single most important Mexican American intellectual between the Great Depression and the Great Society." Blanton, *George I. Sánchez*, x. Yet, because of personal jealousies and party-political animosities, Sánchez's achievements and work in New Mexico went largely unacknowledged, even into recent times. (See Russell Contreras, "Celebrated Scholar Remains Unrecognized in Home State," *Santa Fe New Mexican*, February 11, 2012. Fortunately, Blanton's book has gone a long way toward correcting this oversight.

20. A. C. De Cola, "Use of the Word 'Mexican' Is Criticized by Professor," *Albuquerque Tribune*, November 1958(?). A Xerox copy of the article can be found in Faculty Files Collection (UNMA 152, box 23, folder: Frank Reeve), CSWR.

21. A. C. De Cola, "Use of 'Mexican' Word Is Backed," *Albuquerque Tribune*, n.d. (UNMA 152, box 23, folder: Frank Reeve), CSWR.

22. ES [Ernest Sanchez?], "A Matter of Semantics and Animosity," *New Mexico Lobo*, November 20, 1958.

Chapter One

1. Gerdes, "Department of Modern & Classical Languages," 257.

2. Welsh, "Often Out of Sight," 107–14.

3. For additional details, see Noel, *Debating American Identity*, 59–60.

4. Ian Frazier, "The Magic of the Old Southwest," *New York Review of Books* 63, no. 16 (October 2016): 58.

5. Karl Schwerin, "History of the Department of Anthropology," chap. on "Biographical Sketches" (unpublished manuscript), in University of New Mexico College of Arts and Sciences, Centennial Histories Collection (UNMA 139, box 1), CSWR.

6. In discussing the actions of UNM's presidents, from William Tight through David Spence Hill, I have occasionally drawn on the information provided by Michael Welsh in his article "Often Out of Sight," 113–30.

7. From an article titled "Wm. Tight: An Appreciation," by Frank W. Shepardson. Repr. from *Granville Times* [Granville, OH], 3 February 1910, contained in UNMR (UNMA 001, box 3, folder 37: Tight, William: Correspondence, 1901–1909), CSWR.

8. "Pueblo Architecture Adopted to Modern Needs in New Mexico," *The Craftsman* 19, no. 4 (January 1, 1911): 404.

9. "Pueblo Architecture Adopted," 406.

10. Hodgin, "Dr. Tight," 73.

11. As reported in the 15 April 1908, issue of the newsletter of the university, UNMR (UNMA 001, box 1, folder: 16A), CSWR.

12. Two such articles were "A Revival of Old Pueblo Architecture," *Architects and Builders Magazine* 41, no. 7 (April 1909), and E. Dana Johnson, "A University Pueblo," *World's Work* 14 (October 1907).

13. Dabney, "History of the Department of History," 191.

14. Aurelio Espinosa to J. H. Wroth, Albuquerque, 22 March 1910, UNMR (UNMA 001, box 5, folder 20: Modern and Classical Languages—Faculty, 1910–1911), CSWR.

15. For Espinosa's reactions to the position taken by the Board of Regents, see his memo to J. H. Wroth, Albuquerque, 12 April 1910, UNMR (UNMA 001, box 5, folder 20: Modern and Classical Languages—Faculty, 1910–1911), CSWR.

16. *University of New Mexico Newsletter*, 20 March 1908, UNMR (UNMA 001, box 1, folder 16A: General Correspondence, 1906–1913), CSWR.

17. *University of New Mexico Newsletter*, 20 March 1908, UNMR.

18. These statements about Gray's feelings for New Mexico are based on the recollections of E. Dana Johnson in his "Dr. Gray," 117.

19. "Pueblo Architecture Adopted," 405.

20. Edward McQ. Gray to James L. Rodgers, Albuquerque, 15 August 1911, UNMR (UNMA 001, box 5, folder 1: President Edward Gray, Correspondence and Reports, 8/9/1911–8/17/1911), CSWR.

21. Gray, "Spanish Language."

22. Gray, "Spanish Language," 49.

23. Gray probably had these conversations in early February 1911, when New Mexico's territorial governor, William J. Mills, urged Gray to go to Washington,

DC, when the Pan-American Conference was in session and Gray, Mills believed, had the "possibility of accomplishing something of the sort which [he] desires." See Frank Clancy [head of the Board of Regents] to J. H. Wroth, Albuquerque, 4 February 1911. UNMR (UNMA 001, box 1, folder 1: Clancy, Frank—Correspondence, 1894–1911), CSWR.

24. Gray, "Spanish Language," 51–52.
25. Gray, "Spanish Language," 52.
26. MWHUNM, chap. 5, p. 12.
27. MWHUNM, chap. 5, p. 12.
28. David Ross Boyd to M. C. Allaben, Albuquerque, 1 October 1912, UNMR (UNMA 001, box 5, folder 27: David Boyd, President, Correspondence, September–October 1912), CSWR.
29. Boyd to Allaben, Albuquerque, 5 March 1914, UNMR (UNMA 001, box 5, folder 35: Correspondence, March–December 1914), CSWR.
30. David Ross Boyd to Katherine N. Birdsall, Albuquerque, 13 September 1912, UNMR (UNMA 001, box 5, folder 27: David Boyd, President, Correspondence, September–October 1912), CSWR.
31. David Ross Boyd to J. O. Notestein, Albuquerque, 19 May 1915, UNMR (UNMA 001, box 6, folder 1: David Ross Boyd, Correspondence, January–September 1915), CSWR.
32. Boyd to Notestein, 19 May 1915, UNMR. Espinosa's piece was published in the "Forum Section" of an unidentified newspaper; the clipping is dated 11 May 1915.
33. David Ross Boyd to Ralph Campbell, Albuquerque, 12 July 1913, UNMR (UNMA 001, box 5, folder 30: David Ross Boyd, Correspondence, 2 June–14 July 1913), CSWR.
34. MWHUNM, chap. 5.
35. On this matter, see the correspondence between Boyd and Clara True, an influential business woman in the Española Valley and a nominee, in 1913, for assistant commissioner of Indian Affairs, in UNMR (UNMA 001, box 5, folder 32: David Ross Boyd, Correspondence, September–November 1913), CSWR.
36. David Ross Boyd to Ralph Twitchell, Albuquerque, 25 July 1913, UNMR (UNMA 001, box 5, folder 31: David Ross Boyd, President, Correspondence, 16 July–30 August 1913), CSWR.
37. See a comparison of course offerings in Dabney, "History of the Department of History," 195.
38. Roscoe Hill to David Spence Hill, El Rito, NM, 23 July 1919, Faculty Files Collection (UNMA 152, box 13, folder: Roscoe Hill), CSWR.
39. Dabney, "History of the Department of History," 21–22.
40. MWHUNM, chap. 5, p. 52.

41. Reeve, "History of the University of New Mexico," 132.
42. MWHUNM, chap. 6, p. 18.
43. MWHUNM, chap. 6, p. 18.
44. MWHUNM, chap. 6, p. 61.
45. The thought was expressed in an undated letter to Roscoe Hill, as quoted in MWHUNM, chap. 6, p. 61.
46. MWHUNM, chap. 6, pp. 56, 60.
47. Charles Coan to David Spence Hill, Berkeley, CA, 2 August 1920, UNMR (UNMA 001, box 7, folder 38: Coan, Charles F., 1920–1928), CSWR.
48. For the correspondence between Hill and Osuna Carr, see UNMR (UNMA 001, box 8, folder 33: Osuna, Anita, 1921–1933), CSWR.
49. All of the course-related data cited in this paragraph will be found in UNMR (UNMA 001, box 10, folder 40: Committees, Schedules & Curriculum, 1920–1927), CSWR.
50. David Spence Hill in memo to Lansing Bloom and John Clark, 20 February 1920, "School Of American Research, 1920–26," UNMR (UNMA 001, box 13, folder 27: New Mexico—School of American Research, 1920–1926), CSWR.
51. Again, Native Americans were categorically overlooked. Enrollment was not broken down by race or ethnicity, making it very difficult to know whether Native Americans were represented in the student body. If they were, however, their numbers would have been negligible.
52. *Annual Report of the University of New Mexico*, in UNMR (UNMA 001, box 13, folder 22: New Mexico—Governor Larrazolo, 1919–1920), CSWR.
53. *Annual Report of the University of New Mexico*, in UNMR (UNMA 001, box 14, folders 25 and 26: "Senior Classes, 1921, 1922, and 1923" and "Senior Classes, 1924, 1925, 1926, and 1927"), CSWR.
54. David Spence Hill to Henry S. Pritchett, Albuquerque, 10 November 1922, UNMR (UNMA 001, box 10, folder 19: Carnegie Corporation—Proposed School of Spanish Literature, 1922).
55. A. A. Sedillo to David Spence Hill, Albuquerque, 10 November 1922, UNMR (UNMA 001, box 10, folder 19: Carnegie Corporation—Proposed School of Spanish Literature), 1922.

Chapter Two

1. Ortega, "James Fulton Zimmerman," n.p.
2. "Inauguration of James Fulton Zimmerman," *University of New Mexico Bulletin*, 21–22.
3. This targeted expansion can be traced and quantified in the university's catalogs and biennial reports.

4. Faculty Files Collection (UNMA 152, box 24, folder: Lloyd Tireman), CSWR.

5. For more on the school, see chap. 2, sec. titled "Confronting Ethnic Tensions and Divisions Within the University."

6. Campa's claim to this effect is quoted in Weigle and White, *Lore of New Mexico*, 498n23.

7. Faculty Files Collection (UNMA 152, box 4, folder: Donald Brand), CSWR.

8. That is, as part of expanding and deepening the Southwest–Latin America focus, Zimmerman wanted to increase the Hispanic presence on campus and integrate Hispanic students into the full life of the university, leading to "a consensual ethnic arrangement." But this drive produced what Phillip Gonzales calls the "paradox of integrationist protest," whereby the more Hispanos called for inclusion into UNM, the more their efforts served "to crystallize social boundaries between themselves and the Anglo student body." Phillip B. Gonzales, *Forced Sacrifice*, 75–76.

9. MWHUNM, chap. 7, p. 30.

10. For more on the negotiations between Zimmerman, Hewett, and Paul Walter, see the letters they exchanged between 12 May 1927 and 31 July 1928, Faculty Files Collection (UNMA 152, box 12, folder: Edgar L. Hewett), CSWR.

11. The university gradually divested itself of these properties until it was reduced to holding only Chaco Canyon, which it relinquished to the National Park Service in 1941. See Karl Schwerin, "History of the Department of Anthropology," chap. on "The Hewett Regency, 1928–1935," 6 (unpublished manuscript), in University of New Mexico College of Arts and Sciences, Centennial Histories Collection (UNMA 139, box 1), CSWR.

12. See, e.g., *University of New Mexico Bulletin, Biennial Report of the University of New Mexico 1931 to 1933*, Catalog Series 46, no. 1 (January 1, 1933): 18, where Zimmerman describes some particular university initiatives as illustrative of UNM's "central purpose to become an institution not slavishly following the programs of similar institutions in other states, but seeking to build around a program so definitely New Mexican."

13. Karl Schwerin, "History of the Department of Anthropology," chap. on "The Hewett Regency, 1928–1935," 5 (unpublished manuscript), in University of New Mexico College of Arts and Sciences, Centennial Histories Collection (UNMA 139, box 1), CSWR.

14. Kluckhohn, "Field of Higher Education," 28.

15. See, e.g., France Scholes to George Hammond, Cambridge, MA, 5 February 1936; (BANC MSS 70/89 c, series 2, correspondence carton 16, folder 18: France Scholes) GHP.

16. MWHUNM, chap. 7, 39–40.

17. Clyde Kluckhohn to James Zimmerman, Cambridge, MA, 23 May 1935, Faculty

Files Collection (UNMA 152, box 16, folder: Clyde Kluckhohn), CSWR.

18. James Zimmerman to Clyde Kluckhohn, Albuquerque, 14 June 1935, Faculty Files Collection (UNMA 152, box 16, folder: Clyde Kluckhohn), CSWR.

19. Herbert Bolton to George Hammond, Berkeley, CA, 3 December 1935 (BANC MSS 70/89 c, series 2, correspondence, carton 9, folder 32: Herbert Eugene Bolton, 1930–1935), GHP.

20. George Hammond to James Zimmerman, Los Angeles, 6 June 1935, Faculty Files Collection (UNMA 152, box 12, folder: George P. Hammond), CSWR.

21. James Zimmerman to George Hammond, Los Angeles, letters of 2 July and 23 August 1935; and Carlos Castañeda to James Zimmerman, Austin, TX, 6 August 1935, Faculty Files Collection (UNMA 152, box 12, folder: George P. Hammond), CSWR.

22. George Hammond to Herbert Bolton, Los Angeles, 28 June 1935 (BANC MSS 70/89 c, series 2, correspondence, carton 9, folder 32: Herbert Eugene Bolton, 1930–1935), GHP.

23. George Hammond to James Zimmerman, Los Angeles, 18 July 1935, Faculty Files Collection (UNMA 152, box 12, folder: George P. Hammond), CSWR.

24. Early evidence of this intent will be found in the university bulletin for 1936–1937, where, under the section titled "Additional Schools or Colleges to Be Considered in the Future," it is stated that "recently there has been some discussion of a School of Public Service with special relation to Latin America." *University of New Mexico Bulletin: Biennial Report of the University of New Mexico 1935–1937*, Catalog Series 50, no. 1 (January 1, 1937): 8.

25. UNMFSR (UNMA 010, box 13, folder: Courses of Study, 1937–1940), CSWR. Overall, in 1939, a total of thirty-seven Latin American or Latin American–related content courses (exclusive of language courses) were being taught in ten academic departments.

26. George Hammond to Henry Wagner, Albuquerque, 20 January 1937 (BANC MSS 70/89 c, series 2, correspondence, carton 18, folder 1: Henry Raup Wagner), GHP.

27. JFZP (UNMA 008, box 3, folder: Department of History–Political Science, 1928–34), CSWR.

28. James Zimmerman, 28 February 1934, to Members of the Graduate Committee, UNMFSR (UNMA 010, box 18, folder: Graduate Committee, 1932–1940), CSWR.

29. Zimmerman to Graduate Committee, 28 February, 1934, UNMFSR.

30. For the full report, see "For the Committee on Expansion of Upper Division Courses," January 1937, UNMFSR (UNMA 010, box 17, folder: Expansion on Upper Division Committee, 1936–37), CSWR.

31. "For the Committee on Expansion," January 1937, UNMFSR.

32. George Hammond to Herbert Bolton, Albuquerque, 10 May 1937 (BANC MSS

70/89 c, Series 2, Correspondence, carton 9.31, folder: Herbert Bolton), GHP.

33. MWHUNM, chap. 7, p. 23.

34. MWHUNM, chap. 8, p. 9.

35. Phillip B. Gonzales, *Forced Sacrifice*, 117.

36. Zimmerman, "Social and Cultural Elements," 65–71.

37. Zimmerman, "Social and Cultural Elements," 69.

38. Zimmerman, "Social and Cultural Elements," 69

39. Phillip B. Gonzales, *Forced Sacrifice*, 75.

40. Sánchez, "Good Neighbors—at Home," 4. Interestingly, the version of this article that Sánchez wrote in Mexico (to which he gave the title "Pan-Americanism Begins at Home") for a Mexican readership, struck a much more critical, even embittered tone. See the appendix in this book for extracts from it, with an accompanying translation into English. In a 1964 presentation, some twenty-five years after he wrote this piece, Sánchez had much the same to say about the Peace Corps and the federal government's renewed interest in Latin America. Our neighbors to the south, he reflected, were neither blind nor naïve; they easily grasped the abysmal failure of the US government to deal constructively with its Spanish-speaking population (then still concentrated in the Southwest and California). See George I. Sánchez, "Past and Present Inter-American Relations—A Personal Memoir," *Proceedings*, Fourth Western Regional Conference on Comparative Education, Inter-American Relations (Los Angeles, October 8–10, 1964).

41. Lowitt, *Bronson Cutting*, 195.

42. Lowitt, *Bronson Cutting*, 195.

43. Lowitt, *Bronson Cutting*, 195.

44. MWHUNM, chap. 7, p. 31.

45. For the full program of the 1932 conference, see JFZP (UNMA, box 3, folder: Department of Modern Languages, 1927–38), CSWR.

46. Hoffman and Galaz, "Bi-Lingualism at Work," 225.

47. Hoffman and Galaz, "Bi-Lingualism at Work," 225.

48. Zeleny, "Relations," 291–92.

49. Zeleny, "Relations," 291–92. Zeleny based these claims both on her personal observations and on the information she was given during interviews. The fraternities denied that such rules existed.

50. Zeleny, "Relations," 317.

51. The phenomenon of the *junta de indignación* is well described by Phillip B. Gonzales in his article "La Junta de Indignación."

52. George Sánchez to Frank Angel, Austin, TX, 19 September 1970, GISP, Series II, Correspondence and Subject Files, box 5, folder: Frank Angel.

53. One such incident took place in 1929, when a group of Anglo students decided to publish a literary magazine about the Southwest. They chose to name this publication *The Morada*, after the small chapels in northern New Mexico constructed by the lay Roman Catholic confraternities known as the Penitentes. When word of the publication spread, acrimonious debate broke out on the campus over the symbolism of its title and the intent of its student publishers. Some interpreted the use of the term *Morada* as slighting Hispanic people, as linking them—intentionally or not—to the stereotype of a dark, primitive Catholic past. Faced with this opposition (which he frankly thought misplaced), Zimmerman ruled that the publication needed a different name. MWHUNM, chap. 7, pp. 85–86.

54. For a full history and analysis of all aspects of this episode, see Phillip B. Gonzales's *Forced Sacrifice*. The proceedings of the investigation of the racial-attitude survey are in JFZP (UNMA 008, box 4, folder: Department of Psychology—Race Questionnaire, 1933, and correspondence and other documents relating to it are in JFZP (UNMA 008, box 3, folder: Department of Psychology), CSWR.

55. MWHUNM, chap. 8, p. 30.

56. MWHUNM, chap. 8, p. 30.

57. MWHUNM, chap. 8, p. 33.

58. Mary Austin to James Zimmerman, Santa Fe, NM, 2 May 1933, Mary Hunter Austin Papers (MSS 31 BC, box 3, folder 8: Correspondence Between Dr. Zimmerman and Mary Austin, April–July 1933), CSWR.

59. H. R. Wagner to George Hammond, San Marino, CA, 16 December 1935 (BANC MSS 70/89 c, series 2, correspondence, carton 18, folder 1: Henry Raup Wagner), GHP.

60. George Hammond to Henry R. Wagner, Albuquerque, 20 December 1935 (BANC MSS 70/89 c, series 2, correspondence, carton 18, folder 1: Henry Raup Wagner), GHP. The ten years that Hammond spent at UNM appear to have left him unshaken in this opinion. Writing to France Scholes in 1976, he stated, "As for segregation in New Mexico that ended about the time Juan de Oñate brought his men to the Rio Grande Valley and began to beget (wow, what alliteration) if it did not start with Coronado's Army!" George Hammond to France Scholes, Berkeley, 23 December 1976 (BANC MSS 70/89 c, series 2, ca correspondence, carton 16, folder 2: France Scholes,), GHP.

61. While Nancie Gonzalez states, "as late as 1940, over half the population . . . was of Spanish descent" (*Spanish-Americans*, xi), it is extremely difficult if not impossible to know with any exactitude the percentage of Hispanos within New Mexico's total population in the 1930s and 1940s, because the US Census

Bureau did not specifically ask about or track Hispanic origin until 1970.

62. Montgomery, *Spanish Redemption*, 11.

63. Zeleny, "Relations," 187.

64. In this connection, Zeleny also reasons that the practice generally followed by Anglos and Hispanos of keeping within their own social group was another strategy for minimizing conflict and ethnic tension: "Separatism in social relations minimized contact and conflict between the ethnic societies. Prejudice on the part of the Anglo aims to maintain their position of social and economic advantage, but the strength of the Spanish-American group enforces a strict taboo on overt display or discussion of the existence of prejudice. These mechanisms have established a modus vivendi between the groups under which hostilities are for the most part successfully controlled." Zeleny, "Relations," 329.

65. Zeleny, "Relations," 317–19.

66. Phillip B. Gonzales, *Forced Sacrifice*, 142–44.

67. Gilberto Espinosa to James Zimmerman, Albuquerque, 27 April 1933, JFZP (UNMA 008, box 5, folder: New Mexico–Department of Psychology, Racial Questionnaire, 1933), CSWR.

68. The history is in the form of an untitled, thirteen-page typescript: CCCC (UNMA 007, box 1, folder: CCC-Coronado Celebration History, 1931–1935), CSWR.

69. MWHUNM, chap. 6, pp. 21–22.

70. From "Speech of Senator Dennis Chávez, . . . the Senate Floor," 10 August 1937, mimeograph, CCCC (UNMA 007, box 2, folder: Dennis Chávez Correspondence, 1937–38), CSWR.

71. R. H. Faxon to James Zimmerman, Raton, NM, 29 November 1938, CCCC (UNMA 007, box 2, folder: James F. Zimmerman Correspondence, 1936–40), CSWR.

72. James Zimmerman to R. H. Faxon, Albuquerque, 5 December 1938, CCCC (UNMA 007, box 2, folder: James F. Zimmerman Correspondence, 1936–40), CSWR.

73. James Zimmerman to Dennis Chávez, Albuquerque, 30 November 1937, CCCC (UNMA 007, box 1, folder: Chávez, Dennis—US Senator—Correspondence 1936–1940), CSWR.

74. James Zimmerman to Clinton P. Anderson, 18 August 1939, New York, CCCC (UNMA 007, box 2, James F. Zimmerman Correspondence, 1936–1940), CSWR.

75. Zimmerman to Anderson, 18 August 1939, CCCC.

76. Zimmerman to Anderson, 18 August 1939, CCCC (UNMA 007, box 4, folder: Conferences—Education and Inter-American Cultural Relations, 1939), CSWR.

77. Phillip B. Gonzales, *Forced Sacrifice*, 219.

78. "Here [referring to a new book she proposed to write about New Mexico] is

the rich, deep, and varied background of country, races, and cultures, but here at last it is presented not as static, laboratory material, museum exhibits, but as part of a living, changing community: modern, American in many senses, but forever modified and colored by that background which has made people call New Mexico 'the most interesting state in the Union.'" Erna Fergusson to Herbert Weinstock, Albuquerque, 11 March 1949, Erna Fergusson Papers (MSS 45 BC, box 5, folder 21: Correspondence with Knopf re: New Mexico and miscellaneous, 1936, 1946–50), CSWR.

79. MWHUNM, chap. 6, p. 106.
80. "Possibilities of offering the PhD degree in Spanish, or Hispanic Studies," Francis Kercheville to James Zimmerman, 1 March 1936, JFZP (UNMA 008, box 3, folder: Department of Modern Languages, 1927–1938), CSWR.
81. Sánchez, *Forgotten People*, 13–14.
82. Sánchez, *Forgotten People*, 28.
83. Reid, *It Happened in Taos*, 12.
84. For this and following statistics and facts, see the project prospectus, "The Taos County Adult Education Project of the University of New Mexico, Albuquerque, 1 April 1936," JFZP (UNMA 008, box 5, folder: Harwood Foundation, Adult Education Program, 1936/37–40), CSWR; and Reid, *It Happened in Taos*, 10–11.
85. The Works Progress Administration, established through executive order by President Roosevelt in 1935, was the largest of the New Deal agencies, at its height employing millions of people (primarily unemployed and unskilled men) on a wide range of public works projects. It lasted until 1943.
86. Along with J. T. Reid, director of the university's Extension Division, Arthur Campa had played a key role in working with the Harwood Foundation Board during fall 1935 to draw up a preliminary plan for the project. See Mrs. O. E. Berninghaus to J. F. Zimmerman, Taos, NM, 15 December 1935, "The Taos County Adult Education Project of the University of New Mexico, Albuquerque, 1 April 1936," JFZP (UNMA 008, box 5, folder: Harwood Foundation, Adult Education Program, 1936/37–40), CSWR.
87. Berninghaus to Zimmerman, 15 December 1935, JFZP.
88. The view that resources allocated to higher education worked to the detriment of the public schools went back decades and was in fact widespread and hardly confined to the Hispanic community. In 1908, for example, the university wanted the US Congress to approve issuance of territorial bonds, in the amount of $30,000, to fund the construction of new buildings. There was a perception, however, that UNM already drained away too many dollars, a view shared to some extent within the territorial administration in Santa Fe. As C. H. Olsen, the private secretary to territorial governor George Curry, explained to J. H.

Wroth, the UNM Board of Regents secretary: "The department of Education in Washington has been gathering some data, and is of the opinion that New Mexico spends fortunes on the education of a handful of students, while the public schools of the territory are being neglected. In this, of course, there is more truth than fiction." C. H. Olsen to J. H. Wroth, Santa Fe, 11 March 1908, UNMR (UNMA 001, box 1, folder 5: Regents' Materials, 1893–1912), CSWR.

89. Dennis Chávez to David Chávez Jr., 29 April 1939, Dennis Chávez Papers (MSS 394 BC, Part I, Series 1: Correspondence, box 5, folder 30: David Chávez, 1939–40), CSWR.

90. "The League of United Latin American Citizens, Albuquerque, New Mexico. Resolution, December 23, 1936," JFZP (UNMA 008, box 3, folder: Department of Latin American Studies Major, 1939–1941), CSWR.

91. "League of United Latin American Citizens, Albuquerque, New Mexico. Resolution, December 23, 1936," JFZP.

92. J. T. Reid to Morse A. Cartwright, Albuquerque, 12 February 1938, JFZP (UNMA 008, box 5, folder: Harwood Foundation Adult Education Program, 1936/37–40), CSWR.

93. Reid to Cartwright, 12 February 1938, JFZP.

94. Reid to Cartwright, 12 February 1938, JFZP.

95. James Zimmerman to F. P. Keppel, Albuquerque, 3 March 1938, JFZP (UNMA 008, box 5, folder: Harwood Foundation Adult Education Program, 1936/7–40.), CSWR.

96. George Sánchez to Dr. J. F. Zimmerman, Caracas, Venezuela, 3 January 1938, Faculty Files Collection (UNMA 152, box 24, folder: George I. Sánchez), CSWR. Charles Montgomery observes that regionalist thought in the Southwest was not typically connected to social scientific research, to studies of caste and class, poverty, and social deprivation, but rather remained the province of novelists, poets, and literary scholars. He finds "an absence of social depth" (*Spanish Redemption*, 201), but does credit George Sánchez with breaking out of this mold—a recognition that Sánchez definitely merits. In his letter to Zimmerman, Sánchez cited Howard Odum's *Southern Regions of the United States* (Chapel Hill: University of North Carolina Press, 1936), or Charles Sturgeon Johnson, Edwin Embree, and Will Winton Alexander's, *The Collapse of Cotton Tenancy: Summary of Field Studies & Statistical Surveys, 1933–35* (Chapel Hill: University of North Carolina Press, 1935) as representative of the type of work for which the Southwest was crying out.

97. James Zimmerman to George Sánchez, Albuquerque, 8 January 1938, Faculty Files Collection (UNMA 152, box 24, folder: George I. Sánchez), CSWR.

98. Francis Kercheville to James Zimmerman, Albuquerque, 27 July 1938, Faculty Files Collection (UNMA 152, box 15, folder: Francis M. Kercheville), CSWR.

99. Sánchez does not indicate how he came to refer to the population group he researched as "forgotten people." There are any number of possibilities. He may have invented the phrase himself. It is also possible that he borrowed it from J. T. Reid, who in his above-referenced February 1938 letter to Morse Cartwright refers to the Spanish-speaking population of Taos County as "forgotten people."

100. Nieto-Phillips, *Language of Blood*, 3.

101. Apropos of the many complimentary reviews the book had received, Sánchez wrote to Zimmerman: "[Arturo] Torres-Rioseco of the University of California writes: 'it is a courageous and noble work, written with a clear insight of the problem discussed and with a plainly elegant style.'" George Sánchez to James Zimmerman, Austin, TX, 8 January 1941, Faculty Files Collection (UNMA 152, box 24, folder: George I. Sánchez), CSWR. Other keen admirers of the book were Herbert Priestly, Sánchez to Zimmerman, 8 January 1941, Faculty Files Collection, and Carey McWilliams. The latter described *Forgotten People* as an "extraordinarily fine, sensitive, and perceptive study of Spanish American culture" (McWilliams, *North from Mexico*, 285.) The book, he wrote many years later, had "made a deep and lasting impression on me" (McWilliams, "George Sánchez," 116). For a less adulatory appreciation of *Forgotten People*, see Carlos Kevin Blanton's recent book, *George I. Sánchez*, 62–66. Blanton provides a corrective to the "victimization," anti-"human agency" slant of Sánchez, an interpretive angle that he believes Sánchez overstated. Blanton also provides an excellent summary of Sánchez's fieldwork and research project in Taos County.

102. Zeleny, "Relations," 328. In addition, while working on the Taos County Project, Sánchez—never one to disguise his feelings or opt for the diplomatic course—had made known his disdain for the Taos art colony, whose members, he felt, romanticized Native Americans and made light of Hispanos in their depictions of life in northern New Mexico. The art colony in turn had no fondness for Sánchez. It was an influential voice on the Harwood Foundation Governing Board and within the community more broadly, and Zimmerman could not afford to jeopardize its support. Thus the antipathy the board members (and many political officials) felt for Sánchez was still another factor that Zimmerman had to take into account.

103. Because of his advocacy for educational reforms and the time he spent in fieldwork, Sánchez had won the affection and loyalty of New Mexicans in the northern half of the state to an exceptional degree. When it became known that he was leaving UNM, an organized effort was mounted to retain him. Petitions (located in Faculty Files Collection, UNMA 152, box 24, folder: George I. Sánchez) were received by the UNM Board of Regents and President Zimmerman from several communities and from educators—teachers,

superintendents, principals, administrators—as well as PTAs, up and down the Rio Grande Valley (Taos, Las Vegas, Chama, Tierra Amarilla, Belen, Los Lunas), signed by Hispanos and Anglos alike, in the hundreds, asking that they take whatever steps might be necessary to keep him. LULAC Council No. 34 likewise petitioned the regents.

104. George Sánchez to Frank Angel, Austin, TX, 19 September 1970, GISP, Series II, Correspondence and Subject Files, box 5, folder 6: Frank Angel, 1948–72.

105. Morse Cartwright to James Zimmerman, New York, 23 March 1940, JFZP (UNMA 008, box 5, folder: Harwood Foundation Adult Education Program, 1936/40), CSWR.

106. Sánchez, "New Mexicans and Acculturation," 61.

Chapter Three

1. "Trip to Washington," UNMBRR (UNMA 011, box 2, folder: Agenda and Memoranda for the Regents . . . , October 14, 1939), CSWR.

2. Mills, "Origins of Latin American Programs," 65–66.

3. The five were George Hammond, Donald Brand, Dorothy Woodward, Francis Kercheville, and Victor Kleven. James F. Zimmerman to Isaiah Bowman, Albuquerque, 27 December 1940, UNMFSR (UNMA 010, box 13, folder: Cultural Relations with Latin America Committee, 1940–41), CSWR.

4. "Suggested Program of Studies, Cultural Relations with Latin America," Faculty Files Collection (UNMA 152, box 21, folder: Joaquín Ortega), CSWR.

5. *University of New Mexico Bulletin. Commencement Address,* 2 June 1941, Catalog Series 54, no. 6 (October 1, 1941): 16. Kelly had served as president of Earlham College from 1903 to 1917. Joaquín Ortega was one of three individuals to receive the honorary doctor of literature awarded at UNM's 1941 commencement ceremony.

6. "Agenda and Memoranda for the Regents, November 30, 1940," UNMBRR (UNMA 011, box 2, folder: Agendas, 1940), CSWR.

7. "Memorandum to the Regents, April 30, 1941," UNMBRR (UNMA 011, box 2, folder: Agendas, 1941), CSWR.

8. "Agenda and Memorandum for the Regents of the University of New Mexico, May 31, 1941," UNMBRR (UNMA 011, box 2, folder: Agendas, 1941), CSWR.

9. Concha Ortiz y Pino de Kleven Papers (MSS 457 BC, box 1, folder 1: Biographical Information), CSWR. Ortiz y Pino had also introduced and carried the legislation that allocated special funding to enable the university to acquire the Paul Van de Velde Collection.

10. UNMBRR (UNMA 011, box 2, folder: Minutes, Regents, 1941), CSWR.

11. UNMBRR (UNMA 011, box 2, folder: Minutes, Regents, 1941, section: New Faculty 1941–42), CSWR.

12. While some in the university community may have found Ortega to be too aggressive in his style and approach, no one seems to have doubted his intellectual powers and solid record of academic success. The high regard in which he was held and the appreciation that was felt for the great interest he had shown over the years for the welfare of the university and the state were reflected in the honorary degree he was awarded at the June 1941 commencement exercises.

13. Mills, "Origins of Latin American Programs," 36–49.

14. "News Service—University of New Mexico—Ortega, Joaquín, 3-4-41," Faculty Files Collection (UNMA 152, box 21, folder: Joaquín Ortega), CSWR.

15. "News Service—University of New Mexico—Ortega, Joaquín, 3-4-41," (UNMA).

16. "News Service—University of New Mexico—Ortega, Joaquín, 3-4-41," (UNMA).

17. For these and other details of Ortega's time at Wisconsin, I am indebted to David Null, former head of the UW Archives and Records Management Department, UWUA, Admission Papers and Faculty Employment Cards. (no series or box numbers).

18. For more on the origins of the seminary, see Orstein, "Medieval Spanish Studies," 88–89.

19. See "Letters and Science," p. 125, accessible at http://digital.library.wisc.edu/1711.dl/UW.UWYearBk1949.

20. Joaquín Ortega to G. C. Sellery, Madison, WI, 7 May 1940, UWUA, Series 7/1/13–1, College of Letters and Science, Dean's Office, General Correspondence, George C. Sellery, box 43.

21. The letter to Mauricio Miera is mentioned in a July 17, 1939, letter from Dennis Chávez to his brother, David Chávez. Dennis Chávez Papers (MSS 394 BC, Part I, Series 1: Correspondence, box 5, folder 30: David Chávez, Jr.), CSWR.

22. Francis Kercheville to James Zimmerman, Albuquerque, 21 September 1940, JFZP (UNMA 008, box 3, folder: Department of Modern Languages, 1939–44), CSWR.

23. Kercheville to Zimmerman, Albuquerque, 3 September 1940, JFZP (UNMA 008, box 3, folder: Department of Modern Languages, 1939–44), CSWR.

24. Kercheville was on leave, traveling and conducting research in Latin America, during the first half of 1941. To this point (probably to the relief of Hammond, who was overburdened with administrative duties and also burrowed into scholarly work far more than Kercheville), he had taken the lead in developing UNM's academic program in Latin American studies and chaired the committee that administered the interdisciplinary major in the field. In late May 1941,

Zimmerman officially conveyed to Kercheville that he had chosen Ortega to be director of the SIAA. Ortega, he indicated, had given the plans a sharper, expanded focus: "As I wrote you last December, it was planned for you to continue heading up this important work. In the meantime, Dr. Ortega's stay with us has developed many phases in connection with our plans, and with the approval of Dean Hammond, Dean Knode, and myself, Dr. Ortega has outlined a very comprehensive program for a division of Latin American studies, or inter-American studies, in the University of New Mexico, and I have offered him the headship of this division." James Zimmerman to Francis Kercheville, Albuquerque, 24 May 1941, Faculty Files Collection (UNMA 152, box 15, folder: Francis M. Kercheville). Kercheville had already learned informally of this decision in a letter written to him by Ortega and was deeply offended by the news, because he believed that Zimmerman had gone behind his back and betrayed him while he was away. He responded (prior to receiving Zimmerman's official word) with a turgid, self-piteous, and semithreatening ten-page single-spaced letter protesting against the injustice done to him but also professing his great affection and admiration for Ortega. Francis Kercheville to James Zimmerman, Mexico City, 23 May 1941, Faculty Files Collection (UNMA 152, box 15, folder: Francis M. Kercheville). After Zimmerman's letter reached him, he wrote again on May 29, 1941, repeating his points, albeit in a somewhat more restrained tone. Kercheville to Zimmerman, 23 May 1941 (UNMA). After this, relations between Kercheville, Ortega's erstwhile great booster in New Mexico, and Ortega, Kercheville's academic mentor, could never be quite the same.

25. Kercheville to Zimmerman, 23 May 1941 (UNMA).

26. G. C. Sellery to James F. Zimmerman, Madison, WI, 22 August 1941, Faculty Files Collection (UNMA 152, box 21, folder: Joaquín Ortega), CSWR.

27. Joaquín Ortega to James Zimmerman, Albuquerque, 5 May 1941, Faculty Files Collection (UNMA 152, box 21, folder: Joaquín Ortega), CSWR.

28. Ortega to Zimmerman, 5 May 1941 (UNMA). One again wonders how George Hammond could have been so unaware of this situation and whether, by this time, his eyes had been opened. In Ortega's view, the situation was serious enough that he withdrew a proposal he had drafted for Zimmerman, to fund scholarships and fellowships for students from Latin America to attend UNM, because "it may prove dangerous to bring distinguished Latin American students to the campus with the present racial discrimination prevalent among our students." See Joaquín Ortega to James Zimmerman, Albuquerque, 1 June 1941, Faculty Files Collection (UNMA 152, box 21, folder: Joaquin Ortega), CSWR. Yet only nine months later he went against his own assessment when he learned that the Council of National Defense had shown a strong interest

in promoting student exchange between the United States and the Latin American republics.

29. "An Interested Observer of the Alumni Association" to Concha Ortiz y Pino, Albuquerque (?), 10 February 1941, Ortiz y Pino Family Papers, 1696–1984 (MSS 336 BC, box 1: scrapbook), CSWR.

30. "To the President, Deans, and Librarian of the University of New Mexico: Preliminary Report," Faculty Files Collection (UNMA 152, box 15, folder: Francis M. Kercheville), CSWR.

31. Francis M. Kercheville to James Zimmerman, Mexico City, 10 May 1941, Faculty Files Collection (UNMA 152, box 15, folder: Francis M. Kercheville), CSWR.

32. In arguing that the study of inter-American affairs at UNM should be vocationally oriented, Kercheville was invoking (or borrowing) one of the basic ideas behind New Deal–era reform efforts to promote education among the Hispanic population in New Mexico. The belief that such education should be tailored to and help ensure the survival of traditional arts and crafts and forms of manual and agrarian-based labor was widespread among professional educators across the state at this time. For more on this point, see Getz, *Education of Hispanos*, 103–17.

33. MWHUNM chap. 7, p. 25.

34. Joaquín Ortega to James Zimmerman, Albuquerque, 8 January 1941, Faculty Files Collection (UNMA 152, box 21, folder: Joaquín Ortega), CSWR.

35. James Zimmerman to Joaquín Ortega, Albuquerque, 3 June 1941, Faculty Files Collection (UNMA 152, box 21, folder: Joaquín Ortega), CSWR. Based on his own research and fieldwork during the 1940s, Carey McWilliams made the interesting claim that Ortega's ability to relate so well on such a grassroots level to the Hispanic community was unusual for an immigrant from Spain: "It is a rare case, indeed, when a Spanish immigrant has established any sort of contact with the Spanish-speaking people of the Southwest." McWilliams, *North from Mexico*, 46.

36. McWilliams, *North from Mexico*, 46.

37. Joaquín Ortega to James Zimmerman, Madison, WI, 8 January 1941, Faculty Files Collection (UNMA 152, box 21, folder: Joaquín Ortega), CSWR. Just ten days later, in a letter to Sánchez, Zimmerman stressed how complimentary Ortega had been about *Forgotten People*.

38. Ortega to Zimmerman, 8 January 1941 (UNMA).

39. Ortega to Zimmerman, 8 January 1941 (UNMA).

40. Donald Brand to James Zimmerman, Coyuca de Catalán (Guerrero, Mexico), 2 August 1941, Faculty Files Collection (UNMA 152, box 4, folder: Donald Brand), CSWR.

41. Arthur Campa to George Sánchez, Albuquerque, 6 September 1941, GISP, Series II, Correspondence and Subject Files, box 9, folder 8: Arthur L. Campa.

42. Karl Schwerin, "History of the Department of Anthropology," chap. on "Depression and War, 1935–1948": 4 (unpublished manuscript), in University of New Mexico College of Arts and Sciences, Centennial Histories Collection (UNMA 139), CSWR.

43. Donald Brand to Dean Knode, et al., Albuquerque, 24 January 1942, JFZP (UNMA 008, box 4, folder: Department of the School of Inter-American Affairs, 1941–42), CSWR.

44. "Inter-departmental Cooperation," Joaquín Ortega to Donald Brand, Albuquerque, 28 January 1942, JFZP (UNMA 008, box 4, folder: Department of the School of Inter-American Affairs, 1941–42), CSWR.

45. On Saunders's views see Mills, "Origins of Latin American Programs," 94, and on those of Wisconsin and UNM colleagues, see the conclusion.

46. Of course, we don't know what Campa's motive may have been in putting things to Sánchez in this light. It is possible that Campa, a potential contender passed over as modern-languages department chair, was planting a seed of hostility toward Ortega. Ortega also admired Sánchez's work ethic. Campa reports him, in this same letter, as saying, "A man isn't worth too much under contract. There is a certain work to be done, and all you can do is get the man who can do it. I can pick two men working in that same field whose combined salary would bring Sánchez, but whose combined efforts can't do one fourth of his work." Arthur Campa to George I. Sánchez, Albuquerque, 6 September 1941, GISP, Series II, Correspondence and Subject Files, box 9, folder 8: Arthur L. Campa.

47. Joaquín Ortega, "A Preliminary Survey of the Academic Setup of the University of New Mexico from the Point of View of Inter-American Relations," Faculty Files Collection (UNMA 152, folder 21: Joaquín Ortega), CSWR.

48. Joaquín Ortega to James Zimmerman, Albuquerque, 23 April 1941, JFZP (UNMA 008, box 4, folder: Department of the School of Inter-American Affairs, 1941–42), CSWR.

49. The addition of Latin American and inter-American related courses and the full span of offerings can easily be traced through the university's annual catalog of courses. A more detailed picture of the expansion of this curriculum and the rationale for adding particular courses is available in the "Courses of Study" folders in the records of the UNM Faculty Senate, housed in the university archives (UNMA).

50. *University of New Mexico Bulletin, Biennial Report of the University of New Mexico 1941–43*, Catalog Series 56, no. 2 (January 1, 1943): 57.

51. *University of New Mexico Bulletin, Biennial Report of the University of New Mexico 1943–45,* Catalog Series 57, no. 6 (February 1945): 75. All of the material that follows, relative to the school's activities during the 1943–1945 biennium, will be found in this same report.

52. Ina Sizer Cassidy to George Emerson, Santa Fe, NM, 29 April 1941, JFZP (UNMA 008, box 3, folder: Department of Fine Arts Festivals, 1937–41), CSWR.

53. See "Request for a Grant-in-Aid for a Latin American Artist in Residence ...June, 1941," JFZP (UNMA 008, box 5, folder: Grant Proposals, 1938–1942), CSWR.

54. "Request for a Grant-in-Aid," JFZP.

55. "Acceptance for the University," JFZP (UNMA 008, box 4, folder: Department of the School of Inter-American Affairs, 1942–43), CSWR. The fresco had been commissioned through a grant from the Committee for Inter-American Artistic and Intellectual Relations of the Office of the Coordinator of Inter-American Affairs.

56. For more on the activities and contributions of Gálvez Suárez, see *University of New Mexico Bulletin, Biennial Report of the University of New Mexico 1945–47,* Catalog Series 59, no. 4 (January 1947): 91–92. The artist-in-residence program ended at the conclusion of Mendoza's appointment in 1946—doubtless the result (or victim) of new priorities in the postwar development of federally funded area-studies programs. Valuable as it was, Mendoza's contribution would have been much reduced in scope and content were it not for the groundbreaking work begun more than a decade earlier by Arthur Campa. Supported initially with financial assistance from Bronson Cutting and the Rockefeller Foundation, Campa traversed the state to research, record, and transcribe folk songs. His efforts reaped great rewards, leading to the claim that "nowhere else in the United States was the study of Spanish-American music more seriously pursued than at the University of New Mexico." Lowitt, *Bronson Cutting,* 188.

57. Saunders, "Alumni at Barelas Center," 5. As noted in my introduction, it might make sense in the local context to refer to three main population groups, because the representation of African Americans in the population of New Mexico in this period was exceedingly small—around 1 percent. Here, however, Saunders commits an error that many others, Ortega included, also frequently made—namely, omitting people of African ancestry when referring to "the Americas" as a whole.

58. Zeleny, "Relations," 157.

59. Zeleny, "Relations," 160.

60. See US Department of Agriculture, Bureau of Agricultural Economics/The

University of New Mexico, School of Inter-American Affairs, "School for the Rio Grande Valley on The War and Cultural Relations in the Rio Grande Valley," Albuquerque: University of New Mexico. JFZP (UNMA 008, box 4, folder: Dept. of School of Inter-American Affairs, 1941–42), CSWR.

61. As quoted in a letter from Joaquín Ortega to James F. Zimmerman, Albuquerque, 17 December 1941, JFZP (UNMA 008, box 4, folder: Department of the School of Inter-American Affairs, 1941–42), CSWR.
62. Saunders, "Alumni at Barelas Center," 5.
63. "A Project for the Rehabilitation of Spanish-Speaking People Based on the Barelas Community Center of Albuquerque, New Mexico . . . Submitted to the Coordinator of Inter-American Affairs," 1. JFZP (UNMA 008, box 5, folder: New Mexico—Barelas Community Center, April, 1942), CSWR.
64. "A Project for the Rehabilitation of Spanish-Speaking People," 2, JFZP.
65. "A Project for the Rehabilitation of Spanish-Speaking People," 5, JFZP.
66. Burma, *Spanish-Speaking Groups*, 4.
67. I am grateful to William Stanley for drawing out these disconnects.
68. "A Project for the Rehabilitation of Spanish-Speaking People," 5–6, JFZP.
69. "School of Inter-American Affairs—The University of New Mexico: Community Program," JFZP (UNMA 008, box 3, folder: Department of the School Inter-American Affairs, 1942–1947), CSWR. The grant was actually made by a subentity within the office: the Division of Inter-American Activities in the United States. The very name of this division validated the insistence of Ortega (and others) that implementation of the Good Neighbor Policy needed to begin "at home."
70. "School of Inter-American Affairs," JFZP.
71. "School of Inter-American Affairs," JFZP.
72. Mills, "Origins of Latin American Programs," 75.
73. "School of Inter-American Affairs: The University of New Mexico: Community Program, p. 3," JFZP (UNMA 008, box 4, folder: Department of the School of Inter-American Affairs, 1943–44), CSWR.

Chapter Four

1. Gonzales-Berry, "Which Language Will Our Children Speak?," 170. In reviewing developments affecting language and public-school education in the period 1891–1930, I have drawn on the information provided in Gonzales-Berry's essay.
2. Zeleny, "Relations," 269.
3. Nieto-Phillips, *Language of Blood*, 80.
4. New Mexico's push for statehood, already delayed by decades, gave further

impetus to the English-only policy and, conversely, discouraged the retention
of Spanish. One of its most fervent advocates was the US senator from Indiana
and chairman of Congress's Committee on Territories, Albert Beveridge. In
1902, Beveridge led a subcommittee to the territory to hold hearings on the
question of New Mexico's readiness for joining the union. Beveridge blocked
statehood for the territory (and for Arizona) because he considered it too
sparsely populated by white persons and its residents far too reliant on Spanish.
For Beveridge, "American" meant English-speaking whites. By definition,
"Mexicans" were excluded. For more on Beveridge's role in delaying statehood
for New Mexico and his view of Nuevomexicanos, see David. V. Holtby, *Forty-
Seventh Star: New Mexico's Struggle for Statehood* (Norman: University of
Oklahoma Press, 2012), 39–63, 220–23.

5. Zeleny, "Relations," 281.
6. On this point, see Gonzales-Berry, "Which Language Will Our Children
   Speak?," 178–80.
7. The quoted material is from a *New York Times* article, cited by Gonzales-Berry,
   "Which Language Will Our Children Speak?," 181.
8. Lozano, "Managing the 'Priceless Gift,'" 271.
9. Nieto-Phillips, *Language of Blood*, 197.
10. *University of New Mexico Bulletin, The Summer Session Announcements 1932*,
    Catalog Series 45, nos. 2–3 (February 15 and March 1, 1932), 12.
11. Zeleny, "Relations," 283–84.
12. "Outline of General Plans for the Department of Modern Languages (Spanish
    and Hispanic Studies)," Francis Kercheville to James F. Zimmerman,
    Albuquerque, 15 February 1938, JFZP (UNMA 008, box 3, folder: Department of
    Modern Languages, 1927–38), CSWR.
13. Kercheville to Zimmerman, 15 February 1938, JFZP.
14. McWilliams, *North from Mexico*, 299.
15. UNMFSR (UNMA 010, box 23, folder: Post-War Planning Committee, 1940–44),
    CSWR.
16. That cause is still being pursued, with the arguments on its behalf having
    changed little, if at all, since Edward Gray's day: "Our multilingualism is
    a valuable asset, which we risk losing unless we invest boldly in building
    a bilingual teaching force and a dual-language early childhood education
    system. . . . It's time for New Mexico to leverage one of our people's greatest
    assets, our bilingualism, to become the national leader in dual-language . . .
    education." See Adrián Pedroza and Edward Tabet-Cubero, "NM Should Take
    Advantage of Its Bilingualism," *Albuquerque Journal*, June 8, 2016, A9. Equally
    little changed, in contrast, is the belief held by many that the use of Spanish
    threatens American national identity. For how recent debates about language

and the place of bilingualism in the United States are playing out in a specific New Mexico context, see Simon Romero, "Savoring the Spanish of My Youth," *New York Times*, August 23, 2017. Romero returns to his hometown, Las Vegas (population thirteen thousand), located in the north central part of the state, where he hears "the Spanish of newcomers eclipsing the old Spanish of New Mexico."

17. Kluckhohn, "Field of Higher Education," 29.

18. Joaquín Ortega to Concha Ortiz y Pino, Albuquerque, 11 February 1941, Concha Ortiz y Pino de Kleven Papers (MSS 457 BC, box 2, Scrapbook, 73a), CSWR.

19. Chávez's reversal on the question of whether the teaching of Spanish should be required in the public schools is one example of how, as Carlos Kevin Blanton states, he "shifted definitions of himself in order to advance his political agenda." Blanton, *George I. Sánchez*, 15.

20. Dennis Chávez to Concha Ortiz y Pino, Washington, DC (?), 6 February 1941, Concha Ortiz y Pino de Kleven Papers (MSS 457 BC, box 2, Scrapbook, 76b), CSWR.

21. Chávez to Ortiz y Pino, 6 February 1941, CSWR.

22. "Miss Ortiz Hits Back at LULAC Group," in undated newspaper clipping (paper not identified), Concha Ortiz y Pino de Kleven Papers (MSS 457 BC, box 2, folder 15: Newspaper Clippings, 1940s and 1950s.

23. "Miss Ortiz Hits Back," Concha Ortiz y Pino de Kleven Papers.

24. "Amador in Defense of Teaching Spanish," Santa Fe, February 5 [1941?], clipping from unidentified newspaper, in Concha Ortiz y Pino de Kleven Papers (MSS 457 BC, box 2, folder 15: Newspaper Clippings, 1940s and 1950s), CSWR.

25. This percentage is taken from Sánchez, *Forgotten People*, 30.

26. Joaquín Ortega to Concha Ortiz y Pino, Albuquerque, 9 April 1941, Concha Ortiz y Pino de Kleven Papers (MSS 457, box 2, Scrapbook, 70c–70e), CSWR.

27. For this and the following provisions, see Ortega to Ortiz y Pino, 9 April 1941, CSWR. All of the quotes in this paragraph are from Ortega's 9 April 1941 letter to Ortiz y Pino.

28. Unless otherwise indicated, all of the quoted material down to the beginning of the section on the bilingual conference proposed by Ortega and George Sánchez is from Ortega's *Compulsory Teaching*.

29. Indicative of how the political climate had changed, on April 16, 1941, the bill, "after some campaigning by Chávez," [Lozano, "Managing the 'Priceless Gift,'" 282] was approved and passed in the Senate and then later signed into law by the governor. It required Spanish instruction in schools with at least three teachers or ninety regularly attending students. Parents who objected, however,

were allowed to remove their children from Spanish classes. In addition, the "Governing Boards of Education" were granted the right to exempt particular schools at the start of each school year [Lozano, "Managing the 'Priceless Gift,'" 282–83]. For the law's specific terms and provisions, see New Mexico, *New Mexico Statutes, 1941: Containing the General Laws of New Mexico . . .* (Indianapolis: Bobbs-Merrill, 1942), chap. 143, pp. 250–51.

30. The same impulses and practices that Otis and Ortega identified—e.g., the "lack of unity," and the desire to "win acceptance from Anglo society," are seen by some in the New Mexico Hispanic community as still operating today: "We fail to coalesce as a group and fight injustice when it is directed toward Hispanics. We accept our station in life and do want so much to be accepted. . . . [T]hose of us who have 'made it' forget about those that are still struggling in poverty to achieve the American dream and in some instances to be accepted as Americans." Frank H. Luna, "Hispanic History Could Be Marginalized Again," *Albuquerque Journal*, May 1, 2012, A11.

31. In this instance, although the parallels were obvious (and perhaps because he was dealing specifically with the language issue), Ortega made no mention of Native Americans, whose ancestry in the land long predated the Hispanic population.

32. García, "Foreword," xi–xxx.

33. Joaquín Ortega to James Zimmerman, Albuquerque, 5 May 1941, Faculty Files Collection (UNMA 152, box 21, folder: Joaquín Ortega), CSWR.

34. Joaquín Ortega to Concha Ortiz y Pino, Albuquerque, 28 May 1941, Concha Ortiz y Pino de Kleven Papers (MSS 457, box 2, Scrapbook, 71b), CSWR.

35. Ortega to Ortiz y Pino, 28 May 1941, CSWR.

36. Joaquín Ortega to James Zimmerman, Albuquerque, 8 September 1941, Faculty Files Collection (UNMA 152, box 21, folder: Joaquín Ortega), CSWR.

37. "Request for Co-Sponsorship and Financial Support of an American Conference on Bilingualism, Presented by the University of New Mexico, June 1941," JFZP (UNMA 008, box 5, folder: Grant Proposals, 1938–1942), CSWR.

38. "Request for Co-Sponsorship," JFZP.

39. "Request for Co-Sponsorship," JFZP.

40. Campa, *Hispanic Culture*, 221.

41. Ortega, *Intangible Resources*, 6n4.

42. An example of this phenomenon on the UNM campus was the "Swastika Club," formed during the 1920s to promote the social and academic life of Spanish American students. Membership in the club was open to "any white male person duly registered at UNM." As Michael Welsh notes, the imposition of this racial qualifier reflected "the desire of many Hispanics to be considered the equals of their Anglo counterparts, and the standard racial distinctions in

1920s fraternities between 'white' and 'Negro' students." MWHUNM, chap. 7, pp. 85–86.

43. Montgomery, *Spanish Redemption*, 15.

44. Montgomery, *Spanish Redemption*, 63–72.

45. See Maciel and Gonzales-Berry, "Introduction," 57; Noel, *Debating American Identity*, 14–15; García, *Mexican Americans*, 282; Montgomery, *Spanish Redemption*, 222.

46. Leff, "George I. Sánchez," 69.

47. Campa, "Spanish, Mexican, Native: The Problem of Nomenclature" [excerpt from his *Spanish Folk-Poetry in New Mexico*], 3, Faculty Files Collection (UNMA 152, box 4, folder: Arthur L. Campa), CSWR.

48. As quoted in Montgomery, *Spanish Redemption*, 222. George Hammond found documentary evidence of this fact—that the earliest settlers, from the Oñate expedition, did not bring their wives with them—through his research in Spanish archives. See George Hammond to J. H. Watkins, Albuquerque, 19 July 1938, Eleanor Adams Papers (MSS 826 BC, box 2, folder 15, George P. Hammond, 1938–1974), CSWR. On the notion of purity of blood, Joaquín Ortega drew his own blunt conclusion, in referring the concept back to Spain itself. He is quoted by Campa as follows: "Professor Joaquín Ortega gave the following opinion: 'We the Spanish are an international cocktail.'" See Campa, *Arthur Campa*, 35.

49. Gonzalez, *The Spanish-Americans*, x.

50. Sexton, "New Mexico," 53.

51. For an excellent review of the different schools of thought, see Phillip B. Gonzales, "Whither the Nuevomexicanos." Likewise very useful is Rodríguez, "Hispano Homeland Debate."

52. *Southwest Review* 14, no. 4 (Summer 1929).

53. Pearce, "Southwestern Culture," 196.

54. Pearce, "Southwestern Culture," 198. Pearce's mention of the year 1680 refers to the uprising of the indigenous Pueblo people against their Spanish overlords, resulting in the death of several hundred colonists and the flight of two thousand others south to El Paso. The province was reconquered in 1692.

55. Pearce, "Southwestern Culture," 199. The quotes from Pearce in the paragraph that follows are from this same source.

56. Guérard, "A Mosaic," 126,

57. Guérard, "A Mosaic," 127.

58. Ortega, *New Mexico's Opportunity*, 2.

59. Ortega, *New Mexico's Opportunity*, 8.

60. It may be stretching a point, but the pluralistic society that Ortega had in mind would have had much in common with the Canadian model, wherein Canadian national identity is (in principle) not fractured by the existence of

separate groups and does not require their assimilation to a majority culture. The different ways in which ideas about national identity, pluralism, and assimilation operate in the Canadian system versus the United States' and its "melting pot" culture" (in the context of current debates over immigration) are summarized in an article by Amanda Taub, "Canada Shows How to Thwart A Populist Tide," *New York Times*, June 27, 2017, A1, A6.

61. Ortega, *New Mexico's Opportunity*, 19.

62. Ortega, *Intangible Resources*, 6.

63. Ortega, *Intangible Resources*, 6.

64. Further on, somewhat in passing, he does finally mention "the Negro" as one part of the New Mexican commonwealth. Ortega, *Intangible Resources*, 12.

65. García, *Mexican Americans*, 289.

66. García, *Mexican Americans*, 289–90.

67. García, "Foreword," xvi. A nineteenth-century predecessor in New Mexico, Charles Lummis, seems to have cultivated a very similar idea of what New Mexico could become: "The Lummis model for New Mexico, that it be a land not only of enchantment, but also of brotherhood; that is, a successful tricultural laboratory to demonstrate tolerance, understanding, and mutual respect." From Sexton, "New Mexico," 148.

68. Nieto-Phillips, *Language of Blood*, 120.

69. Wilson, "Ethnic/Sexual Personas," 29.

70. Wilson, "Ethnic/Sexual Personas," 29.

71. Ortega, "Factionalism in New Mexico," 12.

Chapter Five

1. "More on the *New Mexico Quarterly*," 2, UNMFSR (UNMA 010, box 23, folder: Publications Committee, 1946–47), CSWR.

2. "More on the *New Mexico Quarterly*," 2, UNMFSR.

3. "Graduate Committee Minutes, October 15, 1948," UNMFSR (UNMA 010, box 18, folder: Graduate Committee, 1948–49), CSWR.

4. Joaquín Ortega to James Zimmerman, Albuquerque, 12 October 1942, JFZP (UNMA 008, box 4, folder: Department of the School of Inter-American Affairs, 1941–42), CSWR. There is a nice symmetry in Ortega having written this letter— the undertone of which is all about forging new horizons—on Columbus Day.

5. D. D. Brand to George Peterson, Albuquerque, 19 November 1946, UNMFSR (UNMA 010, box 14, folder: Curricula Committee, 1946–47), CSWR.

6. Miguel Jorrín to George Peterson, Albuquerque, 6 October 1945, UNMFSR (UNMA 010, box 14, folder: Curricula Committee, 1945–46), CSWR.

7. James Zimmerman to Joaquín Ortega, Albuquerque, 26 February 1942, JFZP

(UNMA 008, box 4, folder: Department of the School of Inter-American Affairs, 1941–42), CSWR.

8. The address was titled "Toward an Inter-American Ideal." The transcription is in JFZP (UNMA 008, box 4, folder: Department of the School of Inter-American Affairs, 1942–47), CSWR. All of the quotes in this and the following paragraph are from this same source.

9. Popejoy's handwritten marginal note to President Zimmerman can be found on p. 1 of the transcription in JFZP (UNMA 008, box 4, folder: Department of the School of Inter-American Affairs, 1942–47).

10. Joaquín Ortega to James Zimmerman, Albuquerque, 20 April 1942 (JFZP (UNMA 008, box 4, folder: Department of the School of Inter-American Affairs, 1941–42), CSWR.

11. Arthur L. Campa to Keen Rafferty [UNM Public Affairs Office], Albuquerque, Faculty Files Collection (UNMA 152, box 4, folder: Arthur L. Campa), CSWR.

12. J. P. Wernette to George P. Hammond, Albuquerque, 24 April 1946, Faculty Files Collection (UNMA 152, box 12, folder: George P. Hammond), CSWR.

13. J. P. Wernette to Lloyd Tireman, Albuquerque, 3 April 1947, Faculty Files Collection (UNMA 152, box 28, folder: Lloyd Tireman), CSWR.

14. Mills, "Origins of Latin American Programs," 77.

15. A list of new university programs and divisions adopted in the period 1945–1947 is given in *University of New Mexico Bulletin, Biennial Report of the University of New Mexico 1945–47*, Catalog Series 59, no. 4 (January 1947): 11.

16. Charles Judah to Professors Seed and Fellows, Albuquerque, 3 April 1951, UNMFSR (UNMA 010, box 14, folder: Curricula Committee, 1950–51), CSWR.

17. Joaquín Ortega to Concha Ortiz y Pino, Albuquerque, 28 May 1941, Concha Ortiz y Pino de Kleven Papers (MSS 457 BC, box 2, Scrapbook, 71b), CSWR.

18. The memo and attached report were dated 18 April 1947, Faculty Files Collection (UNMA 152, box 21, folder: Joaquín Ortega), CSWR.

19. Memo and report, 18 April 1947 (UNMA).

20. Thomas Donnelly to Joaquín Ortega, Albuquerque, 1 August 1947, Faculty Files Collection (UNMA 152, box 21, folder: Joaquín Ortega), CSWR.

21. Quoted in Francis Kercheville to Thomas Donnelly, Albuquerque, 20 May 1949, Faculty Files Collection (UNMA 152, box 15, folder: Francis M. Kercheville), CSWR.

22. "Inauguration of Thomas Lafayette Popejoy," 38.

23. In 1952 it was decided to discontinue the secretarial training component of the school's program. UNMFSR (UNMA 010, box 14, folder: Curricula Committee, 1951–52), CSWR.

24. UNMFSR (UNMA 010, box 2, folder: Faculty Meetings, 1939–51), CSWR.

25. "U Council to Hear Report on Racial Questionnaire Tomorrow," *Albuquerque Tribune*, April 22, 1947.

26. "Race Quiz Probe to Report Today," *Albuquerque Journal*, April 23, 1947, p. 2.

27. "Race Quiz Probe to Report Today," April 23, 1947, p. 2.

28. "UNM Regents Refuse to Expel Students for Racial Questionnaire," *Albuquerque Journal*, April 26, 1947, p. 1.

29. "UNM Regents Refuse to Expel Students," April 26, 1947, p. 1.

30. "Chávez Says Students Condemned Too Much in Racial Questionnaire," *Albuquerque Journal*, May 1, 1947, p. 1.

31. Gonzales, *Forced Sacrifice*, 227.

32. Gonzales, *Forced Sacrifice*, 227.

33. See bibliography for full citations.

34. Ortega, "Rethinking Cervantes."

35. Ortega, "Doctor Chimera." This piece reproduces an address he gave in February 1935 to the Madison, Wisconsin, Literary Club.

36. Ortega, "Professor and the University."

37. "Minutes of the Meeting of the Publications Committee, July 16, 1947," Albuquerque, UNMFSR (UNMA 010, box 23, folder: Publications Committee, 1947–48), CSWR.

38. T. M. Pearce to Lincoln La Paz (Publications Committee chair), Albuquerque, 17 December 1947, UNMFSR (UNMA 010, box 23, folder: Publications Committee, 1947–48), CSWR.

39. Joaquín Ortega, "*The New Mexico Quarterly Review*: Editorial Statement," 492–95.

40. Joaquín Ortega, "*The New Mexico Quarterly Review*: Editorial Policy," UNMFSR (UNMA 010, box 23, folder: Publications Committee, 1947–48), CSWR.

41. Lyle Saunders to George Sánchez, Albuquerque, 20 February 1951, GISP, Series II, box 32, folder 9: Lyle Saunders, 1951.

42. *The Alumnus*, June 15, 1952, p. 13.

43. Lyle Saunders to George Sánchez, Albuquerque, 23 March 1955, GISP, Series II, box 32, folder 9: Lyle Saunders, 1952–1970.

Chapter Six

1. Ortega clearly stated that, of all the reasons that led him to move to the state, this "promise" was at the forefront. It acted as a powerful motivator: "New Mexico is a land of promise, promise of the fusion . . . [;] because I felt this promise I came seven years ago to sink my roots in New Mexico." Ortega, "Factionalism in New Mexico," 12.

2. Ortega, "Professor and the University," 331.

3. Ortega, "Professor and the University," 331.

4. A good explanation and analysis of this breed of intellectual will be found in Kirkendall, "Franklin D. Roosevelt," 456–71.

5. France Scholes, "In Memoriam." Scholes's appreciation was prepared for the *News Bulletin* of the Rocky Mountain Modern Language Association. A copy is contained in the Faculty Files Collection (UNMA 152, box 21, folder: Joaquín Ortega), CSWR.

6. Zimmerman, "Meaning of Memorial Day," 7.

7. Quoted by McWilliams, *North from Mexico*, 284.

8. McWilliams, *North from Mexico*, 285.

9. Joaquín Ortega to Tom Popejoy, Albuquerque, 31 October 1951, Faculty Files Collection (UNMA 152, box 21, folder: Joaquín Ortega), CSWR.

10. Ortega to Popejoy, 31 October 1951 (UNMA). A copy of the November 26, 1958 *Albuquerque Tribune* article is found in the Faculty Files Collection (UNMA 152, box 21, folder: Joaquín Ortega, CSWR). In 1966, the College of St. Joseph on the Rio Grande became the University of Albuquerque, which in turn closed its doors in 1986.

11. *Albuquerque Tribune*, November 26, 1958, Faculty Files Collection (UNMA).

12. The titles of their addresses were Scholes: "The New Mexican Heritage"; Jorrín: "The School of Inter-American Affairs in New Mexico"; and Popejoy: "Joaquín Ortega and the University of New Mexico." Many official records and documents for the decade of the fifties are currently unprocessed in the university archives, and so I was unable to read the remarks of Scholes, Jorrín, and Popejoy—assuming copies still exist.

13. These extracts from William Roberts's remarks and those from Duncan's are found in Inventory of the University of New Mexico. Dept. of Facility Planning Records, 1889–[ongoing] (UNMA 028, box 84, folder: Ortega Hall #79 1971), CSWR.

14. Ortega, *Intangible Resources*, 2n.

Epilogue

1. The running controversy over the seal was covered by the local press and the UNM student newspaper for more than half of 2016. A sampling includes: Ted Jojola, "UNM Seal Minimizes Pueblo People," *Albuquerque Journal*, May 1, 2016, A11; Chris Quintana, "Discussions Start on a New Seal for UNM," *Albuquerque Journal*, May 14, 2016, A1–2; Chris Quintana, "Criticism of UNM Seal Continues at Forum," *Albuquerque Journal*, June 18, 2016, C2; Russell Contreras, "NM Needs Reconciliation, Author Says," *Albuquerque Journal*, July 30, 2016, C2;

Carlos Melendrez, "Reconciling Past Historical Atrocities," *Albuquerque Journal*, August 15, 2016, A7; Elizabeth Sanchez, "UNM Seal to Remain Unchanged for Now," *Daily Lobo*, November 17, 2016, 2.

2. Jojola, "UNM Seal," May 1, 2016.

3. "In Consideration of UNM's Official Seal: Historical Review by Pamina M. Deutsch, Director of UNM Policy Office and Jozi De Leon, Vice President for Equity and Inclusion," n.d., Vertical Files (UNMA 006, drawer 6, folder: School Banners/UNM Seal), CSWR.

4. "Abolish the Racist Seal: UNM Kiva Club, the Red Nation Statement to the Board of Regents," May 5, 2016, therednation.org/2016/05/05/abolish-the-racist-seal-unm-kiva-club-the-red-nation-statement-to-board-of-regents.

5. As quoted in Quintana, Discussions Start on a New Seal," May 14, 2016.

6. Sanchez, "UNM Seal to Remain," November 17, 2016.

7. Sanchez, "UNM Seal to Remain," November 17, 2016.

8. A prominent advocate for this viewpoint was the Mexican American writer Sandra Cisneros. See Contreras, "NM Needs Reconciliation," July 30, 2016.

9. Contreras, "NM Needs Reconciliation," July 30, 2016. Marley's rejection of the tricultural myth in fact anticipated a more general sense, or recognition, of its unsuitability. In September 2019, for example, New Mexico's governor, Michelle Lujan Grisham, issued an apology to the black community for referring to the state's "tricultural heritage" in a state visitor guide that came out very soon after she began her governorship in January 2019. She stipulated that the word *multicultural*, not *tricultural*, should henceforth be used in all official state communication, correspondence, and publications. See Dan Boyd, "Lujan Grisham Apologizes for 'Tricultural' Reference," in his *Albuquerque Journal* article, September 12, 2019, accessible at https://www.abqjournal.com/1364920/lujan-grisham-apologizes-tricultural-reference-html.

10. See Interim Provost and Executive Vice President Richard L. Woods's communique of October 4, 2018, accessible at https://provost.unm.edu/academic-dispatch/archive/2018/10-4-2018_wednesday-communique_final.pdf.

11. Bellmore, "The University of New Mexico's Zimmerman Library," 152. Bellmore's article provides an excellent overview of the Adams mural, placing it in broad historical and aesthetic context.

12. See, e.g., Joann Santiago, "Racism in Zimmerman," *Daily Lobo*, October 22, 1970; Emiliano Aranda, "Seeds of Racism," *Daily Lobo*, December 10, 1970.

13. "Zimmerman Library Mural Damaged During Holidays," *Daily Lobo*, November 30, 1970; Denise Tessier, "'Racist' Mural Splattered," *Daily Lobo*, January 28, 1974.

14. Neri Holguin, "UNM Students Fight for Non-Racist Murals," *Voces Unidas* 4, no. 2 (1994): 7.

15. These included mounting a permanent exhibit in the library to explain the murals, organizing a symposium on the murals and issues relating to them, producing a brochure on the murals, and pursuing the idea of commissioning a new mural in the library.

16. Quoted in Jessica Dyer, "New Course for an Old Conflict," *Albuquerque Journal*, August 28, 2018.

17. Strikingly similar to the murals controversy at UNM is the case of Washington High School in San Francisco. After contentious public hearings, the city's school board initially voted, unanimously in June 2019, to paint over a series of thirteen murals. (The board has since decided to reconsider its action.) The murals, called *The Life of Washington* and created by the Russian-born artist Victor Arnautoff for the WPA, include a dead Native American and slaves at work in the fields as key elements in depicting the life of George Washington and his support for the "genocidal Western expansion." See Roberta Smith, "The Case for Keeping San Francisco's Disputed George Washington Murals," *New York Times*, July 26, 2019, C1.

18. Details about the planning group, minutes of its initial meetings, the murals class schedule, and recorded lectures are accessible at https://provost.unm.edu/offices/faculty-develop.

19. As reported in the September 5, 2019, issue of the *Daily Lobo*. See the article by Megan Holman, "New Proposals for Controversial Murals Considered," accessible at https://www.dailylobo.com/article/2019/09/zimmerman-murals-new-preposal.

Bibliography

Barker, Ruth Laughlin. *Caballeros: The Romance of Santa Fe and the Southwest.* New York: D. Appleton, 1931.

Bellmore, Audra. "The University of New Mexico's Zimmerman Library: A New Deal Landmark Articulates the Ideals of the PWA." *New Mexico Historical Review* 88, no. 2 (Spring 2013): 123–63.

Blanton, Carlos Kevin. *George I. Sánchez: The Long Fight for Mexican American Integration.* New Haven, CT: Yale University Press, 2014.

Burma, John H. *Spanish-Speaking Groups in the United States.* Durham, NC: Duke University Press, 1954.

Campa, Arthur L. *Arthur Campa and the Coronado Cuarto Centennial.* Edited by Anselmo F. Arellano and Julian Vigil. Las Vegas, NV: Editorial Teleràna, 1980.

———. *Hispanic Culture in the Southwest.* Foreword by Richard L. Nostrand. Norman and London: University of Oklahoma Press, 1979.

———. Review of *Old Spain in the Southwest*, by Nina Otero-Warren. *New Mexico Quarterly* 6, no. 12 (May 1936): 149–51.

Cather, Willa. *Death Comes for the Archbishop.* Lincoln: University of Nebraska Press, 1999.

Dabney, William. "History of the Department of History," in *The College of Arts and Sciences: A Centennial History*, edited by Robert E. Fleming, 189–211. Albuquerque: College of Arts and Sciences, University of New Mexico, 1990.

Fairbrother, Anne. "Mexicans in New Mexico: Deconstructing the Tri-Cultural Trope." *Perspectives in Mexican American Studies* 7 (2000): 111–30.

Fergusson, Erna. *Our Southwest.* New York: Alfred A. Knopf, 1946.

Fincher, E. B. *Spanish-Americans as a Political Factor in New Mexico, 1912–1950.* The Mexican American. New York: Arno Press, 1974.

Fowler, Dan. "E. L. Hewett, J. F. Zimmerman, and the Beginnings of Anthropology at the University of New Mexico, 1927–1946." *Journal of Anthropological Research* 59, no. 3: 305–27.

García, Mario T. "Foreword," in *Forgotten People: A Study of New Mexicans*, by George I. Sánchez, xi–xxx. Albuquerque: University of New Mexico Press, 1996.

———. *Mexican Americans: Leadership, Ideology, & Identity, 1930–1960.* Yale Western Americana, 36. New Haven and London: Yale University Press, 1989.

Gerdes, Dick. "The Department of Modern & Classical Languages: A Comprehensive History," in *The College of Arts and Sciences: A Centennial History*, edited by Robert E. Fleming, 257–87. Albuquerque: [College of Arts and Sciences], 1990.

Getz, Lynne Marie. *The Education of Hispanos in New Mexico, 1850–1940.* Albuquerque: University of New Mexico Press, 1997.

Gonzales, Phillip B., ed. *Expressing New Mexico: Nuevomexicano Creativity, Ritual, and Memory.* Tucson: University of Arizona Press, 2007.

———. *Forced Sacrifice as Ethnic Protest: The Hispano Cause in New Mexico & the Racial Attitude Confrontation of 1933.* Politics, Media, and Popular Culture, vol. 5. New York: Peter Lang, 2001.

———. "La Junta de Indignación: Hispano Repertoire of Collective Protest in New Mexico, 1884–1933." *Western Historical Quarterly* 31, no. 2 (Summer 2000): 161–86.

———. "Spanish Heritage and Ethnic Protest in New Mexico: The Anti-Fraternity Bill of 1933." *New Mexico Historical Review* 61, no. 4 (October 1986): 281–99.

———. "Whither the Nuevomexicanos: The Career of a Southwestern Intellectual Discourse, 1907–2004." *Social Sciences Journal* 43 (2006): 273–86.

Gonzales-Berry, Erlinda. "Which Language Will Our Children Speak? The Spanish Language and Public Education Policy in New Mexico, 1890–1930." In *The Contested Homeland: A Chicano History of New Mexico*, edited by Erlinda Gonzales-Berry and David Maciel, 169–89. Albuquerque: University of New Mexico Press, 2000.

Gonzalez, Nancie L. *The Spanish-Americans of New Mexico.* Albuquerque: University of New Mexico Press, 1969.

Gray, Edward McQ. "The Spanish Language in New Mexico: A National Resource." *University of New Mexico Bulletin.* Sociological Series 1, no. 2 (February 1912): 37–52.

Guérard, Albert. "A Mosaic, Not a Synthesis." In *America in the Southwest: A Regional Anthology*, edited by T. M. Pearce and Telfair Hendon, 126–28. Albuquerque: University of New Mexico Press, 1933.

Hodgin, Charles E. "Dr. Tight—the President and the Man," in *Remembrance Wakes: Memorial Day Exercises of the University of New Mexico*, edited by Lynn B. Mitchell, 70–84. Albuquerque: University of New Mexico Press, 1941.

Hoffman, Harold, and Alfredo Galaz. "Bi-Lingualism at Work (Cultural Bridge-Building in the American Southwest." *New Mexico Quarterly* 3, no. 4 (November 1933): 223–26.

Hurtado, Albert L. *Herbert Eugene Bolton: Historian of the American Borderlands.* Berkeley: University of California Press, 2012.

"Inauguration of James Fulton Zimmerman as President of the University." *University of New Mexico Bulletin* 42, no. 3 (April 1929): 1–39.

"Inauguration of Thomas Lafayette Popejoy as Ninth President of the University of New Mexico." Albuquerque: n.p., 1949.

"Indian Arts at the University of New Mexico." *American Magazine of Arts* 21 (December 1930): 727–28.

Johnson, E. Dana. "Dr. Gray—the Man and the President," in *Remembrance Wakes: Memorial Day Exercises of the University of New Mexico*, edited by Lynn B. Mitchell, 116–22. Albuquerque: University of New Mexico Press, 1941.

Kirkendall, Richard S. "Franklin D. Roosevelt and the Service Intellectual." *Mississippi Valley Historical Review* 49, no. 3 (December 1962): 456–71.

Kluckhohn, Clyde. "The Field of Higher Education in the Southwest." *New Mexico Quarterly* 7, no. 1 (February 1937): 23–37.

Leff, Gladys R. "George I. Sánchez: Don Quixote of the Southwest." PhD diss., North Texas State University, 1976.

Lowitt, Richard. *Bronson Cutting: Progressive Politician*. Albuquerque: University of New Mexico Press, 1992.

Lozano, Rosina A. "Managing the 'Priceless Gift': Debating Spanish Language Instruction in New Mexico and Puerto Rico, 1930–1950." *Western Historical Quarterly* 44, no. 3 (Autumn 2013): 271–93.

Maciel, David, and Erlinda Gonzales-Berry, "Introduction," in *The Contested Homeland: A Chicano History of New Mexico*, edited by David Maciel and Erlinda Gonzales-Berry, 1–9. Albuquerque: University of New Mexico Press, 2000.

McWilliams, Carey. "George Sánchez: Teacher, Scholar, Activist," in *Humanidad: Essays in Honor of George I. Sánchez*, edited by Américo Paredes, 116–19. Monograph no. 6. Los Angeles: Chicano Studies Center, University of California–Los Angeles, 1977.

———. *North from Mexico: The Spanish-Speaking People of the United States*. Repr., New York: Greenwood Press, 1968.

Meyer, Doris. *Speaking for Themselves: Neomexicano Cultural Identity and the Spanish-Language Press, 1880–1920*. Pasó Por Aquí. Series on the Nuevomexicano Literary Heritage. Albuquerque: University of New Mexico Press, 1996.

Mills, Nick. "The Origins of Latin American Programs at the University of New Mexico, 1927–1948." Unpublished manuscript. Albuquerque: Latin American Institute, University of New Mexico, 1981.

Mitchell, Pablo. *Coyote Nation: Sexuality, Race, and Conquest in Modernizing New Mexico, 1880–1920*. Worlds of Desire. The Chicago Series on Sexuality, Gender, and Culture. Chicago and London: University of Chicago Press, 2005.

Montgomery, Charles. *The Spanish Redemption: Heritage, Power, and Loss on New Mexico's Upper Rio Grande*. Berkeley: University of California Press, 2002.

Mora, Anthony. *Border Dilemmas: Racial and National Uncertainties in New Mexico, 1848–1912*. Durham and London: Duke University Press, 2011.

Nieto-Phillips, John M. *The Language of Blood: The Making of Spanish-American Identity in New Mexico, 1880s–1930s*. Albuquerque: University of New Mexico Press, 2004.

Noel, Linda C. *Debating American Identity: Southwestern Statehood and Mexican Immigration*. Tucson: University of Arizona Press, 2014.

Orstein, J. "Medieval Spanish Studies at the University of Wisconsin." *Bulletin of Hispanic Studies* 27, no. 106 (April–June 1950): 88–89.

Ortega, Joaquín. "A Colombian Poet in New Mexico." *New Mexico Quarterly Review* 12, no. 2 (May 1942): 179–81.

———. *The Compulsory Teaching of Spanish in the Grade Schools of New Mexico: An Expression of Opinion*. Albuquerque: University of New Mexico Press, 1941.

———. "Doctor Chimera. Story." *New Mexico Quarterly Review* 18, no. 2 (Summer 1948): 165–80.

———. "Factionalism in New Mexico." *Rio Grande Writer* 5, no. 2 (April 1948): 11–14.

———. "Insects on a Pin." 4-part series. *New Mexico Quarterly Review* 11, no. 2 (May 1941): 197–99; *New Mexico Quarterly Review* 11, no. 3 (August 1941): 341–44; *New Mexico Quarterly Review* 11, no. 4 (November 1941): 478–80; *New Mexico Quarterly Review* 12, no. 1 (February 1942): 71–74.

———. *The Intangible Resources of New Mexico*. Repr., Las Vegas, NM: La Galería de los Artesanos, 1978. Repr. January 1978 from *Papers of the School of American Research*. Santa Fe, NM: Archaeological Institute of America, 1945.

———. "James Fulton Zimmerman: An Appreciation." *New Mexico School Review* (December 1944). Copy of article contained in the James F. Zimmerman folder (1887–1944), UNMA, Faculty Files.

———. "*The New Mexico Quarterly Review*: Editorial Statement." *New Mexico Quarterly Review* 18, no. 4 (Winter 1948): 492–95.

———. *New Mexico's Opportunity: A Message to My Fellow New Mexicans*. Albuquerque: University of New Press, 1942.

———. "The Professor and the University." *New Mexico Quarterly Review* 18, no. 3 (Autumn 1948): 319–37.

———. "Remarks on Modern Mexican Art," *New Mexico Quarterly Review* 11, no. 2 (May 1941): 133–38.

———. "Rethinking Cervantes." *New Mexico Quarterly Review* 17, no. 4 (Winter 1947): 405–19.

Otis, Raymond. *Fire in the Night*. New York: Farrar and Rinehart, 1934.

Paredes, Américo. *Humanidad: Essays in Honor of George I. Sánchez*. Los Angeles: Chicano Studies Center, University of California–Los Angeles, 1977.

Pearce, T. M. "Southwestern Culture: An Artificial or a Natural Growth?" *New Mexico Quarterly* 1, no. 2 (May 1931): 195–209.

Reeve, Frank. "History of the University of New Mexico." Master's thesis, University of New Mexico, 1928.

Reid, J. T. *It Happened in Taos*. Albuquerque: University of New Mexico Press, 1946.

Rodríguez, Sylvia. "The Hispano Homeland Debate." Working Paper Series no. 17, Stanford, CA: Stanford Center for Chicano Research, 1986.

Sánchez, George I. *Forgotten People: A Study of New Mexicans*. Albuquerque: University of New Mexico Press, 1940.

———. "Good Neighbors—at Home." Unpublished manuscript, University of Texas, Benson Latin American Collection. GISP, Series II, Correspondence and Subject Files, box 70, folder 18.

———. "New Mexicans and Acculturation." *New Mexico Quarterly Review* 11, no. 1 (February 1941): 61–68.

Saunders, Lyle. "Alumni at Barelas Center: Two of Them Are at Work in Spanish-American Teaching and Clinics with Aid of School of Inter-American Affairs." *The Alumnus* (University of New Mexico, January 1943): 5–7.

Sexton, Joseph Franklin. "New Mexico: Intellectual and Cultural Developments, 1885–1925: Conflict Among Ideas and Institutions." PhD diss., University of Oklahoma, 1982.

Weber, David J. *Myth and the History of the Hispanic Southwest: Essays*. The Calvin P. Horn Lectures in Western History and Culture. Albuquerque: University of New Mexico Press, 1988.

Welsh, Michael. "Often Out of Sight, Rarely Out of Mind: Race and Ethnicity at the University of New Mexico, 1889–1927." *New Mexico Historical Review* 71 (April 1996): 105–34.

———. "A Prophet Without Honor: George I. Sánchez and Bilingualism in New Mexico." *New Mexico Historical Review* 69, no. 1 (January 1994): 19–34.

Weigle, Martha, and Peter White. *The Lore of New Mexico*. Albuquerque: University of New Mexico, 1988.

Wilson, Chris. "Ethnic/Sexual Personas in Tricultural New Mexico," in *The Culture of Tourism, the Tourism of Culture: Selling the Past to the Present in the American Southwest*, edited by Hal K. Rothman, 12–37. Albuquerque: University of New Mexico Press, 2003.

Zeleny, Carolyn. *Relations Between the Spanish Americans and Anglo-Americans in New Mexico: A Study of Conflict and Accommodation in a Dual-Ethnic Situation*. The Mexican American. New York: Arno Press, 1974.

Zimmerman, James F. "Social and Cultural Elements of Pan-Americanism," *New Mexico Quarterly* 3, no. 2 (May 1933): 65–71.

———. "The Meaning of Memorial Day," in *Remembrance Wakes: Memorial Day Exercises of the University of New Mexico, 1928–1941*, edited by Lynn B. Mitchell, 5–8. Albuquerque: University of New Mexico Press, 1941.

Index

Page numbers in italic text indicate illustrations.

three cultures, 140; land of, 63; meeting ground of, 68, 105

three cultures motif, 79, 104, 139

Three Peoples mural, 167–69, 204nn15–17

Thurstone scale, 58, 152–53

Tight, William, 24; ambitions of, 42; goals of, 49; presidency of, 19–21

Tireman, Lloyd S., 10, 55, 56, 59, 113; career of, 40–41; collaboration with, 128; presentation by, 56

Tolle, Vincent, 59

tourism, 68

Tozzer, Alfred, 45

traditions, 2, 4, 73; commonality of, 135; of competition, 69; customs and, 9; folkloric, 36; indigenous, 28

transculturation, 134

Treaty of Guadalupe Hidalgo, 8, 69–70

tricultural formulation, 103, 132; credibility of, 61; as cultural reference point, 135; Hammond and, 65; manipulation of, 65; Ortega and, 9; synthesis of the Americas and, 162; Zimmerman description of, 44–45

tricultural heritage, 130

tricultural image, 11, 175n14

tricultural myth, 203n9

Twitchell, Ralph, 28

Union of the Americas, 103

United States (US): citizenship in, 8; commercial opportunities sought by, 47; Department of Agriculture, 106–7; government agencies, 107; Latin America relations with, 48, 52, 65–66, 93

University of New Mexico (UNM), 1; architecture of, 27–28; athletic park for, 26; Bi-Lingual Club at, 55–57; Board of Regents at, 17, 21, 35, 177n15; budgets for, 30; campus, 9; at center of community-based projects, 54; cleansing of, 53; Committee on the Expansion of Upper Division Courses at, 50; concentration in inter-

American field, 48; cultural relations at, 41; Department of Anthropology and Archaeology at, 42–43, 100; Department of Economics and Business Administration at, 100; Department of History at, 29; Department of Modern Languages at, 119, 151; Department of Romance Languages at, 41, 56; Department of Sociology at, 76, 100; distinctive identity for, 44; division between Hispanic and Anglo students at, 51–55, 61; early leaders of, 17; history and growth of, 14; implementation of programs at, 40–41; inter-American studies at, 11; Latin American studies at, 80–82; Latin American studies commitment of, 31; leadership at, 69; library collection of, 48–49; mission and purpose of, 89; modernization of, 30–31; new era for, 38; *New Mexico Lobo*, 12; outreach examples at, 80; Pan-American Society at, 91; promotion of, 22; reputation of, 97, 100; Research Bureau in Social Sciences at, 101; role in lifting poverty, 94; SAR alliance with, 42–43; Scholes visiting, 45; School of Latin American Affairs at, 29–30; School of Spanish Literature and Life at, 35; seal of, *166*; SIAA at, 2; Spanish American College established by, 24–25; Taos County Adult Education Project at, 56, 71–78; Tight presidency at, 19–21; as venue for bilingual conference, 130–31

University of Oklahoma, 26

University of Texas, 47, 78

University of Vienna, 44

University of Wisconsin–Madison, 1, 41, 85–86, 102, 141

UNM. *See* University of New Mexico

US. *See* United States

Van Hise, Charles R., 160

Vázquez de Coronado, Francisco, 64–65

veterans, Hispanic, 11–12

Vierra, Carlos, 18
The Voice of the Southwest, 112

Wagner, Henry, 48, 61
Wallace, Henry, 67
Wallis, Marie Pope, 111–13
Walter, Paul, Jr., 10, 36, 69, 76, 110, *111*, 113, 153
Walter, Paul A. F., 42, 65, 111
war psychology, 127
Weinstock, Herbert, 68
Wernette, John Phillip, 147–48, 150–51, 155
whitening, 132
Whitman, Walt, 6
Wilson, Chris, 140
Wilson, Woodrow, 12
Women's Board of Home Missions, 26
Woodward, Dorothy, 48
Works Progress Administration (WPA), 71, 185n85
World War I, 12, 30, 116
World War II, 9, 13, 82, 97, 133
WPA. *See* Works Progress Administration
Wynn, Dudley, 155–56

Zeleny, Carolyn, 57–58, 60–62, 106, 125, 133, 182n49; on *Forgotten People*, 77–78; on language handicap, 118; separatism and, 184n64

Zimmerman, James Fulton, 1, 9, *40*, 74–76, 144–45, 161; administrative skills of, 51; advice given to, 104; alliances forged by, 42–43; CCCC and, 63–68; commitment to Southwest-focused research, 50–51; conviction applauded by, 94; criticism of, 55–56, 105; death of, 146–47, 150; dedication of, 160; faculty increased by, 40; Hewett agreement with, 19; Hispanic presence and inclusion increased by, 180n8; hostility expressed toward, 53–54; inauguration of, 39, 117; initiatives of, 180n12; Institute of World Affairs speech by, 57; inter-cultural problem awareness of, 52; interrogation of, 63; Kluckhohn and, 44–46; networking by, 82; *The New Mexico Quarterly* publication by, 52, 54–55; opposition to plans of, 95; Ortega appointment by, 89–90; Ortega following progress of, 80; Ortega meeting with, 38–39, 52; Pan-Americanism and, 68–69; presidency of, 10, 14, 24; protest against, 59; recruitment trip of, 82–83; Scholes and, 46; strategies employed by, 15, 122; transparency of, 90; tricultural formulation description by, 44–45